STEEL FROM
THE SKY

Also by Roger Ford

Fire from the Forest

STEEL FROM THE SKY

The Jedburgh Raiders, France 1944

ROGER FORD

WEIDENFELD & NICOLSON
LONDON

Weidenfeld & Nicolson

The Orion Publishing Group Ltd
Orion House
5 Upper Saint Martin's Lane
London WC2H 9EA

British Library Cataloguing-in-Publication Data
A catalogue record for this book is available
from the British Library

ISBN 0-297-84680-9

Distributed in the USA by
Sterling Publishing Co Inc
387 Park Avenue South
New York NY 10016-8810

Printed and bound in Great Britain by
Clays Ltd, St Ives plc

To MMZ, who was the first to jump

The sky is darkening like a stain;
Something is going to fall like rain,
And it won't be flowers.

WH Auden, *The Two/The Witnesses*, 1935

CONTENTS

LIST OF MAPS

INTRODUCTION

The Jedburgh programme, brainchild of Britain's 'fourth armed service' – the Special Operations Executive – and brought to life thanks to an active collaboration between it, the United States' Office of Strategic Services and the Free French *Bureau Central de Renseignements et d'Action*, occupies a special place in the history of unconventional forces in World War Two. Its role, which focused on assisting partisan leaders to organise, train and arm their men, was an entirely new one, and very different from that of the *coup de main* 'commando' parties, the SAS parties and Operational Groups who established bases in enemy-held territory, or even the clandestine organisers and agents sent in by all three parent bodies.

The Jedburgh teams operated in the space between the military and the paramilitary, co-ordinating activities with the former and assisting the latter. It was an entirely new game, the rules of which were made up as they went along. The teams, moreover, were integrated at the operational level, made up of at least two and sometimes all three nationalities; in this respect they were unique. There was no question of any one nationality dominating the programme, and while it was SOE-led at the very beginning, during the training phase, that was only due to the British having more relevant experience than the other partners at that time. Personnel were actively encouraged to choose their partners for themselves, and an officer of any nationality could emerge as leader of a team. Volunteers kept their individual identities as members of a particular regiment or corps. They wore no distinguishing badge, although one of their number designed the so-called Special Force 'wings' – more in the nature of a qualification badge – which they shared with other uniformed SOE and OSS personnel.

Each Jedburgh operation had a code-name, and the team which carried it out took it as its own. All the individual Jedburghs also had code-names, and all but two of the French volunteers used *noms de guerre*. I have used actual names throughout, except in quotations from after-action reports, which appear verbatim [with any comments added in square brackets]. Other individuals are identified by their code-names, by their *noms de guerre*, and by their actual names where possible, and in this case I have used their code-names or *noms de guerre* throughout. Their ranks were often figments of individual imagination. Jedburgh's ranks are those applicable at the start of an operation, as far as I could ascertain – some individuals were promoted while in the field, others immediately upon their return, before after-action reports were written. I have not differentiated between grades of lieutenants among American and British personnel (which former are distinguished, where possible, from the latter by the use of their middle initial). The French rank of *aspirant* does not occur in either of the other nations' armed services, and is that of an officer-cadet, who was assumed to be on a par with a senior NCO; *commandant* is equivalent to major. Many reports misspell place-names, and I have provided what I believe to be the correct version, although some locations proved impossible to identify from even the most detailed modern gazetteer.

I decided to group the Jedburgh operations according to the area in which they operated, rather than along chronological lines, because to have done otherwise would have introduced more anomolies than it resolved. It could be argued that the regions I have chosen are too large – particularly, perhaps, the Seine basin which, by my definition, stretches from the Ardennes to the Côte-d'Or – but frankly, since most operations are treated in isolation, this was an 'administrative' procedure in any event.

When I began work on the book which became *Fire from the Forest*, my intention was to examine the Jedburgh teams' role in the liberation of France in 1944 along with those of the SAS Brigade, the OSS Operational Groups and the Inter-Allied Missions. It soon became obvious that such an undertaking could not be accomplished in a single volume, and thus *Fire from the Forest* was restricted to the activities of the Special Air Service Brigade, and except for occasional references – where their tracks crossed those of the SAS parties – I set aside the Jedburghs' after-action reports, thinking to combine an analysis of them with those of the OGs and the Missions. It soon became clear, however, that the Jedburghs must have a work of their own, all the more so because, almost unbelievably, no comprehensive history of them or their activities existed.

During my researches for *Fire from the Forest* I made a decision to rely on contemporaneous material, and not to be unduly influenced either by individuals' published accounts, most of which were written long after the fact and all of which reflect a very personal view, or by equally individual memories of events which took place six decades in the past; and I saw no need to adopt a different principle when I turned my attention to the Jedburghs. Once again, however, I was able to speak to many people in Britain, France and the United States, and once again, I thank them all for their co-operation. Inevitably, if only for reasons of space, I have had to abbreviate the accounts of some Jedburgh operations to the point of near-dismissal. That should not imply that the men who undertook those operations were in any way inferior to others whose activities have been dealt with more fully, but rather to acknowledge that some teams were simply sent into action far too late ever to have been able to have fulfilled the role they were so arduously trained to perform. As with the reports I used as my primary sources for *Fire from the Forest*, the after-action reports of Jedburgh operations are of variable quality: some are brief, little more than badly-linked notes, while others are full to the point of verbosity; some are entirely objective, while others were perhaps designed to build or enhance the author's reputation. In some instances, more than one team member submitted a report (and infuriatingly, their accounts do not always tally, one with the other) and many touch upon events in which others – SAS personnel, and men and women who worked for other branches of SOE or OSS, for example – were involved, and on which they, too, reported. Only three Jedburgh teams failed to make more or less comprehensive reports, two because all their personnel were killed or captured, and the other because its leader was killed and it operated with another team; two more teams operated together and combined their reports.

There was, then, a wealth of material on which to draw, all of it held for posterity in the United Kingdom by the National Archives (formerly the Public Record Office) at Kew, and in the United States by the National Archives and Records Adminstration at College Park, Maryland; the staff of both have been of enormous help. In addition, a surprising number of Jedburghs – at least nine that I could trace – have written accounts of their service, while one has compiled a valuable short history of the programme, to which another contributed a postscript in which he provided short biographies of many of the men involved as well as some information relating to their later activities in the Far East.

My surprise upon discovering that no attempt had previously been made to produce a comprehensive history of the Jedburgh teams and their activities was tempered by gratitude for the opportunity this gave me to analyse and present material which had not been worked over and interpreted by others to any measurable extent. Thus, such mistakes – of fact or of interpretation – as there are in the work which follows are most definitely my own, and so, too, are the opinions expressed therein. As well as to the Jedburghs themselves, my thanks are due in particular to Clive Bassett, a leading light in the Carpetbaggers Aviation Museum at Harrington Airfield in Northamptonshire, for his unselfish help and enthusiastic support.

St-Paul-Cap-de-Joux,
July 2003

Part One

THE ORIGINS OF THE
JEDBURGH PROGRAMME

Following the fall of France in June 1940, newly installed Prime Minister Winston Churchill's first priority was to rebuild the shattered British Army, but he understood that during the time it took to regroup, even small acts of aggression would be important to morale. He adopted a two-pronged approach: firstly, reorganised 'commando' forces were to make 'butcher and bolt' raids into enemy territory, and secondly the 'fourth armed service', the Special Operations Executive, would be created 'to set Europe ablaze' at a time when it looked very much as if the flame of resistance would be smothered entirely by the blanket of occupation.

SOE was formed by the relatively simple (at least, on the surface) expedient of combining Section D of the Secret Intelligence Service (MI6), which dealt in sabotage; a semi-secret Foreign Office department (EH), which existed to disseminate propaganda, and a War Office research department known as MI(R), which was concerned with finding ways of undertaking and supporting partisan operations. Churchill was determined to keep SOE apart from the existing military and intelligence communities – the former he considered hide-bound, without any spark of strategic creativity, while the latter were lazy and self-serving – and he bypassed the claims of both, giving ultimate responsibility for it to Hugh Dalton, Minister for Economic Warfare.

An important landmark in SOE's development came in November 1940 when Brigadier-General Colin McVean Gubbins was appointed to head its operational and training section, SO2. He became more powerful within the Executive when SO1, which controlled the propaganda aspect of its operations, was hived off to become the Political Warfare Executive, nine months later, and became its head in September 1943. Gubbins had been commissioned into the Royal Artillery at the outbreak of World War One and served through it with distinction, winning a Military Cross. He later served in Russia during the 1919 campaign, in Ireland during 'The Troubles', on the North-West Frontier in India, and had personal experience of guerrilla warfare. He joined MI(R) in 1938, and before returning to the British army to command Independent Companies in the Norwegian campaign, literally 'wrote the book' on irregular warfare, in the form of three pamphlets entitled *The Art of Guerilla Warfare*, *Partisan Leader's Handbook* and *How to Use High Explosives*. In the first of these he hinted at a scheme containing seeds which grew into the Jedburgh programme. It was to him that Churchill had entrusted the establishment of the British Resistance Organisation, the ultra-secret network which would have waged a paramilitary campaign against the Germans, should they have invaded the British Isles. Part of his responsibilities involved producing a realistic evaluation of the likely effect of such a war of sabotage and ambush. Naturally, when he came to SOE he applied the yardstick he had formerly devised to the partisan movement which the Executive was supporting in Europe.

Although there was never any question as to how committed were SOE's clandestine paramilitaries, there was always a nagging doubt concerning the real effectiveness of the partisans with whom they were operating, particularly in France. The doubt was partially well-founded, and partially the result of a certain arrogance: important factions in Whitehall could not forget the sudden and catastrophic collapse in 1940 of what had widely been thought a world-class military power, with the ability to field an enormous and well-equipped army. They simply could not believe that the very same people they held reponsible for that collapse would or could now live up to very demanding military expectations, particularly after years of occupation had sapped both their strength and their confidence still further. This attitude became hardened, if anything, with the entry of the United States of America into the war in Europe at the end of 1941.

At that point, SOE still had few friends in Whitehall, but it soon found itself with a powerful ally when the US government, which possessed no formal intelligence-gathering organisation, established one as the Office of Strategic Services on 13 June 1942, under the direction of Gen William ('Wild Bill') Donovan; this was a very happy choice as far as the British were concerned, for Donovan was a confirmed anglophile. Collaboration between SOE and OSS began immediately after the latter's creation, when a week-long conference resulted in a detailed agreement covering all possible spheres of interest. When OSS established a London-based Special Operations (SO) Branch in the second week of January, 1943, it 'shadowed' SOE, having a section which corresponded to each of the Executive's own.

Roughly contemporaneously with the creation of OSS, Gubbins became SOE's Deputy Director, Operations, and coincidentally a new concept was developed within the Executive. It called for a mobile tactical reserve, a 'flying squad' of small teams of military personnel, to be inserted deep inside enemy-occupied territory to assist with the organisation of armed resistance in specific areas, or to perform predetermined (military) tasks. The notion was first voiced at a meeting held in May, to discuss suggestions for defining the Executive's role in any forthcoming invasion of France, specifically that contained in an over-optimistic plan of American origin known as Sledgehammer. Sledgehammer called for the seizure and retention, in September that year, of either the Cotentin Peninsula or, more ambitiously still, western Brittany, both as the precursor to a full invasion in 1943 and to pull German divisions out of the Soviet Union and at least partially assuage Stalin's demands for a second front.

The responsibility for drafting briefing papers for this meeting fell to Robin Brook, a senior staff officer. Brook nominated Peter Wilkinson, Gubbins' long-time aide, and now his GSO 2, who had had an important role in setting up the British Resistance Organisation, to examine the problems and possibilities of co-ordinating the activities of armed *résistants* with the overall Allied military strategy. Wilkinson wrote:

> As and when the invasion commences, SOE will drop small teams of French-speaking [military] personnel carrying arms for some forty men each. The role of these teams will be to make contact with local authorities or existing SOE organisations, to distribute the arms, to start off the action of the patriots, and most particularly, to arrange by W/T communication dropping points and reception committees for further arms and equipment on the normal SOE system. Each team will consist of one British officer, one W/T operator with set and possibly one guide.

Sledgehammer was soon abandoned, but Wilkinson's proposal was deemed to have some wider merit, for on 6 July 1942 Gubbins wrote to the chief of SOE's Security Section:

> A project is under consideration for the dropping behind enemy lines, in co-operation with an Allied invasion of the Continent, of small

parties of officers and men to raise and arm the civilian population to carry out guerrilla activities against the enemy's lines of communication. These men are to be recruited and trained by SOE. It is requested that 'Jumpers' or some other appropriate code name be allotted to this personnel.

In the event it was felt that Jumpers was a too-obvious, and therefore insecure, code-name, and they eventually became Jedburgh teams instead. The code-name, it is held by some, suggested itself to Gubbins during a train journey which took him through the small Scottish town of the same name, a place associated with the 'border reivers', bandit groups which had raided settlements in England during the sixteenth century, and the birthplace of a judicial system which saw such individuals executed first and tried afterwards, which became known as 'Jedburgh Justice'; others, including more than one ex-Jedburgh, discount Gubbins' involvement but hold to the connection between the teams, the town and the reivers, while a few claim that the Jedburghs trained near that town and took its name for their own. All these notions are fanciful; 'Jedburgh' was simply the next entry on a list of meaningless words.

Wilkinson's original proposal was for the teams to be composed of two men – a British officer with some knowledge of France and the French language, with a non-commissioned officer to act as his wireless operator – to be augmented by a locally recruited guide. A meeting held on 24 December 1942 decided that the Jedburgh teams – by now expanded to include American personnel – should include a French officer, rather than a local guide. In principle the Frenchman would have responsibility for liaison with local groups, while the team leader would both control the operation and provide security for the radio operator; but the distinction became blurred when some of the French officers emerged as team leaders. There was never any intention to field teams consisting of one American, one Briton and one Frenchman, as many writers have suggested (in fact, the original plan was to pair British officers with British signallers, and Americans with American), and in only seven of the Jedburgh teams eventually dropped into France were the three nationalities represented.

It was also decided at that Christmas Eve meeting that the teams would operate in uniform. This decision was apparently conditioned by a belief that if they were captured in uniform they would be protected by the Geneva Convention of 1929. This would not have been the case, German troops being under orders (the *Sonderbehandlung* or *Kommando-befehl*, issued on 18 October 1942 after three German soldiers were executed while bound during an operation the SOE-sponsored Small Scale Raiding Force mounted on the island of Sark) to kill all 'commandos' out of hand or pass them over to the *Sicherheitsdienst* (SD) for disposal. In the event, during the liberation of France one Jedburgh was unlawfully executed after having been reported as a prisoner of war, and four more were killed when they could probably have been taken prisoner (six men died in combat, or of wounds they received in combat, and three more died as the result of accidents), while two were captured and survived. Other documentary evidence suggests the decision that they were to be uniformed was aimed at boosting the morale of the *Maquis* groups with which they would operate, and this seems at least an equally valid reason. There were certain areas where this was a completely impractical arrangement; in consequence, some teams were dropped in civilian clothing, and some wore it throughout their time in enemy-occupied territory.

At midnight on 3 March 1943, there began in southern England a week-long exercise known as Spartan. Spartan pitted British troops against Canadian, the former being tasked to push across Salisbury Plain in a northerly direction towards the town of Hungerford, to simulate the breakout from an invasion bridgehead. It seems that SOE got to hear of Spartan late on in the planning process, but decided that it presented a useful opportunity to test the Jedburgh concept under something like operational conditions. Eleven teams recruited from SOE personnel were added to the offensive force, to be parachuted in ahead of it; they were to liaise with a partisan force (played by men from 8 Battalion, Royal Welch Fusiliers), carry out a set task each – five teams were given demolition targets; three were to secure and prevent the destruction of targets of strategic value; two were tasked with disrupting communications and the last was to attack a tactical headquarters – and establish radio links with 'headquarters' located in Scotland, far enough away to create the sort of communications problems the teams would later experience in France, in order to receive further instructions. OSS personnel did not participate, but SO Branch sent observers.

A comprehensive after-exercise analysis was carried out swiftly, and on 6 April a report, in the form of a paper entitled 'Coordination of activities behind the enemy lines with the actions of Allied military forces invading NW Europe', was submitted by SOE to Lt-Gen Sir Frederick Morgan, Chief of Staff to the Supreme Allied Commander (COSSAC). In fact, the commander in question, Dwight Eisenhower, had yet to be appointed, and so Morgan had greater powers even than his title suggests. It was followed on 23 April by another report with the same title and virtually identical contents, prepared by the senior OSS observer, Capt Franklin Canfield, for Lt-Gen Jacob Devers, the Commanding General, European Theater of Operations, United States Army (ETOUSA). The two papers carried the same recommendation as to the overall size of the effort – just seventy teams were deemed to be sufficient to undertake the task of liaising with, and perhaps organising, training and leading, the Resistance movement in France. In fact, before the Jedburgh programme actually came to life, the total was expanded by thirty additional teams, who were to constitute a reserve (the distinction between 'first team' and 'reserve' status soon disappeared), and the concept was extended to cover other territories. There is no indication in the surviving records as to how the planners arrived at the total number of teams, and it may in fact have been arbitrary, but the number was actually realistic, and a higher figure would have been difficult to attain, simply because men with the right qualifications were not available in substantially greater numbers. The plan was approved by the British Chiefs of Staff Committee on 21 July, and by Devers on 24 August, by which time SOE/SO had been aware of the Overlord plan for a fortnight. On 16 October a directive was issued enabling OSS to begin recruiting formally, although it had actually started doing so a fortnight earlier.

Until that point, the Jedburgh initiative was still essentially British, and command and control of the operation was solely in British hands. Even after the formal decision to include American personnel had been made, all the Jedburgh teams, be they 'British' or 'American' in origin, were still to have been run by SOE – rather uncharacteristically, Devers had agreed to that without demur – but as soon as senior OSS staffers became involved on a day-to-day basis they began to put pressure on their Director to lobby for a change. Donovan objected most strenuously to the arrangement, saying that to accept it would be tantamount to selling out his own service. The least he would accept was equal status and joint control, and much as some of the less pragmatic at SOE's headquarters baulked at the idea, this was no sooner demanded than accepted. In fact, although an official Jedburgh Section with both American and British personnel was set up before the end of 1943, it was tacitly understood that SOE would actually remain in charge until the Jedburghs became theoretically operational on 8 April 1944 – and that was reflected in the relatively lowly rank of the two initial 'co-commanders' of the Jedburgh programme, Maj Henry Coombe-Tennant and Maj Henry B Coxe.

This unvoiced acceptance that the Jedburgh programme would remain under British control until the teams were ready for operational employment sprang from the realisation, in the OSS, that SOE was hugely more able in this area than it was itself. In July 1943 – by which time SO was supposed to have been self-supporting – the SO Branch's newly appointed Chief Training Officer, Maj John Tyson, spent his first three weeks in post on a familiarisation tour of SOE training establishments. At that time, Jedburgh operations were still some way short of authorisation, and he was primarily concerned with the training of clandestine paramilitaries, but his conclusions were to affect Jedburgh training too. In his report to Col Charles Vanderblue, by that time Chief of Special Operations, he said:

> It should be definitely understood that the training any prospective SO agent has received in our Washington Schools prior to his arrival in this theater is entirely inadequate and no trainee should be considered for field operations until they have had further training in this theater...
>
> The quality of the training given, the manner of handling the men and caliber of instructors in the SOE schools is far superior in every detail to anything we have to offer in our training centers in the USA. This superiority ... is the direct result of 3 hard and confusing years of trial and error.

He went on to say that while he had received an undertaking that SOE's Training Section would be happy to 'have all or any of our recruits go through their schools', it had been made clear to him that the Executive would also welcome the attachment of as many competent instructors and training personnel as could be provided, offering to put them through instructors' courses where necessary, after which they could either be returned to OSS or used in joint operational training schemes or indeed, in joint operations proper. That, of course, would include the Jedburgh training programme.

By the end of 1943, then, the Jedburgh concept was largely in place and recruitment of personnel was well advanced, though there still seems to have been some confusion – or perhaps some argument – about their precise function. Wilkinson's outline description of their task had been somewhat refined, though little changed, in the basic Jedburgh Directive, issued on 20 December, 1943. It said (in its American version) that they were to:

provide the strategic reserve with which SOE/SO can create and control offensive action behind the enemy lines on and after D Day where existing communications, leadership, organization or supplies are inadequate, or to carry out specific tasks demanded by the military situation.

It then went straight on to note that while their primary function was to liaise with resistance groups, and that they would be dropped by parachute only to areas where there were actual or potential resistance elements, well behind the German front lines ('at least forty miles'; this was one of the lessons learned from Operation Spartan), together with arms, explosives and stores, they were to represent the Supreme Allied Commander and bring the latest orders from Allied Head- quarters and from SOE/SO HQ, and from that point on to act as the focus for resistance in the area. 'It is NOT', the Directive said, 'the intention that Jedburgh teams will necessarily usurp the authority of local leaders, but it is felt that the arrival of Allied soldiers, in uniform, behind the enemy lines, will have a marked effect on patriotic morale and that these teams, representing as they do the Allied High Command, will act as a focus for local resistance.' As we shall see, this optimistic 'feeling' was often to prove illusory, but a deeper conceptual flaw also lay hidden in the Jedburgh Directive: the timing of the teams' deployment.

This is a subject to which we shall return in due course, but for now the priority was to take the most precious commodity of the entire scheme – the men themselves – and set up a training programme which would at least give them a sporting chance of succeeding. The OSS/SO War Diary tells us that Jedburgh officers were to be:

> picked for qualities of leadership and daring, ability to speak and understand French, and all-round physical condition. They should be experienced in handling men, preferably in an active theater of opera- tions, and be prepared to be parachuted in uniform behind enemy lines and operate on their own for some time. They must have at least basic military training and preferably have aptitude for use of small arms weapons.

> Qualifications for radio operators are not so high as for leaders and seconds-in-command, and a fair working knowledge of French is suf- ficient. In addition to normal requirements for good radio operators they must be of exceptionally good physique to stand up to training and be prepared to be parachuted behind enemy lines to operate their

sets in open [sic] under war conditions. They should attain a speed of 15 words per minute before being shipped to the UK.

It was Franklin Canfield, by now promoted major, who had been given the job of locating and seducing these paragons of military virtue in the USA, and he had returned to Washington within days of Devers approving American involvement. It was 1 October before he actually got agreement to recruit the fifty Jedburgh officers and fifty enlisted men to work as radio operators but little more than another week had passed before the first of around a hundred ostensibly suitable officer candidates – the majority of them from Fort Benning and Camp Mackall, which were Airborne bases – had received orders to report to Washington for a twenty-one-day temporary assignment.

In fact, seven of the American officers who were to go on to become Jedburghs had already been recruited by OSS to join what were to be known as Operational Groups (OGs), essentially platoon-sized commando units composed of first- or second-generation immigrants from European countries or men who had lived in Europe and spoke the language of an occupied land with some degree of fluency. Like the Jedburghs, they were to be inserted into enemy-held territory, but unlike them they were to operate independently of local partisans, and in this respect they were more akin to the Anglo-Franco-Belgian SAS Brigade. In their books *No Bridges Blown* and *From OSS to Green Berets*, William Dreux, who went on to jump into France as a member of Jedburgh team Gavin, and Aaron Bank, of team Packard, relate how they volunteered for service with the OGs in June 1943, and were ordered to report to the 'Q' Building, at 2340 E Street, Washington DC, the following month. They were redirected to the Congressional Country Club, known officially as Area F, six miles out of the city to the west, in Potomac, Maryland. This establishment, with its luxurious clubhouse, golf course and swimming pool – drained, Dreux complained – had been taken over by OSS ostensibly as a training area for the OGs, but more realistically to be an assembly- and dispersal-point. Volunteers filled their time with mild exercise in the form of cross-country runs and calesthenics interspersed with lectures on unconventional aspects of warfare, apparently delivered exclusively by men who had no personal experience of it. When a party was up to strength it moved to a more remote training area, where the men were taught the rudiments of demolition, improved their skills with various types of firearm and took part in mock attacks and raids. There was a widespread feeling that the instruction they received there was inadequate and unrealistic – as those who crossed over to the Jedburgh programme would discover when they made the move to the United Kingdom, and were placed in the care of hard-bitten men who had been operating as commandos since 1940.

Clearly, someone realised that the OG officer training programme might also function as a selection course for the instructors SOE had offered to train. Dreux and Banks were among those chosen. By their accounts they were soon told the bare bones of the Jedburgh plan and were invited to transfer into this alternative programme, though curiously neither mentions that they were to act as instructors. In fact they were two of a group of seven who did; all of them (and two more, recruited later) subsequently became operational Jedburghs themselves. The seven, plus a more senior officer, Maj Harry Dorsey, who was to be one of the three company commanders at the Jedburgh school, were ordered to Fort Hamilton, a holding area adjacent to the Brooklyn Navy Yard, late in October, to await the next available fast transport to the United Kingdom (it turned out to be RMS *Aquitania*), and little over a fortnight later they were in the very different surroundings of the Western Highlands of Scotland.

They spent six weeks at SOE's Commando School at Arisaig, then, at around the turn of the year, were sent to what Dreux calls 'a testing school' in southern England, where their suitability for Jedburgh operations was assessed. Bank says that during this period he also passed through a number of specialist schools – intelligence-gathering and agent-running; sabotage; fighting in built-up areas including house clearing, and communications – before attending the parachute school near Manchester with Dreux. His recollection and Dreux's are not necessarily at odds – the files show that only a very small number of Jedburghs attended the special schools.

In the meantime, the hundred or so American officers who had volunteered as potential Jedburghs in October and November had been whittled down to around fifty during an assessment period at the Country Club. Those who passed the test received orders posting them to the Office of Strategic Services on detached duty, and moved on to a requisitioned hunting lodge near Thurmont, in the Catoctin Mountains of northern Maryland, which was known as Area B. It was later to become Camp David, the country retreat of the President of the United States. Here they received basic instruction in map reading and navigation; explosives and demolition; hand-to-hand fighting and the use and care of firearms. They remained at Area B for six weeks and were then sent off, in their turn, to Fort Hamilton, to await transport to the UK;

one instructor from the course, Lt Lawrence Swank, a demolitions specialist and one of only four Jedburgh 'West Pointers', joined them. The facility's commanding officer, Maj Horace 'Hod' Fuller, also became an operational Jedburgh, and led team Bugatti; a US Marine, Fuller was the only non-army Jedburgh officer.

The men boarded the liner RMS *Queen Elizabeth* on 17 December, arrived at Gourock near Glasgow on 23 December, and were transported to Arisaig where they were given a short period over Christmas to acclimatise before being put through SOE's more rigorous Student Assessment Board (SAB) – a collection of military men, old SOE hands and behaviourists, including a psychologist and two psychiatrists. The SAB was located at Winterfold, near Cranleigh in Surrey (to SOE it was a Special Training School, like all of its out-stations – STS-7), but it seems that for the purposes of assessing Jedburgh officers, both British and American, a temporary subsidiary board known as the 205 Selection Board was convened at STS-3, Stodham Park, at Liss, near Petersfield in Hampshire. It dealt with the American would-be Jedburghs in three groups, between 28 December and 8 January. On their arrival the men completed written tests and were then interviewed extensively (and at least once, aggressively) by both behaviourists and military officers, which latter also put them through a series of practical tests of their problem-solving abilities, initiative and resourcefulness. This included the infamous 'brook test', for which they were led off to a shallow stream in the grounds. Here they were given a variety of short boards, none of them long enough to bridge the stream – which they were told was a raging torrent, too deep to ford and too wide to jump – as well as three lengths of rope, a pulley block, a log and a small boulder, the last of these representing fragile loads – a range finder and a box of detonators – which had to be transported across the stream. A solution had to be devised in ten minutes or less, and there were extra marks for demonstrating leadership.

At the end of the assessment, all were told they had failed, although that was actually the final test; in fact thirty-seven were accepted for Jedburgh training. There was considerable concern over the rejection rate, especially since most failures were attributed to lack of motivation which, it was felt, should have been detected during the initial screening in Washington; additional volunteers were found among American officers already in the United Kingdom, but there was a steady further loss through men who dropped out during training, and even with the addition of the nine instructors the numbers never came up to the establishment figure.

The men who had passed the assessment board were then ordered to one of three SOE 'schools': STS-6 at West Court, Finchampstead, near Wokingham in Berkshire; STS-41 at Gumley Hall, near Market Harborough in Leicestershire and STS-45 at Hatherop Castle, near Fairford in Gloucestershire. Over the next four weeks they underwent preliminary training very similar in nature to that which they had received at Area B, before moving to more permanent quarters from early February. Their temporary dispersal to Operational Holding Schools, normally home to SOE paramilitaries who had finished their training and were awaiting deployment, was necessary because conversion work at the location earmarked as the Jedburgh training establishment, Milton Hall near Peterborough in northern Cambridgeshire (ME-65, but also known to Americans as Area D; it did not receive an STS designation as an extra security measure) was running behind schedule, and there was no single available secure location suitable – or perhaps big enough – for them all.

Even before the coming of the American Jedburgh Officers, the first of their British counterparts had started arriving at the Operational Holding Schools having responded to recruiting circulars. By late 1943, such circulars had made the rounds many times and unit commanders were heartily sick of losing trained officers; considerable persuasive pressure had to be applied before enough suitably qualified men were released, though some candidates were more freely available: Capts John Marchant of the Wiltshire Regiment and Victor Gough of the Somerset Light Infantry, for example, had only recently been released from serving as Intelligence Officers with the British Resistance Organisation, and their parent units had not yet had time to reassimilate them, while others, like Stanley Cannicott, had been square pegs in round holes for years, he having joined up in 1940 and passed through infantry, armoured and artillery regiments, being trained and retrained without ever seeing active service. Awaiting reassignment yet again, he tells us in his autobiographical fragment *Journey of a Jed*, he spied a request on the Battery notice board for 'Volunteers who are interested in parachuting and guerrilla warfare and with a knowledge of French', and duly responded, even though the only one of those criteria he actually met was the last, having been born and brought up in Paris.

Eventually, fifty-five were passed by the selection board and detached for Jedburgh training, and most stayed the course thereafter. The Royal Armoured Corps provided at least eight of the officers dropped into France and the Royal Artillery six. Officers already serving with SOE volunteered, too, including Maj Henry Coombe-Tennant, who was replaced as the head of the Jedburgh Section initially by Maj F O'Brien and then, when that post took on a new importance with the Jeds' transition to operational status, by Lt-Col DLG Carleton-Smith (Henry Coxe stayed on as his deputy, and was soon promoted to equal him in rank). The most senior (and by far the oldest, at fifty-something) Jedburgh, Lt-Col Jim Hutchinson, came from SOE too, where he had been head of RF Section, although there is some confusion about his true role – he was trained at Milton Hall and inserted as a member of team, Isaac, which was soon converted into an Inter-Allied Mission, Verveine, with broader responsibilities. Hutchinson, who had reason to believe that the German security services knew his identity and perhaps even had photographs of him, went to considerable lengths to alter his appearance, including plastic surgery which changed the profile of his nose and chin, reducing the former and augmenting the latter by a piece of bone removed from his hip. He claimed in his autobiographical *That Drug Danger* to have been successful to the point that his own son did not recognise him but colleagues at SOE disagreed. Even the man appointed as deputy commandant of the selection board at Stodham Park, Maj Mike 'Bing' Crosby, volunteered, and led team Graham in Provence; one of his Testing Officers, Capt David Stern, who went on to become an instructor at Milton Hall, did likewise, and led team John. Crosby also wrote about his experiences as a Jedburgh, in *Irregular Soldier*, as did three other Americans, Stewart Alsop (*Sub Rosa*), William Colby (*Honourable Men*) and John Singlaub (*Hazardous Duty*).

It was accepted that the training of suitable radio operators would take longer than that of Jedburgh officers, for they had a much more complex task to perform. In addition to the combat and fieldcraft skills they would need to survive in enemy-held territory, they had to know how to site, set up and operate their sets, to be able to repair them using such materials as they could find and, if necessary, adapt other equipment to their needs. They had also to master the art of coding and decoding, though that was simplified by the decision to adopt one-time pads, the safest and surest non-mechanical method of translating clear-text messages into cypher and vice-versa.

Canfield had imposed on himself a deadline of 1 December for the US signallers to arrive in the UK, but missed it by a month, due to the difficulties he had had in recruiting sufficient men. A visit by recruiters to the High-Speed Radio Operator School at Fort Monmouth, New Jersey, produced six candidates; the USAAF's Radio Operator and Mechanic School at Scott Field, Illinois, produced nine, and six US

Navy signallers then training at the OSS Communications School also volunteered. More came from the very much larger Signals Corps Morse Code School at Camp Crowder, Missouri, but, as one student of the Jedburgh programme was to observe, 'when the nature of the assignment was made clear, three-fourths [of the two hundred or so who had expressed an interest] decided that parachute training and operating behind enemy lines were not for them'. Robert Kehoe, then twenty years old and in the US Army since September 1942, who was to become team Frederick's radio operator, was one of those recruited at Camp Crowder:

> One lunch hour an announcement came over the loudspeaker requesting qualified radio operators interested in volunteering for immediate overseas assignment. Many responded, but the numbers dwindled as details emerged: two years of college preferred; some training in French or another European language; willingness and ability to qualify as a parachutist; and the likelihood of a dangerous assignment. For those still interested, there was a personal interview. Some 25 of those who passed through this gauntlet were selected. Friends made during these months at Camp Crowder generally agreed I was a fool – but with some hint of envy. The haze of mystery surrounding the assignment provoked interest as well as annoyance. We soon found ourselves en route to Washington, where a few more people were added – from the Signal Corps, the Air Force, and even from the Navy – bringing the total to about 40 qualified radio operator volunteers. Twenty-eight continued on to complete the training program and become members of the Jedburgh teams.

From the surviving records it is clear that Kehoe actually underestimated the success of the recruitment effort, for the records show that the total selected for training came to sixty-two, and that over forty of them stayed the course.

They boarded RMS *Queen Mary* on 23 December, together with around 15,000 other American troops, and spent a very uncomfortable Christmas crossing the North Atlantic at high speed to arrive in a foggy Glasgow on New Year's Eve. If they thought of celebrating Hogmanay in its public houses they were to be disappointed, for they were put aboard a southbound train immediately, and arrived next day at Henley-on-Thames, where they were accommodated in huts in the grounds of a large house named Countess Gardens. Their technical instruction took place at nearby Fawley Court, SOE's STS-54, which was not only a training school but also an operational communications centre. It began within days of their arrival, when they were introduced to the newly developed Type B3 Mk II (known as the B2) and Type 46/1 (the Jedset) radio transceivers, the MCR 1 receiver, and the variety of accessories, especially generators, which went with them. Already established at Fawley Court were the forty-five British signallers who remained, out of some sixty who had volunteered two months earlier. Sgt Arthur Brown, who deployed as radio operator of team Quinine, and who wrote a short history of the Jedburghs in 1991, tells us that all save one from the Royal Air Force, a lone infantryman from the Royal Berkshires and four from the Royal Corps of Signals came from the Royal Armoured Corps. While at Fawley Court, where they remained for a month, the American signallers were subjected to a simplified version of the assessment course, and sixteen were rejected as unsuitable, while ten more dropped out following a general slump in morale. One W/T instructor at Fawley Court and later at Milton Hall – Sgt Maurice Whittle, who had been a Post Office telegraphist before the war – volunteered to serve with the Jedburghs, and became the radio operator of team Nicholas.

By mid-January, the situation among the signallers had become most serious – the project was short of more than twenty radio operators, and recruiters were finding it very difficult to locate sufficient numbers of potential replacements who had even a smattering of French, let alone the 'fair working knowledge' of the language called for in the original criteria. The solution was to expand the search into the ranks of the Free French, and an initial trawl produced enough to make up the deficit. When recruited, these men were all NCOs, but all were commissioned as *Sous-Lieutenants* before going into action. The same procedure was not followed with British and American signallers, although the former, many of whom had been lance-corporals when they volunteered, had all been made up to sergeant or the equivalent early in March.

Thus, by early February, when the officers and their radio men were to be united at Milton Hall, the latter were up to strength (though there were still comings and goings as men continued to drop out in small numbers and were replaced; the last one left late in March, and was replaced by the sole Canadian Jedburgh, Sgt Durocher). The same, however, could not be said for the officers, who, largely thanks to the shortfall in the American contingent, were some fifteen per cent below establishment. A few additional Americans were recruited from units already stationed in the UK in preparation for the invasion –

and two supposedly British Jedburghs, Stewart Alsop and George Thompson, who had both enlisted in the élite King's Royal Rifle Corps, were revealed as Americans, transferred to the US Army and helped to swell their nominal roll – but there were still not enough, and neither was the recruitment of the French liaison officers going according to plan.

SOE/SO had been quite confident that the hundred men they required to fill those spots would be provided effortlessly by the London-based Free French Committee, and though suitable men had begun arriving for training in small numbers from late November (they went to Arisaig, along with the American instructors-to-be), by the end of January it was clear that this would not be the case. A direct approach to General de Gaulle's *Bureau Central de Renseignements et d'Action* (BCRA) and a subsequent trawl through units in training provided a few more, but the shortfall at the end of February was around fifty per cent, and the entire project was in danger of collapse as a result. At this point SOE/SO HQ took a direct hand, and despatched two officers, one American and one British, to Algeria. The result was quite dramatic, and it must be concluded that French attempts to recruit their own countrymen had been at best half-hearted. (There were 'issues' at stake here, of course, starting with de Gaulle's general attitude to his 'poor cousin' status in the alliance and the distrust in which he was held, particularly in Washington. His staffers were chosen largely for their intense personal loyalty to him, and if he showed a tendency to slow his step, they immediately dragged their feet.)

In any event, this second recruiting campaign in North Africa resulted in no less than seventy men signing up. The newcomers did not arrive at Milton Hall until late in March, and thus missed much of the training period, but since virtually all of them were combat veterans, this was less important than it might have been. With the British and American contingents by now putting themselves through their paces, they received concentrated instruction in the areas in which they had little or no experience, such as W/T procedures and morse code – all officers had to attain a basic proficiency, at least in theory, in case the team's radio operator was killed or incapacitated; few were called upon to practise this skill, which was probably just as well – and other specialities such as the preparation of demolition charges and the proper placing of them. That, and the fact that the date of the invasion had slipped from early May to early June, meant that by the time they came to be deployed they had all reached the desired standard.

*

Milton Hall, at Longthorpe on the outskirts of Peterborough in Cambridgeshire, some ninety miles north of London, was built by Humphrey Repton for the second Earl Fitzwilliam in 1791, and enlarged and improved in the nineteenth century. It was an important house, set in a six-hundred-acre park, including thirty acres of formal gardens, and had a nine-hole golf course, added in the 1920s. On October 16 1943, Maj Tyson and Lt-Col Frank Spooner, who had already been identified as the commandant of the Jedburgh Training School, were taken to visit the estate by Col James Young of SOE. They decided it would be suitable for the purpose, and SOE was asked to requisition the property. (In fact, it had long been taken over by the British Government, and at the time of Tyson's and Spooner's first visit was in use as an anti-aircraft training school and home to the 2nd AA Division.) The Executive gained possession, and Spooner and his staff began to move in, in late November. It had been hoped to open the Jedburgh Training School from 1 January, but the necessary conversion work, although minimal, was hampered by lack of materials, and the inauguration slipped by a month.

Extensive though it was, Milton Hall was never going to be big enough for all the Jedburghs and the training staff, and huts were erected in the grounds to provide additional living accommodation. Dreux reports that one of the British Jeds made his own arrangements, and asked the commandant if he could set up a tent in the woods, far away from the house, pointing out that they would have to rough it in France, and should start to get used to it now. (Bank and Cannicott confirm this; the latter embroidered the tale somewhat, saying the campsite was situated on an island in a lake, and that the officer in question would swim there and back, night and morning, his kit and personal weapons on his head.) It transpired that 'Major Whitley' (Dreux changed the names of his *dramatis personae*, and to muddy the water further, mixed up their character traits and histories) or 'Capt Reggie Carlton' actually had an ulterior motive, and shared his campsite with a woman friend on a regular basis.

The staff establishment of the Jedburgh Training School stuck to the accepted pattern, with a British officer in the leading role, seconded by an American. Lt-Col Spooner, whose pre-war career had been in the Indian Cavalry – 'a Pukka Sahib type in his early sixties, with a craggy face and a bristling mustache. When he wasn't sure of what to say, which was often, he emitted a loud, prolonged grunt ...', said Dreux – was to prove a bad choice as commanding officer, largely because the American contingent treated him with far less respect than he believed he deserved. He was eventually replaced, from 8 April, by Lt-Col Richard

Musgrave, a big-game hunter of some note, pre-war, who had less of a 'spit-and-polish' mentality and proved immediately popular. There seems to have been a persistent belief among Jedburghs that they engineered Spooner's premature dismissal by behaving badly during a parade – both Dreux and Cannicott recount the episode, though without agreement even as to the period at which it is supposed to have taken place; Dreux says it was during a visit by a senior figure from OSS, relatively late on in the training programme, Cannicot that it took place during a drill parade soon after Milton Hall opened. In fact, 8 April was a pivotal date, and indeed the change-over to operational status marked the end of the training which Spooner had been appointed to supervise. Certainly, if a change had to be made at the top, for any reason, this was the logical date on which to do it.

The 'bad behaviour' involved the closest thing the Jedburghs had to a battle cry, which, perhaps not too surprisingly, had its origins with the American contingent. In Dreux's version of its genesis, an Airborne officer at Fort Benning, late on parade, was told by the sergeant-instructor to 'drop and give me fifty' press-ups, and counted them off, culminating in a heartfelt 'Some shit!' It came to Milton Hall with the volunteers from the American Airborne Divisions and got a new lease of life as a 'hazing' response to unrealistic demands or anything considered to be bullshit or pomposity: someone would call out 'Forty-eight!'; others would respond with 'Forty-nine!'; more would add 'Fifty!', and the entire group would then shout 'Some shit!' in unison.

Spooner's deputy was the US marine, 'Hod' Fuller, who had already seen action in France as a volunteer in 1940, and in the Pacific. When he departed for Algeria with fifteen Jedburgh teams which were to be deployed from there, in early May, he was replaced by a US Army major, Richard V McLallen, who had previously been Deputy Chief Instructor. There were fifteen staff and administrative posts, ten of them filled by British officers and five, including that of PX (Post Exchange, the American equivalent of the NAAFI (Navy, Army and Air Force Institute) officer, by Americans. There were twenty-six instructors under Maj Oliver Brown and his deputy, seventeen of them British and nine American. All but ten of the instructors, including Oliver Brown, later became operational.

If William Dreux is to be believed, the Jeds-in-training followed their national stereotypes almost to the letter. The Americans were:

a hell-for-leather bunch, gregarious, tough, unruly, and very sure of themselves ... including another lawyer [Dreux was one himself], two high-school teachers, two insurance salesmen, a young bank vice-president, a Wisconsin dairy farmer, the assistant chef of a French restaurant in New York and a stunt man [René Dussaq, the self-styled 'Human Fly'; Dussaq was pulled out of Milton Hall while still in training, to run an OSS circuit near Lyon] who had once done a hand-stand on a ledge at the top of the Empire State Building.

The British and French were more reserved, a quality which he attributed at least in part to their countries having been at war for four years and many of them having experienced the realities of combat for themselves.

Training followed the model devised during the latter part of 1943, and included six weeks of basic instruction in combat skills, a parachute course and six weeks' operational training, though in practice the latter stretched out to at least ten weeks, and in some cases – for those teams not committed to action until near the end of the campaign – much more. Any basic 'commando' training the American contingent had undergone in the United States was discounted. Although there was considerable demand for places at the Army Parachute School at Ringway Airport, Manchester, Jedburgh trainees had priority. They went to STS-51, the SOE facility at Altrincham, adjacent to the airport, from the last week of January, each Operational Holding School sending its entire complement of Jedburgh trainees together, and STS-54 sending the signallers in groups. In order to qualify from the Parachute School, each man had to make three jumps: from a tethered balloon in daylight, then from the balloon again, but this time by night, and the third from an aircraft; the course took three days, weather permitting, and the men could then wear parachutists' wings and draw jump pay. They also got three days' leave, and rejoined the course at Milton Hall, where they completed their basic training. All Jedburghs subsequently made further jumps under rather more realistic conditions, though surprisingly some had never jumped from an aircraft at night until they went into action. Americans who had been through the parachute course at Fort Benning before coming to the UK were not exempt from the Ringway course; there was a very good reason for this – they had learned to jump from the side door of a C-47 Skytrain/Dakota, and that was a very different experience from going out through a 'joe hole' (so named because all SOE agents – even the women – were known anonymously as 'Joe') in the floor of a bomber or, worse still, down the exit slide which led to the ventral hatch of a Lockheed Hudson.

Basic training was to include demolition; physical training; map reading and fieldcraft; weapon training on British, American, German and French small arms; appreciation and orders; tactics, both guerrilla and German; identification of dropping zones and reception committee work; anti-tank mines; street fighting; motor cycle and car driving; intelligence training, with special reference to recognition of German uniforms and armoured fighting vehicles, and codes and cyphers. Some instruction was to be given in the general history of the resistance movement, the geography and culture of France and the Low Countries, first aid and W/T procedures, plus observation and memory training.

During the third stage of their training, which began on 21 February, the volunteers were grouped into three-man teams for the first time. This allowed individuals to form impressions as to with whom they did and did not want to work, and this self-selection was actively encouraged; in practice, all the officers paired off and 'got married' in this way, and many chose their own signallers. Spooner and McLallen reviewed the pairings, but seem seldom to have interfered, though they did have a hand in the reallocation of some W/T operators. As Stanley Cannicott was to observe, 'there were a few divorces', but most of the teams formed in March were to go into action together. Banks tells us more about the courtship process; when it began, the French contingent was still under strength, and since every pair had to include one Frenchman, competition was stiff. He relates that his attempts to woo his partner-to-be, Henri Denis, cost him a weekend in London, including a night at a top-class hotel and meals in several expensive restaurants, plus the company of a number of *femmes de joie*.

Much of the operational training took the form of 'schemes' or exercises; most involved small-scale attacks on local targets – airfields, factories and railway lines, in particular – but teams were also dropped by parachute to remote areas, instructed to link up with local 'partisan' elements and operate with them. These exercises were run with an eye to strict realism, and teams were required to evade security forces, set up and maintain radio contact, and locate and lay out suitable drop zones (DZs) for resupply operations from the air. There were also initiative tests, which saw teams transported some way from Milton Hall and told to make their way back within a specified period, and exercises in living rough in which, after a long cross-country march, they would set up a makeshift camp and then have to kill and butcher a sheep (delivered by truck, not stolen from the nearest flock) if they wanted to eat. Some did, and were proud of the achievement, no doubt, but others bartered their live animals for cooked meals and more comfortable accommodation at isolated farms.

In addition to small-scale schemes, the Jedburghs also took part in bigger exercises. The first of these was Spill Out, which lasted for six days and tried in general to simulate the sort of conditions the men could expect to meet in occupied territory. The second, Sally, tested command, control and communications between headquarters in London and Jedburgh teams in the field, while the third, Spur, was something of a showpiece, and involved groups of partisans led by Jedburgh teams attempting to kidnap a high-ranking German officer. It was mounted during a visit by Gen Pierre Koenig, de Gaulle's deputy, to Milton Hall near the end of April.

By then the Jedburghs were considered to be fully trained and ready for operational deployment, but the invasion had been put back a month, and it was essential to keep the men occupied, so training and exercising continued. For fifteen teams, however, there was to be a change of scene, when in late March, SHAEF authorised SOE/SO HQ to work with Allied Forces HQ in Algeria to co-ordinate support operations in southern France. Since the region was outside the range of UK-based aircraft, it was decided, early in April, to base some Jedburgh teams in North Africa; approval was granted during the last week of the month, and forty-five Jedburghs, plus some administrative personnel, under the command of Majs Hod Fuller and Bing Crosby, left Milton Hall on seven days' embarkation leave. They reassembled on 2 May to board the liner *Capetown Castle* at Glasgow, and travelled to Algiers in some comfort (although the American officers were sucked into taking part in a boxing tournament aboard, and came off decidedly second best against a team which included several Royal Marines and Royal Navy representatives). The teams were run from a base at Guyotville, outside Algiers, with the code-name 'Massingham' – and the Jedburgh missions launched from there, by way of airfields at Blida and Maison Blanche, were usually known by that name – and lodged at nearby El Riath, where they were joined by ten more teams in June.

Domestic staff at El Riath were locally employed, and in some cases their hygiene left something to be desired; Aaron Bank described the nectarine grove behind the house, where 'scraps of toilet paper were dotting the landscape, indicating that they relieved themselves alfresco rather than at a common latrine'. The result was an outbreak of NYD ('Not Yet Diagnosed') fever, which Bing Crosby described as 'half malaria and half dysentery', lasting three or four days. The outbreak reached its peak in July and then subsided, but not before one of the American W/T operators, Sgt Thomas J Tracy, caught such a severe dose that he had to be invalided back to the United States.

During May at Milton Hall (and at El Riath, when the contingent arrived there), the days were filled with more repetitions of lessons which all felt they knew inside-out: small-arms practice; cross-country runs and endurance marches; unarmed combat and silent killing; encoding and decoding; morse code; identification of DZs and setting up resupply operations, guiding aircraft with signal lamps, with the S-phone, a very directional, and thus quite secure, radio telephone and beacon, or with Eureka, a radar transmitter which 'talked' to a Rebecca set aboard the in-bound plane; French grammar and vocabulary, and even – though this proved risky, and more than one man suffered a potentially debilitating last-minute injury – more parachute jumps. And then, on 3 June, as the other teams were in the Charnwood Forest to the north, midway through a major exercise called Lash, the first two Jedburgh teams were ordered to London, to be briefed for Operations Hugh and Harry.

The final composition of the teams sent to France to carry out a total of ninety-three missions (if one omits Isaac, q.v.) was eighty-nine French officers and seventeen French radio operators (all but one of whom adopted pseudonyms in an attempt to spare their families from reprisals, should they be identified or captured), seven of whom were inserted twice; forty-seven British officers and thirty-eight radio operators, of whom five carried out two missions, and forty American officers – one of whom returned for a second mission – and thirty-seven radio operators. Four teams were dropped as pairs – two without a radio operator and two without a second officer – while two later received an extra member each. There was one Canadian W/T operator and one Belgian liaison officer, who took part in an operation mounted near the Franco-Belgian border. Six further missions were later mounted in Holland, and a total of eight Dutchmen, eight Americans and six Britons participated; a small number of men who had operated in France were later inserted in northern Italy and operated there. The teams took the code-name of the operation they were to carry out; those launched from London all used men's forenames, as did some based in Algeria. Others among the twenty-five launched from there carried the names of drugs or spices (Ephedrine and Cinnamon, for example), motor cars (Bugatti, Citroën, Packard, etc), or random terms such as Masque, Minaret, Scion and the like.

By modern standards the Jedburgh teams were hardly well equipped, but by those of their own day they had everything available to help them carry out the task at hand. Those who deployed in uniform – the vast

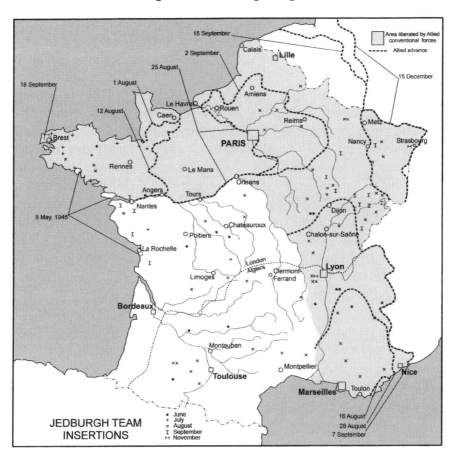

The German strategy to defeat the Allied landings on the Channel coast hinged on containing the would-be liberators within Normandy. For almost two months the Allied armies made little headway, but when American armour succeeding in breaking out in the west, progress was swift. Axis resistance in Brittany, where a substantial number of Jedburgh teams had been installed since soon after D-Day, was soon subdued, and when the Falaise Pocket was closed there was little to hold the Allies back. Long before the end of August they were on the Seine, with the French capital in their hands.

By that time the second phase landings, on the Côte d'Azur, had taken place. Here, progress was rapid from the outset, and thanks largely to Jedburgh teams, not only by way of the major route north, up the Rhône Valley, but also by the more direct 'Route Napoléon', to Grenoble. The success of Operation Anvil/Dragoon meant that large numbers of Axis troops south and west of the Loire and west of the Rhône were effectively trapped, and could only hope to save themselves by headlong retreat. Here the *Forces Françaises de l'Intérieur*, assisted by Jedburghs and others, bore the brunt of the action.

majority – wore standard British 'Dennison' camouflage smocks, as issued to the airborne units, over normal battledress, together with American-issue jump boots; they disdained steel helmets, but their jump helmets were of British origin, as were the parachutists' over-smocks, designed to prevent any of their equipment catching on the exit hatch, which they wore as their outermost garment. Both over-smock and helmet were discarded as soon as they came to earth. Their personal weaponry was American: a .45-calibre Colt M1911 or very occasionally a Browning GP35 Hi-Power or other 9mm semi-automatic pistol – the Spanish Llama, a copy of the Colt but in the lighter calibre, was a favourite – and an M1A1 .30-calibre carbine, the version developed for airborne forces, with a folding stock. Some carried machine-pistols, usually American 9mm UD M42s, known as the Marlin after its manufacturer, instead of the carbine, though some took a British Sten as well as their carbine, as a back-up weapon. A very few swapped their carbines for M1 Garand rifles, despite their extra weight and the resupply of ammunition in .30-06 calibre being problematic. All men were offered a small box containing five Benzedrine tablets, to keep them awake; a similar number of 'knock-out' pills – to be administered to others, and not taken themselves; they had very unpleasant side-effects – and one 'L-pill', a capsule containing cyanide (the poison was enclosed in a glass container covered in rubber which could be held in the mouth for long periods, but which would cause death within minutes if it were crushed and the contents swallowed). No records were kept of how many accepted the offer. Each officer wore a money belt stuffed with 100,000 francs (the radio operators only got 50,000) in small-denomination notes, plus US$50, and each, of course, had his commando dagger, the talismanic Fairbairn-Sykes fighting knife. They dropped carrying little but their personal weapons and escape kit; the rest of their kit, together with the all-important radio, arms and often very large sums of money to be distributed to *maquisards*, was packed into containers or panniers and dropped with them. Many – far *too* many – container parachutes failed to deploy, usually because either the static line was not properly hooked up, or the chute was not secured to its load, and the contents of the packages were smashed in the process.

If the Jedburgh teams had a conceptual flaw we have not yet considered, it was probably the decision to limit them to three members (a serious injury to, or the loss of, one man rendered the team practically ineffective, especially if he happened to be the radio operator). If they had an operational flaw, it was the decision, as noted earlier, not to insert at least some of them before the invasion got under way, and a subsequent delay in inserting others, which can only be attributed to a change at the top of the command structure made even while the Normandy battles were in progress. Operational control of the teams was apparently simplified when OSS's Special Operations branch (SO) and SOE were formally integrated as SOE/SO HQ in January 1944, and even more so when Special Forces Headquarters (SFHQ, in the UK) and Special Project Operations Centre (SPOC, in Algeria) were formed from SOE/SO in May of that year, and were expanded to include French staff officers. SFHQ and SPOC were independent organisations reporting and responsible to SHAEF at the 'G' (staff) level, with Colonel Robin Brook as Liaison Officer. From 1 July, SFHQ and SPOC's French operations were subordinated to the *État-Majeur des Forces Françaises de l'Intérieur* (EMFFI; High Command of French Forces of the Interior), commanded by Lieutenant-General Pierre-Marie Koenig. For security reasons (no Frenchman, not even de Gaulle, was privy to the Neptune/Overlord plan) Anglo-American and French operations could not be integrated before the Normandy landings had taken place, but once the Allies were on French soil it was difficult to refuse de Gaulle's demands that French troops – and the majority of Jedburghs *were* French – be placed under French command.

In fact, there is considerable evidence to support the view that this last change was counter-productive, causing disruption and confusion at a critical time. Credible sources suggest that the new regime did not really begin to be effective, at the operational level, until late July, yet prior to that insertion of Jedburgh teams had been restricted – just thirteen were in place by the end of June, and only eleven more had been added by the end of July. Those in a position to know blame the (tactically inexplicable) delays which occurred after EMFFI assumed control of the operation on the new command structure. At least one accused EMFFI of deliberately holding the teams back, and in the process utterly wasting them; protest at their late insertion is a common, almost ubiquitous, theme in teams' after-action reports.

Most importantly, delay in inserting the Jedburgh teams altered the nature of the primary task they were now expected to carry out. The original plan was for them to disrupt German reinforcement and resupply of the invasion battlefield; by the time the majority of the teams were inserted, however, the battle of Normandy was over. Even a cursory glance at a map which shows where and when they were deployed (see page 27) reveals that most would actually be working to constrain the enemy withdrawal and attempting to limit the damage they could inflict on the civilian population and on the basic infrastructure of France.

This called for very different skills to those required to keep railway lines out of action, for instance, or to disable a power station.

Was there an ulterior motive of some kind impelling Koenig to delay the deployment of the teams? If so, was it a patriotic one? Or was it simply a result of the confusion which followed EMFFI taking over the Jedburgh programme? There is a good and fairly obvious case to be made for suggesting that EMFFI wanted no obstacles put in the way of future claims that the Resistance groups which played a major role in liberating France were wholly French. There is, however, perhaps as sound a case for arguing that the earlier insertion of the remaining Jedburgh teams would have made no real difference to the outcome, that the aircraft needed to transport them were better employed elsewhere on other tasks, and that Koenig and his staff had more important things on their minds than worrying about rushing small groups of lightly armed men into battle behind the lines, to assist in (or as some alleged, take over) the organisation of what *was*, when all is said and done, the *French* Resistance. In the final analysis, and certainly when set in context against the backdrop of the liberation of France, the misuse or poor deployment of the Jedburgh teams probably matters very little; but many of the Jedburghs themselves saw it as an indefensible waste of a precious asset and believed wholeheartedly that they could have contributed even more than they did, had they been committed earlier.

Part Two

WESTERN FRANCE

Hugh, Hamish and Julian

The first Jedburgh teams to go into action left Milton Hall in the back of a 15cwt truck at around 0730 on the morning of Saturday, 3 June without a great deal of ceremony, most of the other volunteers and the school staff being engaged in Exercise Lash in the Charnwood Forest. They arrived three and a half hours later at 46, Devonshire Close, London W1, one of the many small properties that F Section, SOE kept for agents who were about to go into the field. They were briefed over twenty-four hours – although dinner on the Saturday evening was taken at a restaurant and followed by a visit to a night club, a pattern which was to be repeated with other teams – and in the process Capt William Crawshay of the Royal Welch Fusiliers ('Crown'), Capt Louis l'Helgouach, who called himself Louis Legrand ('Franc'), and S/Lt René Meyer, who went by the name of Robert Mersiol ('Yonne'), whose only corporate identity up until that point had been 'Team No. 4', became Hugh. On the Sunday afternoon, accompanied by Capt John Tonkin and Lt Richard Crisp, two officers from B Sqn, 1 SAS who were to go with them to France as the reconnaissance party of Operation Bulbasket, they transferred to SOE's agent assembly area – Station 61, otherwise Hassells Hall, near Sandy in Bedfordshire – arriving just in time for tea. Their Operational Order said they would be parachuted into France just nine hours later, but D-Day was postponed for twenty-four hours, and they passed the night in the peace, quiet and luxury of the Georgian mansion instead of in the fuselage of a stripped-out Halifax bomber.

Hugh's destination was the region between Poitiers and Châteauroux, where it was to liaise with the local *résistants*, assist SAS Operation Bulbasket to establish a base from which rail traffic on the two main lines through the region could be halted, and then carry out such further orders as might be passed from London. Crawshay was not

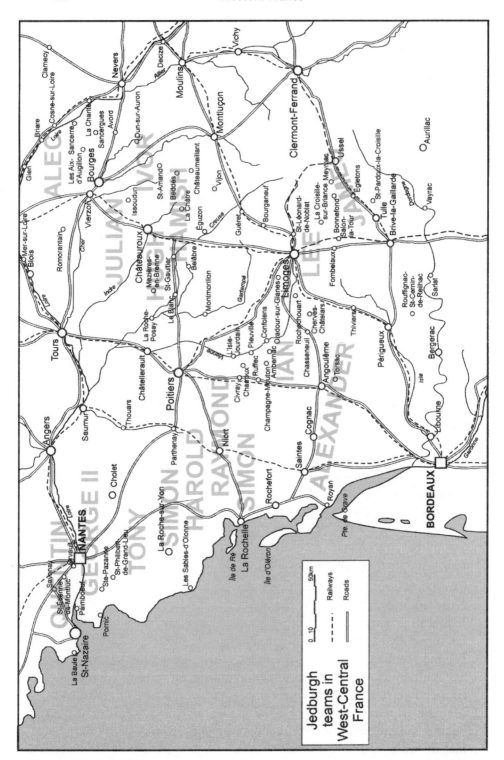

Jedburgh
teams in
West-Central
France

entirely happy at having to support Bulbasket, mistrusting the SAS men's ability to operate effectively and not compromise security, either their own or that of those around them. In his after-action report, his misgivings having been borne out, he was dismissive of the 'Sad Athletic Sacks', as he called them in one signal to London, saying:

As regards the SAS, we never considered that uniformed troops, foreign to the country and its language, could carry out sabotage in better conditions than the resistance. On the contrary, they attract far more remark, and consequently draw danger not only on themselves, but on all the Maquis in the region.

The future was to show that these very factors were to bring catastrophe upon them while their positive achievements were considerably less than were effected by the Maquis in the same period with less facilities at their disposal.

The employment of jeeps by the SAS at that early stage [the Bulbasket party received four jeeps by parachute on 17 June, and used them freely thereafter], showed how little they appreciated the true position.

It is clear that by the evening of his first day in France – if not before – Crawshay had already decided to put as much distance as possible between the SAS and his team. If only in view of the catastrophic outcome of Operation Bulbasket, that decision must be called into question, but in the final analysis Hugh could not have been expected to nursemaid the SAS party, nor would Tonkin, an independent type with a high opinion of his own abilities and a strong desire to forge a reputation for himself, have accepted its interference.

The small party left Tempsford airfield, adjacent to Hassells Hall, at 2300DBST on 5 June, aboard a Handley-Page Halifax of 161 (Special Duties) Sqn, RAF, which – together with the USAAF's 492nd Bombardment Group (H), the 'Carpetbaggers', based at Harrington in Northamptonshire – would play such an important role in the whole Jedburgh programme. Little over two and a half hours later they were falling gently to earth on a DZ known as Sanglier, on the margins of the Brenne Marshes, some five kilometres north-west of the small town of St-Gaultier. They were soon joined by local people, one of whom had connections to a *maquis* group. Dawn brought 'Samuel' (Capt Amédée Maingard), the organiser of SOE F Section's Shipwright/Stationer circuit, and the party moved the short distance to Neuillay-les-Bois and met up with 'Col Surcouf' (Cmdt Paul Mirguet), leader of the *Armée*

Secrète (AS) in the region. Surcouf told Tonkin that to operate as he had been briefed, against both the Montauban–Limoges–Vierzon railway line, which ran through Châteauroux, and that between Bordeaux (or Limoges and points south, via a connecting line) and Tours, which ran through Poitiers, would be impossible since the distance between the two lines – around eighty kilometres – was too great. He promised that *maquisards* could be relied upon to keep the former out of commission permanently, and Tonkin acquiesced to Crawshay's forceful 'suggestion' that he should base himself in the Vienne, nearer to Poitiers, while the Jedburghs operated to the east, in the Indre. The following night the SAS advance party of nine all-ranks arrived safely, and on 9 June the whole ensemble, including Surcouf and Samuel, moved west to Le Blanc, where the colonel was based. The Bulbasket party was detached that evening and given over into the care of a resistance group based near Montmorillon, and from that time on contact between Hugh and Bulbasket was indirect and minimal.

Crawshay and l'Helgouach toured the southern half of the Indre, meeting with *maquisard* leaders and trying to formulate a plan to arm and train the vast numbers of men who were flocking to join the Resistance now that the invasion had come. They estimated that there were over 3,000 would-be partisans in the region; perhaps half of them were armed to some degree, but few had had any training at all. Without even basic discipline they were very vulnerable, and when Axis troops attacked camps in the Forêt de Luant, south of Châteauroux, and near Valençay, further north, they met little resistance, caused large numbers of casualties and made hundreds of arrests.

The initial task was enormous; Crawshay tells us that in the first five days in France they had just six hours' sleep, and that by 11 June exhaustion had set in. Help was soon at hand, however, in the shape of team Hamish – Lt Robert M Anstett ('Alabama'); Lt René Schmitt, alias Lucien Blachère ('Louisiana') and Sgt Lee J Watters ('Kansas') – which parachuted to a DZ near Belâbre, south-west of St-Gaultier, where Hugh had now relocated, on 13 June. Hamish, the first Jedburgh team to be inserted by the Carpetbaggers, was soon despatched to the south-eastern part of the Indre, to operate there and in the neighbouring Cher, leaving Hugh to concentrate on the area to the west, roughly, of the N20, the main north–south route through the area, which links Châteauroux with Limoges.

While Hugh was trying to establish itself, a power struggle was under way between Surcouf and the local chief of the *Organisation de Résistance de l'Armée* (ORA), 'Col Martel' (Raymond Chomel, who unusually for the Resistance was genuinely a colonel) for leadership of the FFI in the Indre; Martel was eventually to prevail, but for the moment the dispute was resolved in Surcouf's favour, largely thanks to Crawshay's ability to convince Martel to become his Chief of Staff.

Crawshay's persuasion of Martel to concentrate on organisation and training was crucial; from that point on Hugh's signals to London took on a more optimistic note, and considerable progress seems to have been made before the end of the month, even if the leftist *Franc Tireurs et Partisans* (FTP) were still being 'rather sticky'. The plan was simple and straightforward: to fit the newcomers into a military framework as members of platoons ('*trentaines*') under trained soldiers who would become their officers and NCOs; and to instil some discipline into them, and give them basic training in weapons handling and simple tactics. All seemed to go well, and by early July Hugh was reporting the existence of five battalion-sized mobile columns in addition to static units distributed across the region.

There was soon to be a set-back, however. On the morning of 3 July the by-now enlarged Bulbasket party's campsite in the Forêt de Verrières was attacked; only eight men, plus ten more who had been out of the camp at the time, escaped, and all the captives, thirty-four officers and men, plus one American flyer who had had the misfortune to have taken refuge with them, were later killed. Over the following week, German forces followed up their success against the SAS by raiding *maquisard* encampments right across the Vienne, and the partisans were driven steadily eastward, into the Indre. On the morning of 10 July, around 2,000 German troops, together with several hundred *miliciens*, (see Appendix A, page 260) attacked a large group near Belâbre. After a prolonged fire-fight they fell back on Hugh's base (much to Crawshay's disgust), and the team, together with Surcouf, Martel and their staffs, had to beat a hasty retreat deeper into the marshes to the north.

At the beginning of August, 'Ellipse' (Eugène Deschelette), the *Délégué Militaire Régional* (DMR), appointed Hugh *Délégué Militaire Départemental* (DMD), not just for the Indre, but also for the Indre-et-Loire to the immediate north; this put a considerable extra strain on the team, especially when L'Helgouach fell sick due to an infected wisdom tooth, but gave it substantially greater authority. Pressure on it was relieved when a third Jedburgh team, Julian, consisting of Maj AH Clutton ('Stafford'); S/Lt Joseph Brouillard alias Marcel Vermot ('Vermont') and CQMS James Menzies of the Royal Corps of Signals ('Essex'), was inserted into the Indre-et-Loire on 11 August with orders to assist. Following the pattern Hugh had set, Julian increased the effectiveness of the Indre-et-Loire *maquisards*, and was able, by means of destroying selected river crossings as well as establishing carefully placed blocking forces, to continue the essential work of channelling the retreating Germans on to specific routes, preventing them from spreading out across the countryside. This both made them vulnerable to air attack and reduced the damage they could cause as they went, and many French lives, and much property, were saved as a result.

American forces reached the Loire by 10 August, and were in control of the right bank to beyond Orléans by 17 August. They did not cross the river, but their presence none the less forced the German columns to stay well south of it, so that their eastward progress took them across the Indre. Facing them, the Resistance forces numbered around 9,000, and were deployed in a wide arc extending northward across the *département* from Châteauroux towards the left bank of the Cher. Heavily outnumbered, their strategy would be not to confront the enemy, but to contain him. All the remaining bridges across the River Creuse were prepared for demolition, and subsequently all save that at La Roche-Posay were destroyed by *maquisards* and the French SAS party engaged on Operation Moses, which had replaced the rump of the Bulbasket party by 9 August and was now operating to the east of Châtellerault. By the end of the month only a few roads across the Indre were left open to the Germans, and on them they would be vulnerable to air strikes throughout the daylight hours.

Crawshay's plan hinged on that factor, and he seems to have feared that his voice would go unheard in the general clamour for air support; on 26 August he and Bobby Anstett returned to London from Le Blanc aboard one of the Dakotas which were by then already running a sporadic shuttle service, intent on convincing SHAEF that there were still up to 100,000 Germans to the west of their position and of the validity of the plan to decimate them by means of air strikes. He got his air support, but a further request, for an American armoured column to cross the Loire and advance as far as Châteauroux, to take the Germans in their left flank and then act as a blocking force, was rejected.

Crawshay returned to the Indre via Limoges on 4 September, by which time the destruction of the German columns was already well under way. That day the FFI liberated Poitiers and Châtellerault, thus effectively putting paid to any chance of escape for German forces who had not already passed those cities. Poitiers had been a staging and assembly point for Axis troops from all over the south-west, and now they were making pitifully slow progress as they struggled eastward. The tail of the column passed through Châteauroux on 9 September and finally ground to a halt near Issoudun the following day. The Elster column, as it became known after the officer in charge, *Generalmajor* Botho Elster, lost many of its number in the process; but most of those who made it as far as Issoudun passed unharmed into captivity thanks to Elster's skill as a negotiator and a shocking misreading of the situation by Maj-Gen Robert C Macon, which is addressed in greater detail in the accounts of teams Julian and Ivor, below.

With the passing of the column, Hugh's job was done. Such Germans as remained in western France – and there were still perhaps as many as 50,000, most of them in the coastal enclaves – showed no signs of moving, and many would in fact hold out to the war's end. On 12 September the team departed for Paris, leaving Hamish in charge in its place.

Hamish

After Hamish separated from Hugh on 16 June, Anstett and Schmitt set out to familiarise themselves with the area in which they were to operate, their briefing having centred on the western part of the Indre. Sgt Watters suffered badly sprained ankles during the team's insertion, and was still only semi-mobile at the end of the operation; throughout it he remained at the locations the team used as headquarters, surrounded by bodyguards (who on one occasion had to carry him to safety when they were surprised by a German search party). The first of these was near La Châtre, but on 8 July Hamish moved to the south-eastern corner of the Indre, at Vijon, near the border with the Creuse, the Allier and the Cher, and from there Anstett set about forming volunteers into three companies, each of which later formed the basis for a battalion. By this time Hamish had become the focus for *maquisards* from the Cher and the northern part of the Creuse, all of them desperate for arms and money, and 'telegrams' to London eventually produced an additional Jedburgh team, Ivor, which was despatched to operate further to the east.

When the Germans in Châteauroux began to evacuate, on 20 August (they were to reoccupy the city a week later, and then held it for two weeks more), the battalions Hamish controlled moved westward, back towards the city, blocking German attempts to use the roads leading out to the south-east. On 21 August they became involved in a relatively major engagement when they denied a reinforced battalion the use of the road towards La Châtre, inflicting over 300 casualties over a period of three days at little cost to the partisans, and eventually driving the Germans back.

Anstett departed for London with Crawshay on 26 August, but did not return with him; it was 9 September before he was back in the Indre, by which time the war there was virtually over. Anstett then involved himself in the Elster affair (as did every other interested person in the entire region, it seems, as well as not a few who had no real business being there at all), and was instrumental in arranging for a plane-load of medical supplies to be flown in to Châteauroux, a gesture which went some way towards alleviating the anti-American feeling the affair generated in the city. Hamish left the area on 20 September, spent the night in Orléans and arrived at the Hotel Cecil, SFHQ's base in the French capital, on 21 September. Three days later the team reached London and was stood down.

Julian

Julian, having arrived in the region relatively late, when the situation had become rather more clear-cut, had a somewhat easier task than Hugh or even Hamish. By mid-August, German forces were interested only in fleeing the area, and were ready to involve themselves in offensive operations only if they were forced to, which made the task of moving around the countryside and establishing training bases for the thousands of *résistants* very much easier. It was the middle of the third week of August before the members of Julian became personally engaged in combat for the first time, and then it was a patchy affair, on the margins of an operation designed to interdict the N76 on the right bank of the Cher; a robust German reaction caused the team to abandon its position, and it was forced to fall back again, on 31 August, when 'imprudent action' by a partisan group sparked a response from a German unit with vastly superior firepower, which turned on them, drove them off and then destroyed an adjacent village as a reprisal.

Julian, too, was involved in the Elster affair, and together with Col Martel was instrumental in setting up the conference at which the arrangements for the Germans' passage into captivity were worked out. Julian encountered the point unit of the US 329th Infantry Regiment, a patrol led by a lieutenant named Magill, at Romorantain in the Loir-et-Cher, seemingly on or about 8 September (this was the first contact between regular Allied troops and the FFI south of the Loire), and Clutton took him to meet Martel. Martel told him that his guerrilla unit of around 6,000 was in contact with a superior German force, and asked for material assistance. Magill, who had no instructions for this eventuality, hedged. The next day Martel met Magill again, and informed him that the ranking German officer, *Generalmajor* Botho Elster, had let it be known that he was willing to surrender, but only to American forces, and not, under any circumstances, to the FFI. This convinced the commanding officer of the US 83rd Infantry Division, Maj-Gen Robert C Macon, to travel south to Issoudun to meet with him when, Julian's report says, Elster 'showed himself to be a very skilled negotiator, and … succeeded in converting the exceedingly unfavourable situation in which he found himself into one of relatively great advantage'.

In fact, Macon agreed to the passage of almost 20,000 fully armed German troops through FFI-controlled territory without any reference to them. The result could have been catastrophic, but thanks in part to the presence of jeep-mounted units of 1 and 4 SAS who acted as military police, there were very few incidents along the line of march, and the so-called Elster column finally crossed the Loire into American-controlled territory at Orléans, Beaugency and Mer-sur-Loire, surrendering on 17 September. From 14 September the column was provided with US rations and even oranges and cigarettes while Frenchmen and women, who had next to nothing themselves, looked on. Worse, from the FFI's point of view, they were not allowed to commandeer the Germans' vehicles (many of which were later sold to individuals at a going price of 500 francs by enterprising GIs – particularly galling since the cars and trucks in question had earlier been seized from the French), bicycles, draught animals (both likewise stolen) or weapons. Macon's behaviour led to American flags being torn down and burned, the appearance of outraged leaders and letters in both local and national French newspapers and a very considerable degree of enduring popular ill-will. On this sour note, Julian made its way to Paris, where it enjoyed some local leave before returning to the United Kingdom on 3 October.

Ivor

By the end of the first week in August, the situation to the east of Hugh's operational area, where Hamish was located, was in its turn becoming more complex, and it asked for, and received, an additional Jedburgh team, Ivor. Team Ivor was tri-national, composed of Capt John Cox ('Monmouth'), Lt Robert Colin, who called himself Yves Dantec ('Selune') and T/Sgt Lewis F Goddard ('Oregon'). The team left Harrington airfield aboard a Carpetbaggers' Liberator on the night of 6 August, to jump to a ground between Beddes and Châteaumeillant, but the insertion went badly wrong. Sgt Goddard's parachute failed to develop correctly, and he died when he hit the ground. He was buried with military honours in Beddes on 7 August. Capt Cox tells us that the parachute had deployed but had not opened, which implies that it was incorrectly packed and that the most common cause of failure – improper attachment of the static line to the aircraft – could be ruled out.

Apart from the emotional impact it had on the other members of the team, the loss of its radio operator put Ivor under considerable extra pressure. Cox and Colin had both been injured in incidents at the DZ; Cox had stumbled in a pothole and sprained an ankle, while the Frenchman had missed his footing too, but with a loaded pistol in his hand, and had shot himself through the fleshy part of his leg, just above the knee. They now had to work the reserve radio themselves, and clearly found it heavy going; urgent messages were sent by courier to Hamish for transmission. However, even if they were of reduced value as a lifeline between the Resistance groups and EMFFI, the Jedburghs could still help to organise and train personnel, and Cox lost no time in meeting with 'Col Benoît' (Col Bertrand, who also called himself 'Dupin' in the Morvan, where he had been sent for a time), who led the best-prepared Resistance group in the *département*. (Benoît had been the commanding officer of the *Premier Régiment de France* until November 1942; two battalions of the regiment, which had not been disbanded when the Germans occupied the *Zone Libre*, were stationed in the Cher, and he was later to be instrumental in causing them to switch sides.) On 8 August the depleted team moved to the Château de Frappon, a few kilometres west of Saulzais-le-Potier and due south of St-Amand, where Benoît had his command post, and began mapping out a scheme to mobilise partisan units across the south of the *département*. On 12 August they received news from Hamish that Sgt Glyn Loosmore, the radio operator of team Andy, whose two officers had both been incapacitated during their insertion, had been reassigned to work with them, and Cox went to fetch him two days later.

Ivor's first priority was to persuade the other Resistance leaders in the *département* to unite under Benoît, and this they achieved rapidly by dint of a mixture of promises and the unvoiced threat of 'reduced' support.

Ivor received its first *parachutage*, organised with the assistance of Hamish, on the night of 14 August, but arranging a reception committee for it and gathering up the large quantity of supplies it brought was apparently the least of the team's worries, for that same day orders had come from the Paris-based *Conseil National de la Résistance*'s *Commission d'Action Militaire* (COMAC) for Benoît. He was to return to the Morvan, whence he had been despatched a month earlier with orders to take over as military commander, and had received short shrift from the DMR there, who resented COMAC attempting to interfere in his affairs. On top of that, a messenger had arrived from the Creuse with orders from *its* military commander, 'Col François' (Georges Fossey) of the *Armée Secrète*, to all the Resistance groups in the southern Cher, placing them under his own command. After some reflection, Cox and Colin decided that the latter instruction, which had no legitimacy at all, was best dealt with simply by disregarding it, and persuaded Benoît that he should do the same with that emanating from COMAC, pending a decision from *their* DMR ('Ellipse'), who had conveniently absented himself and was now nowhere to be found.

In fact, François' courier returned on 17 August, with a message to the effect that the elusive 'Ellipse' would be at Bourganeuf the next day. Colin, who was by now largely recovered from his self-inflicted leg wound, set off to report to the DMR, who concurred with Ivor in both matters. Already, the mobilisation plan Ivor and Benoît had laid was being put into effect, and two FFI *demi-brigades* had been formed. Effective strength stood at around 1,700, but only half were armed. Of the other elements in the *département*, a dissident FTP group, which now styled itself the *Régiment Populaire Berrichon*, had been brought up to a strength of over a thousand; it was still poorly armed, even after raiding an arms dump in the Indre which the AS was maintaining for its own purposes, and coming away with sixty Brens and a large number of rifles. In addition there was the sizeable contingent from the *Premier Régiment de France* which had been swayed by Benoît, some of whom may have joined the *maquisards* in the Indre.

The nature of the task facing the partisans had changed, too, since Ivor had arrived in the area; German forces had left the area south of Bourges, but were still occupying the city as well as a large military camp and airfield close to the village of Avord, some twenty kilometres to the east. Intelligence reports indicated that they intended to begin moving out towards Sancergues and La Charité-sur-Loire any day, and the military commander in the northern Cher had asked Benoît to begin operations against both locations. Benoît was reluctant, reasoning quite correctly that Bourges, in particular, would become a resting place for the flood of Axis troops already moving out of south-western and western France towards Châteauroux and Issoudun, and that even in their depleted state, they would prove too strong for his limited forces.

By the end of August, 'the whole zone was covered with Boche', and Ivor's report tells of skirmishes and small ambuscades which picked off a vehicle here and a vehicle there; but the sheer number of Germans moving through the area clearly made more meaningful operations impossible, even though the partisans' numbers were increasing daily. Against this backdrop there were the perennial supply problems, and here Ivor's experience replicated that of the other Jedburgh teams in the region: very limited – and entirely negative – response from London to more and more heated requests for *parachutages* of arms and ammunition. Ivor received one supply drop during this period – it consisted of Sten SMGs ('unsatisfactory weapons with which to attack columns of lorries and armoured cars') and field dressings – and was promised a share of a consignment of heavier weapons to be delivered to Hugh at Le Blanc by a Dakota flight, which never arrived.

Contact with other Jedburgh teams, save for Hamish, with whom they could speak by telephone, remained somewhat intermittent; it was not until 6 September, for example, that Colin, who had set out in company with one of Bertrand's lieutenants to contact Resistance elements north of Bourges, in the hope of procuring additional manpower, weapons and ammunition, met up with a member of team Alec, which had been dropped into the northern part of the Cher only three days after Ivor's own insertion. Some days prior to Colin's departure Ivor had received a visit from team James, and another arrival at Ivor's base that day was a 'Lt Davidson of 1 SAS'. This is the only reference to the presence in the area of a party from the Special Air Service Brigade: the rest of B Squadron, which mounted Operation Haggard in the area north-west of Bourges during the latter part of August, which was just about to be wound up. Davidson also informed them of the presence of French SAS units at Bourges, and Colin was able to link up with what proved to be Pierre Bourgoin's 4 SAS, also on 6 September. That same day he made the team's first contact with Bertrand's counterpart in the northern Cher, 'Col Colomb' (the Comte de Vogüé), and finally caught up with the organiser of SOE F Section's Ventriloquist circuit there, 'Antoine' (Philippe de Vomécourt, known as Maj St-Paul), who also promised to send arms.

Bourgoin had brought his men to the Loire Valley as soon as his work in Brittany was finished, and his battalion, now expanded from three to four squadrons and completely mechanised, had deployed over a wide area to the west of the river between its base at Briare and Decize; he judged that, with the US Army now east of Briare and the river between there and Nevers impassable to Germans, his work in the northern Cher was over. He was quite happy to bring his men south, but he wanted approval from EMFFI. Colin set off for Paris and was able to extract from Gen Koenig not only orders to that effect, but also a further promise of arms and ammunition.

He returned to the southern Cher on 9 September, just in time to become involved in isolated engagements with the advance elements of a large German column. This – though neither he nor Cox nor even Benoît, whose intelligence sources in the Indre were usually very good, knew it – was the Elster column, soon to pass under the protection of the Americans. The partisans in the Cher, entirely ignorant of this, continued to engage it as and when they could; it was that evening before Benoît received a telephone call from Martel in the Indre, telling him of the deal Maj-Gen Macon had struck and asking him to hold off, and he issued orders to that effect.

The passage of the column through the Cher occupied most of Ivor's time over the next days. On 14 September they and Benoît set out to chart for themselves the progress it was making, and drove past perhaps 5,000 men, some in German vehicles, others in commandeered cars, others on bicycles, all of them in good order, with flank guards manning machine-gun posts at the roadside at regular intervals and truck-mounted AA guns ready for action. Ivor reached the Loire on 15 September, and continued on to Paris, hoping to get new instructions from SFHQ, which was installed in the Hotel Cecil, but was simply told to come back in three or four days time. They returned instead to Bourges, where they received a message from London instructing them to 'organise attack on La Rochelle', and disregarded it as being completely impractical. By that time the Cher was almost back on a peaceful footing, though there were isolated incidents involving small groups of Germans who had been cut off, and were routed out by roving bands of partisans, and a potentially dangerous one involving 'a dissident force of royalist origin (Action Catholique de Charette)', which Benoît dealt with severely. Team Ivor packed its kit and moved to Paris on 21 September, and was back in London two days later.

Summing up his experiences with team Ivor, John Cox was very critical of the support and assistance he received from SFHQ. He said:

From our own reliable sources of information we calculate that approximately 150,000 Germans passed ... between 20th August and

15th September. London was kept continuously informed of the progress of their withdrawal and the movements of the columns, but we received NO ASSISTANCE FROM THEM WHATSOEVER [emphasis in the original], the only occasion when they achieved any results was when they sent three Lightnings [long-range fighters] over which proceeded to shoot up some FTP lorries killing 20 and wounding 30 men, although the lorries were clearly marked with white stars.

In fact, the failure to supply Ivor (and other Jedburgh teams) with arms was not due to overwhelming demand from elsewhere – that was a fiction – or even to inefficiency, but rather it was part of a deliberate policy aimed at limiting the number of weapons in French hands. The reason for this is very straightforward: the British and US governments, which still had little faith in de Gaulle's abilities to unify France, were terrified of the possibility of civil war breaking out, post-liberation, with the attendant risk of delaying the subjugation of Germany and thus either prolonging the war or permitting the Red Army to occupy a much greater part of the *Reich* than it eventually did. The mechanism they chose was the suspension of arms supplies to partisans. This actually prolonged the conflict by permitting many German troops to reach the temporary sanctuary of the *Reich*, regroup and return to the fighting, when they could have been killed or captured comparatively easily while trying to escape from France.

Cox also devoted space to the affair of the Elster column in the conclusion of his report, not so much to complain about the way the Germans were treated by their American 'captors' as to make the very valid point that Macon had run a very grave risk when he allowed Elster's men to withdraw 'with their small arms intact' (though the interpretation of that term was very liberal, and it is difficult to see quite how 3.7cm cannon can fall into that category ...):

We must also point out the fantastic armistice terms which the Americans arranged with the final German column under General Elster. In the cinemas and newspapers the Americans interest themselves with the publicity and took all the glory for this surrender. The Germans were to traverse 100 kms, still fully armed and equipped with transport, 100 kms of territory w[h]ere we [were] forbidden even to set up observation posts ... The least untoward incident could have caused fire and bloodshed over a large area of the countryside, for what could 6,000 Frenchmen, poorly armed and trained, do against

18,000 well armed and properly trained and grouped Germans? The Americans comfortably stationed north of the Loire did not seem to realise this point of view, and the pictures on the cinema showing the incident of a German General handing over his pistol to an American General in Hollywood style, bear out this impression. But all this is very far from reality and from a certain point of view one might say criminal.

Alec

Team Alec – Lt George C Thomson ('Cromarty'), Lt Alain Bordes, who used the name Allet ('Oxford') and Sgt John A White ('Colorado') – left Harrington aboard a B-24 Liberator on the night of 9 August to be dropped to a ground just east of the main Bourges–Gien road, close to the Forêt d'Ivoy. Its aircraft was one of three on the mission, the others carrying seven troopers from 1 SAS, the advance party for Operation Haggard. Alec was probably inserted in the wrong location; its after-action report states that it was 'dropped sixty miles east of area intended in briefing', and it may be that the team somehow became attached to the wrong SAS party. Early on in the Alec report there appears the note, 'Met Antoine [Philippe de Vomécourt, the SOE F Section organiser] 12 August. Decided to remain in present area …', which perhaps supports this notion.

On 21 August, by which time Alec had done little more than meet with the local chiefs and appraise the situation, some 5,000 German troops arrived in Bourges from the south-west, and began to construct defensive installations. As we have seen from Ivor's account, the city was to be a very important feature of the German withdrawal strategy, and was held as a resting place for the following two weeks. It soon became clear to Alec that the partisans' campaign to impede the passage of the Germans and pick off stragglers would have to be maintained for longer than had been envisaged. Leaving aside the question of whether this was the right strategy to have adopted – compared with Hugh's principle of restricting the Germans to the main roads, where they could be targeted by ground-attack aircraft, it ran the risk of encouraging bloody reprisals upon the civilian population – this would require arms and, in particular, fresh supplies of ammunition. Alec had begun requesting *parachutages* of arms and equipment as soon as they had made an appreciation of the situation, to little effect (between 15 August and 21

September, they received arms for 800 men), and on 26 August, Thomson crossed the Loire at Ouzouer, fifteen kilometres north-west of Gien, and met up with the American 35th Infantry Division. He gave them information as to the situation the other side of the river, and they gave him seventeen bazookas, 500 rockets to go with them, 1,000 gallons of petrol and badly needed medical supplies in return. This was useful, but nothing like sufficient to arm enough men to make a real difference, and as a result the partisans in the northern Cher – around 1,500 when Alec arrived on the scene – were much less effective than they might have been.

Somewhat curiously, Thomson's report makes no mention at all of 1 SAS's Haggard party, which had by this time grown to fifty-eight men and was operating in the same area. He does, however, talk of Pierre Bourgoin's 4 SAS, which had begun to arrive in Briare to mount Operation Spenser on 31 August. The Jedburghs and the French SAS soon began working together, he tells us, liberating small towns and villages from German elements which, having come this far, found they could go no further. It was in the course of one such action, at Les Aix-d'Augillon, that Lt Bordes was wounded. Taken to a hospital in Bourges when the city was liberated on 6 September, he underwent surgery but it was not successful, and he later died of his wounds.

The first priority for Thomson after the liberation of Bourges was to put the local airfield back into commission. It had been repeatedly bombed, but the Germans had always managed to repair the runway; when they left, however, they cratered it extensively themselves. Thomson organised a working party, numbering some 2,000 men, and working non-stop from the morning of 7 September, they had the strip usable again in forty-eight hours. Initially the RAF refused to accept that it was suitable for Dakotas, but after some P-38 Lightnings and a fuel-starved B-17 Flying Fortress had put down there and taken off again successfully, supply flights eventually began.

By then, however, Alec too had become embroiled in the issue of the Elster column, although Thomson, perhaps unsurprisingly, was less critical of his compatriots' behaviour than the (British) leaders of teams Hugh, Ivor and Julian, and makes scant reference to the affair in his report. He returned to Bourges after the column had crossed the Loire, left for Paris on 22 September and was back in London three days later. Like Ivor, he was very critical of the support he received from SFHQ while in the field, and like most of the other Jedburghs despatched in August he complained that the team was sent into the field at least a month too late.

Ian

The third Jedburgh team to be dropped into the Poitou-Charente region, Ian, was made up of two Americans – the leader, Major John Gildee ('Oklahoma') and the W/T operator, T/Sgt Lucien Bourgoin ('Mayo') – together with Lt Alexander Desfarges, who used the name Yves Delorme ('Maine'). The team left Harrington aboard a Liberator late on 18 June, but the pilot failed to find the ground, and refused to drop them. They tried again with more success two nights later. The small DZ, about five kilometres east of L'Isle-Jourdain in the south-east corner of the Vienne, was rocky and surrounded by ditches, trees and barbed wire, but all three were dropped safely despite Bourgoin's parachute opening late and causing him to land heavily. Both radios were damaged, but the other containers seem to have arrived intact; in view of the team's orders to concentrate on cutting the rail links in the area, two containers of exposives and accessories had been substituted for one of Brens and one of carbines. The team also brought a million francs for Samuel, the SOE organiser, and emphatic instructions that there was to be no general rising against the Germans for the foreseeable future. Ian makes no mention in its report of the presence, just fifteen kilometres away, of the Bulbasket party from 1 SAS.

One of Samuel's lieutenants was on hand to meet them (though he had been expecting only containers), and they were soon established in a nearby farm. Samuel himself arrived the next day, and passed a message via his own radio operator confirming the team's arrival and requesting two replacement Jedsets. One was dropped five days later, but it too was smashed. Sgt Bourgoin managed to cobble together a set by 26 June, but its performance, particularly reception, was patchy.

It seems that Samuel's original intention was to deploy the team near Châtellerault, but because of intense German activity there it was decided that Ian would move westward instead, to the area due south of Poitiers, close to the meeting point of the Vienne, the Deux-Sèvres and the Charente, so as to be conveniently placed to sabotage the railway line running from Niort north to Poitiers and to organise Resistance groups in an area where Samuel had not been very active. The team seems to have relocated as soon as it had a working radio.

Rather than relying on stealth for their security, Gildee and Desfarges decided they would be better served by force of arms, and travelled from place to place in a car which mounted two LMGs manned by *maquisard* bodyguards (an idea they perhaps appropriated from Samuel, who travelled about in a similarly-equipped vehicle). The operation went smoothly – even, for once, the supply drops – and Gildee seemingly became convinced that it would be possible to isolate a relatively large area and transform it into a bastion of resistance, although how he squared that with his instructions to permit no popular rising is unclear. That was to be some time in the future, however, and throughout the first two weeks of July Ian concentrated on building its forces. By Bastille Day, 14 July, the team was able to tour the region openly, and Desfarges, protected by forty armed men, spoke to public meetings in villages and small towns to tumultuous applause.

By 20 July, Gildee was ready to put his plan into effect:

> We chased the Germans from the zone limited by the towns of Charroux, Confolens, Chasseneuil and Champagne Mouton. This zone was transformed into a fortified bastion. We made barricades of trees and masonry on the roads and the bridges were mined. A complete telephonic network was established and by requisitioning a certain number of lorries we were able to form mobile companies which could be moved to any point which was menaced. In this zone we received all the men who, whether from town or country, wished to join the Maquis. These men were then armed and trained. The principal parachuting grounds were also in this zone …

The exact zone is hard to define, but it formed a roughly triangular area some fifty kilometres from north to south and thirty-five kilometres wide at its base. According to Gildee, a working administration with its own police force (and two 'concentration camps' for suspected collaborators), hospitals and a workshop making uniforms from requisitioned material was established; it had 'outstations' in Angoulême, Ruffec and Civray and a direct telephone connection to the regional *maquisard* HQ in Limoges.

In fact, there is good reason to believe that Gildee was, at best, exaggerating. The signals traffic between Ian and London talks about '800 Germans in Champagne Mouton' on 26 July, '400 Boche at Ambernac' the following day, and '1,000 Boche SS and Milice with armor and guns attacked maquis' on 2 August. The following day, Gildee's report says, German security forces having split the partisans under Ian's command in two, the team made a decision to travel to the south-western Vienne 'in order to learn the needs of our Maquis, give them the order to come down to the south driving back the enemy …'

Gildee's account of the events which followed is, unfortunately but characteristically, disjointed and confused, but a supplement to it, written by Alexander Desfarges, describes the events of that day. It tells us that the Jedburghs left Cherves-Châtelars in the early afternoon in a Citroën *Traction Avant* (whether this was the car mounting light machine-guns is unclear) with two *maquisards*, Louis Mondineau and André Very, bound for Charroux, taking with them all their kit, including the radio, and a satchel containing 1.8m francs; at Alloue they dispensed with an escort from the *corps franc* of the *Maquis* Bir'Hacheim, and continued northward to Pleuville, arriving at about 1500, and running straight into a half-battalion of German troops who, Desfarges says, opened fire on them immediately (it is not clear whether they were in uniform or civilian clothes). He, Gildee and Very got out of the right-hand side of the car, Bourgoin and Mondineau the left; the latter were both shot and killed. The two officers and the *maquisard* found cover behind a wall and managed to get into a barn with a small rear exit which let into a walled garden, and eventually got clear of the village and found shelter in a wood, where they hid for the rest of the day. It took them two days to contact the *Maquis* Bir'Hacheim, who took them back to Cherves-Châtelars.

By Gildee's account, large-scale offensive action against Axis forces (which included many so-called White Russians, as well as Indians, both groups having volunteered from captivity, and also some Italians), continued unchecked throughout the month of August, and he makes substantial claims for the number of dead, wounded and captured as the Charente was liberated, town by town. By the end of the month he estimated that Ian commanded a force which numbered 6,000 men in the south-west Vienne and the Charente, adding, 'We should have been able to get together twenty thousand if arms had been supplied'. The ultimate prize, Angoulême, was taken by forces under Ian's command, says Gildee, before the end of the month. We should note that his report makes no mention of the presence of any other Allied forces; another Jedburgh team (Alexander) was certainly present during the liberation of Angoulême, and team Lee had also been in the area, together with an SAS party and an Operational Group.

By early September, German resistance in the area had dwindled, though the garrison of the town of Royan still held out. (In fact, the entire neck of land between the Gironde and the Seudre rivers – an area some thirty kilometres by ten – the adjacent Île d'Oleron and a large area across the mouth of the Gironde Estuary, the Pointe de Grave, were all still in German hands, and would remain so until a few days before the war's end.) On 15 September Gildee radioed London to say that if he heard nothing in the interim period, the following day he intended to leave for Limoges to hitch a ride back to the United Kingdom on one of the supply flights. Instead, he received orders to report to OSS headquarters at 79 Avenue des Champs-Élysées in Paris, and Desfarges was ordered to Les Invalides, which was once again the seat of the *État-Majeur* of the French Army.

Lee and Andy

Team Lee was dropped on to a much-used ground code-named Framboise on the edge of the Forêt de Châteauneuf in the Haute-Vienne. This was some seventy-five kilometres south-east of the region where team Ian was operating, and roughly the same distance south of Hugh and Hamish. Not inserted until the night of 9 August, it was to operate under the control of an SOE agent, 'Hamlet' (Philippe Liewer, also known as Maj Charles Staunton), of the Salesman circuit, to assist him to arm and organise the Resistance in an area bordering the Massif Central, where there was still a significant German presence, and where outside intervention on anything but a small scale was impossible. Lee accompanied a half-troop from 3 SAS who were engaged on Operation Samson, and an OSS Operational Group, Percy Red, had also been dropped into the area. Lee was actually a somewhat belated replacement for team Andy, which had never become operational after its two officers, Maj Ronald Parkinson ('Fife') and Cmdt J Verneuil, who called himself Vermuelen ('Carlow'), suffered severe injuries as a result of being dropped from too low an altitude during their insertion (in the Indre, by mistake) almost a month earlier. After some adventures, including an escape through a window from the farmhouse where they were hiding, and then the evasion of a German search party – no easy matter, given that Parkinson had a plaster cast on one leg and Verneuil could not put one of his feet to the ground – the two officers were evacuated on 28 July by one of the earliest Dakota flights into Le Blanc. Their W/T operator, Sgt Glyn Loosmore ('Lundy'), joined team Ivor as a replacement for Sgt Lewis Goddard.

Lee's insertion, from one of a pair of RAF Stirlings, went reasonably well despite the sticks of parachutists being dropped from too great an altitude and drifting some distance off target in consequence, but the Jedset that the team's leader, Capt Charles Brown ('Pice'), late of the US Cavalry, carried in his leg bag was smashed. (Jedsets were packed in leg bags – kitbags attached to one of the parachutist's legs by a pair of straps with quick-release buckles – and were freed as soon as the parachute canopy opened, dangling on a twenty-foot line and hitting the ground before the man, thus reducing his mass on landing; many were lost as a result.) Unfortunately, the back-up set, which was packed in a container, was similarly smashed when its parachute failed to open. Moreover, when the containers which did survive the drop were opened, Lee discovered that they had received the personal kit, and one of the Jedsets, of team Tony. Brown, together with Lt Paul Angoulvent, who called himself Viguier ('Sous') and S/Lt Maurice Pierat, who used the name André Chevallier ('Reis'), landed almost three kilometres from the beacons, and it was some time before they were found, but eventually the whole party moved off to the Château de Sussac, near La Croisille-sur-Briance, eight kilometres away, where Hamlet had his base. They would remain there until they moved into Limoges on 22 August.

The following night OG Percy Red, which had been dropped over three nights from 1 to 5 August and had travelled around eighty kilometres on foot to get to La Croisille, and the SAS troopers from the Samson party, left to ambush an armoured train on the Brive-la-Gaillarde–Limoges line. The ambush site was near Salon-la-Tour, some twenty kilometres away from La Croisille; the operation went wrong, costing the lives of the OG's commander and two SAS troopers (a third was captured, later released when Limoges was liberated), but the track was blown and the train retreated to Limoges.

Lee missed the ambush, having remained with Hamlet to begin to map out a plan of operations. Hamlet advised that existing grounds could handle all the supply drops they were likely to receive, and that petrol was a higher priority than arms, for the entire *département* save for Limoges and its environs: and that the town of St-Léonard-de-Noblat – the site of an important deposit of the tungsten ore, wolframite, which was still being extracted and shipped to Germany by rail – was effectively in Resistance hands. (London never did respond to requests for petrol, Brown complained; when the team went to Limoges to negotiate the city's surrender, it barely had enough fuel to get there.) As for the Resistance in the Haute-Vienne, its leadership was in the hands of the Communists, and the FTP chief, a teacher named Georges Guinguoin, was soon to be appointed military commander of the FFI there by Ellipse, the DMR. Guinguoin, the '*Préfet du Maquis*', is widely regarded as one of the most important figures of the entire Resistance movement, and was one of the first (he claimed, *the* first) to take to the *Maquis*. He commanded perhaps as many as 14,000 men in the Limousin in mid-

August (sixty per cent or more were members of the FTP and the rest came from the *Armée Secrète* and the ORA). Brown judged – and Hamlet agreed – that he was the only man worth 'playing' with, and Lee subsequently dealt almost exclusively with him. This decision later brought down considerable criticism on Brown's head, but he never regretted it, saying that 'these were the men who really wanted to fight and who did the work'.

There was no question, then, of Lee organising or training the Resistance fighters – Guinguoin and his lieutenants had already seen to that – and the supply of arms was well in hand too, so in that sense, there was little justification for the team's having been sent in. However, the very fact of its presence, and specifically that of an American officer in uniform, was to have considerable significance when it came to liberating the region.

In the meantime, there were specific tasks to be undertaken: firstly, to destroy the bridge which spanned the Vienne between Limoges and St-Léonard; secondly to inhibit the progress of a German infantry division said by London, in a message received on 16 August, to be moving northward from its bases near the Spanish border. The bridge was blown by the OG party under Brown's supervision on 14 August – though they did not make too good a job of the demolition, and the Germans were still able to use it – and the Jedburghs then turned their attention to the N20, one of the routes the infantry division was said to be taking. A spot just north of the village of Fombelaux, about thirty-five kilometres south of Limoges, was chosen for a road-block, which took the form of a deep ditch the entire width of the road at a point where vehicles could not leave it, supplemented by barricades of felled trees and mines. It was completed on 18 August. The German formation – 159. Infantry Division, which had garrisoned the region between Dax and Bayonne – never did come that way, but actually stayed well to the west, where the going was very much easier; it reached Poitiers in time to form a large part of the Elster column.

Intelligence reports from Limoges – then a city of some 120,000 inhabitants – indicated that the German garrison there was preparing to move out, and Brown and Angoulvent turned their attention to reinforcing the cordon the partisans had thrown around the outskirts and to making overtures to leaders of the large *milice* contingent. A meeting with a colonel was broken up, quite literally, in most spectacular fashion, when a car full of heavily armed *maquisards* drove by at high speed, intent on shooting up any target which offered itself; by the time Brown had recovered his wits, the officer had disappeared. Those negotiations were to bear fruit, however, for the whole of the collaborationist *Garde Mobile* left the city two nights later, and subsequently went over to the Resistance. Lee made a further attempt to intimidate the garrison by calling up an air raid on its barracks. The request was made on 18 August, and the raid scheduled for 21 August, but it was hastily cancelled when Guinguoin brought news, on 20 August, that the German commander had asked the Swiss consul to pass on a request for a meeting with representatives of the Allies.

It was agreed with General Gleiniger next day that the German garrison would surrender at 2000 that evening with arms and supplies intact, in return for assured prisoner of war status. At 1915, however, shooting was heard, and it soon became clear that dissident elements in the garrison had no intention of surrendering, and that a large convoy was leaving the city on the road towards St-Léonard. Gleiniger was never seen again, and it was said that he was shot by an SS officer who objected to his attempts to surrender. In the event, just 341 prisoners were taken, the vast majority of them Russians, out of a garrison estimated at 1,500. By midnight, *résistants* had arrived in the city in force, and the night was given over to an orgy of celebration and recrimination. Brown had well-founded concerns that known collaborators were being roughly treated, but said in his report: 'I will not dwell on this as we remained *completely* [emphasis in the original] aloof from all proceedings since it involved civil administration and politics.'

Lee's work in the Limousin was now finished, and on 27 August, along with Hamlet, the SAS party and the OG, they left Limoges in the direction of Angoulême, which was still in German hands. Brown was clearly eager to get into action; his report says: 'From now on, our activities became more of a purely personal military nature. I was able to do some of the fighting which I had been forced to avoid earlier', and that is indeed how he and Angoulvent occupied themselves, he operating with the OG and the Frenchman with the SAS troopers. Brown's report makes no mention of team Ian being in the area, but it is quite possible that the two Jedburgh parties were actually ignorant of each other's presence. Over the next three days they attempted to mount ambushes on the main road leading north out of Angoulême towards Poitiers but without conspicuous success, largely because there was an almost constant stream of traffic on the road. On 1 September, the entire multi-national party returned to Limoges, where Hamlet received orders to move northward, to Le Blanc, with the SAS party. He suggested that Lee and the OG accompany him, and the party arrived in the town on the edge of the Brenne marshes on 3 September. Almost immediately they were in action again, this time attacking a party of some fifteen Germans sheltering in a small château outside Mezières-en-Brenne. The assault – by the SAS, with Percy Red giving fire support – was successful, but proved to have been somewhat ill-conceived; there were, of course, tens of thousands of German troops passing through the area, and a good few of them turned aside to investigate. The Allied party managed to make good its escape, but was rather more cautious from then on.

On 6 September, they met Lt-Col Obolensky of OSS, who ordered Percy Red to join up with another OG, Patrick, which had been para-chuted into the southern Indre under his command to safeguard the important hydro-electric plant at the Lac du Chambon, near Éguzon; the two OGs returned to the United Kingdom on 12 September. The Samson party had already received orders to join with the Moses party and move towards the Paimboeuf–Pornic pocket, and Lee attached itself briefly to a partisan group which was operating to the south-west of Châteauroux. On 9 September Lee received a message via the BBC which sent the team back to Limoges once more, and there it was decided that Brown should return to the United Kingdom while Angoulvent and Pierat remained to work with the DMR.

James

The second Jedburgh team to operate in the Limousin was originally briefed as team Anthony, to be dropped into Brittany to work alongside Felix and Frederick. That mission was cancelled, and Lt John Singlaub ('Mississippi'), S/Lt Jacques Le Bel de Penguilly, who called himself Leb ('Michigan') and T/Sgt Tony Denneau ('Massachusetts') were rebriefed on 8–9 August to operate as team James, in the Corrèze. The ground to which James was dropped was at the very limit of the range of the Fair-ford-based Stirling which carried them, and had it not been for the requirement to insert an SAS party at the same time, the mission would probably have been mounted from Algeria. The Corrèze is one of the least populous and least exploited *départements* of central France, heavily wooded and mountainous. Its one major road, the N89, runs SW–NE through its centre, and is the principal link between Bordeaux, where there was still a sizeable German presence in mid-August 1944, and Clermont-Ferrand and points east. The Departmental capital, Tulle, was the site of a massacre perpetrated on 9 June 1944 by a reconnaissance unit from 2. SS-Panzer Division *Das Reich*, which hanged ninety-nine of its citizens from the balconies and lamp posts around the main square after FTP partisans led by 'Antoine' had prematurely liberated the town and killed perhaps 100 of the garrison. The following day, a further forty-seven male hostages were shot outside the school in Ussel, and there were other atrocities committed in the region, although none of them approached the magnitude of that at Oradour-sur-Glanes, west of Limoges, where at least 642 men, women and children were murdered.

Two months later, when team James and the SAS party which was to mount Operation Marshall arrived in the area, the situation was very different. There were still German garrisons in Brive-La-Gaillarde, Tulle, Égletons and Ussel, but they seldom ventured off the N89 which links those cities. Like the Creuse to the north, the Corrèze had been an early recipient of an Inter-Allied Mission, Tilleul, inserted at the end of the first week of July; but unlike Bergamotte in the Creuse, Tilleul had not succeeded in imposing a unified command structure on the Corrèze *maquisards*, and there was very considerable friction between the leftist FTP led by Antoine, a warlord by any credible definition, and the rightist AS groups commanded by 'Patrick'. While the latter were more numerous, the former were the better armed; French sources suggest that this was due to the personal preferences of Maj Jacques de Guélis, the leader of Mission Tilleul, and F/Lt André Simon, his deputy, both of whom had dual French and British nationality, and shared a reputation as being somewhat anti-Gaullist. De Guélis had established his headquarters alongside the FTP and as a result of his political leanings it received almost all the arms the Mission requested from London.

In fact, there were very large quantities of weapons and ammunition available to the partisans in the Corrèze. On 14 July, Operation Cadillac had seen a total of 320 B-17 Flying Fortress aircraft of the 8th USAAF's 3rd Bombardment Division drop 3,791 containers to seven areas in France. Thirty-five of them dropped a total of 419 containers to an SOE circuit known as Digger, to a DZ thirty kilometres south-east of Tulle; Patrick's men got the entire consignment and shared it with the AS group from Ussel. An even larger batch – 558 containers – was dropped to the Footman circuit on a ground near Vayrac, forty kilometres south of Brive; all of this consignment, sufficient to arm perhaps 5,000 men, is said to have been gathered up by Antoine's FTP. Cadillac was only one of four massive supply missions flown during this period. To put it into perspective, however, we should note that during the whole of 1944, the Allied air forces dropped 23,324 containers and

10,017 packages into France; they contained, among other things, 159 tons of explosives, 30,972 SMGs, 7,314 LMGs, 26,206 pistols, 7,065 carbines, 35,002 rifles, 241,710 grenades and 1,024 anti-tank weapons, together with 64,652,792 rounds of assorted ammunition.

James and the twenty-six all-ranks of the SAS Marshall party under the command of Capt Claude Wauthier, for which the Jedburghs were to provide a communications link, were dropped in the early hours of 10 August to a reception committee organised by Tilleul at a ground near Bonnefond, about twenty kilometres north-west of Égletons. James and the Marshall party established a base at nearby Chadebec. Reviewing the situation with Tilleul, Singlaub came to the conclusion that James' duty was to 'lead the troops actually engaged in the fight', which was, of course, directly contrary to the terms of the Jedburgh Directive, and he chose Égletons as the battleground. The town had been surrounded and isolated for some time by an AS group from Tulle led by 'Hubert', though his hold on it was precarious due to his men being poorly armed. On 14 August Antoine arrived at the head of a strong FTP contingent, and went straight on to the offensive, apparently without even liaising with Hubert. This prompted the German garrison, which numbered around 300, including fifty SS, to take thirty hostages and retreat with them to a school on the outskirts of the town, a stone-built complex with deep cellars, which was soon turned into a formidable defensive position, thanks not least to the Germans possessing two 3.7cm anti-tank guns and two armoured cars. The Jedburghs duly set out from Chadebec, but arrived at Égletons only after night had fallen, and reconnaissance and an appreciation of the situation had to wait until the next day.

Team James' report suggests that the SAS party did not join them at Égletons until two days later, but the latter's report states that it arrived before them. There is also some dispute regarding the command structure of Allied forces in the prolonged battle which followed. The SAS party's report is scant, but leaves us in no doubt that it was the men of 4 Squadron, 3 French Para (as the 3rd Battalion, The SAS Brigade, was generally known), who bore the brunt of the action, losing a man in the process. James' report is certainly much more complete, but paints a somewhat different picture, implying that Singlaub, who had never been in action before, and who was inferior in rank to the SAS commander, took command. How likely this was, in view of the fact that Wauthier was a professional soldier and a graduate of the St-Cyr military academy, who had seen action for much of the previous four years and was on his own ground, is open to doubt. Singlaub describes Wauthier in his personal account of the adventures of team James, published in his autobiography, as 'cautious', 'a little too prone to do things by the numbers' and 'too traditional for effective guerrilla action' (although this last opinion he attributed to Le Bel).

The first assault on the school seems to have taken place on the morning of 14 August, but achieved little. Singlaub tells us that James became involved some twenty-four hours later, and that air raids also began on 15 August. He states that he and Le Bel organised and commanded two anti-aircraft teams, each armed with three or four Brens, and that thanks to a rudimentary system of fire control, a Heinkel He.111 was downed on the first day. German aircraft returned that afternoon, and again during the next two days, while the attackers kept up sustained fire and never allowed the German garrison to sortie. James' report is rather vague on the subject, but certainly suggests that Wauthier did not become engaged in the fighting at Égletons until 16 August, when 'Captain Wauthiez [sic], head of the SAS decides [sic] to intervene with his trentaine'.

Wauthier's report – which makes no mention of the presence of the Jedburghs – tells a different story. He says:

> On 13 Aug, Comdt Antoine of the FFI, Major de Guelis of the Inter-Allied Mission and Capt Wauthier rendered an ultimatum to the German advance posts at Égletons, which consisted of 300 SS troops and reinforcements. This ultimatum was rejected and on 14 Aug the attack began. The Germans retreated after a short time to L'École Normale ... The paratroopers attacked the school with PIATs, mortars and their normal equipment.

and Wauthier is quite clear in saying that it was his SAS troopers who organised and manned the air defences; that one of his men, Sgt Zemb, was killed 'on the first day' of the fighting (SAS sources give the date and place of Alphonse Zemb's death as 14 August at Égletons, which would seem to reinforce Wauthier's claim); that another, Sgt Rundwasser, brought down the Heinkel with a light machine-gun, and that it was the SAS's two 2in mortar batteries, under the command of S/Lt Collery, Wauthier's 2i/c, and Asp Boye, which were largely responsible for keeping the Germans pinned down and destroying their transport.

Somewhat surprisingly, considering the pivotal role he ascribes to himself in the fighting there, Singlaub then relates how he left Égletons late on the evening of 16 August 'to represent the American Army at the arrangements for the unconditional surrender of the garrisons of Brive and Tulle'. In fact, the former had begun to surrender even before he got there, and the latter put down its weapons the following morning. Singlaub began the return journey to Égletons, arriving in time to learn that a German relief column – it was in fact a specialist anti-partisan unit, the *Kampfgruppe* Jesser – was on its way down the N89 from Clermont-Ferrand via Ussel to lift the siege of the school. Jesser arrived in Ussel that evening, and around that time rumours began to spread that significant numbers of men from the Tulle garrison had not surrendered, but were even then making for Égletons from the south-west, intending to join up with the garrison there to fight their way towards Ussel and the *Kampfgruppe*. Since Singlaub had himself been in Tulle to witness the surrender of the garrison, and since he commented in his report that 'It might be added that these troops were quite cheerful as they brought in their weapons and seemed happy at the thought that the war was finished for them', it is difficult to understand why he was unable to persuade Antoine not to abandon the siege, setting off towards Tulle on a wild goose chase to ambush a non-existent force, just at the time when Antoine should have been heading in the other direction to attempt to counter a threat which was all too real. Had there been less personal animosity between the two, perhaps there might have been greater co-operation.

On the afternoon of 17 August, the remaining civilians in Égletons evacuated the town, and James went too, the team becoming separated in the process. By the time they were reunited just before noon the following day, Jesser's men had entered Égletons and raised the siege. At around 1900 a force of eight RAF Mosquitoes mounted an air raid which Capt Wauthier had requested two days previously. 'While the RAF is to be complimented on the accuracy of this attack it arrived … hours after the Germans had left. As it was, only a few lorries and some equipment were destroyed, and possibly a few guards,' said Singlaub, although the two statements do seem somewhat contradictory.

Its objective achieved, *Kampfgruppe* Jesser, 'which had bivouacked at Égletons for the night', did not turn about and head back to Clermont the next day, but instead continued on down the N89, arriving in Tulle at 1400. Finding the garrison dispersed, it retraced its steps, arriving back in Égletons before night fell. It had come under sniper fire in both directions, and Singlaub tells us that at least one ambush was sprung by partisans, resulting in about twenty-five men being killed and numerous vehicles destroyed. The following day the German column left Égletons bound for Ussel and Clermont-Ferrand; but with the SAS party already installed in suitable ambush positions above the Chabanon Pass east of Ussel, it was to lose more men and vehicles after Wauthier's men mined the road and then rolled boulders down on the halted column.

James knew nothing of this, for during the afternoon of 18 August, while Jesser's men were retracing their steps from Tulle to Égletons, the team was moving in the other direction, towards St-Pardoux-le-Croisille, where it set up camp. It was to remain there for five days 'owing to car trouble', but during that period it instructed the Antoine's FTP guerrillas in the use of 2cm cannon taken from the Brive garrison. Having tried and failed to catch up with Ellipse, the DMR, at Meymac, just north of the Tulle–Égletons road, on 23 August, Singlaub moved the team to Hubert's campsite, north of Tulle, on 25 August, and spent three days instructing his men on the care and use of the PIAT, Bazooka and Bren, as well as small-arms taken at Brive and Tulle, but also sent daily requests to London to secure more weapons for it. 'We receive none,' Singlaub wrote, 'not even a reply or acknowledgement, and gain the depressing impression that London is letting us down'. On 28 August James concluded that its work in the Corrèze was finished, and repaired to Limoges, where the Jedburghs finally located Ellipse.

Ellipse concurred in Singlaub's decision, and decided that James would be best employed at the disposal of the Bergamotte Mission (which seems somewhat bizarre since only ten days earlier he had stripped Bergamotte of Alexander, the team actually assigned to it); James was ordered north, and Hubert's group was to go with it, to operate as a *brigade mobile*. With a more dependable car at its disposal, James returned to Hubert's base, and on 30 August set out to locate Bergamotte's leader, Maj Revez. They found him the following day in Guéret, and were immediately sent north, to reconnoitre the Indre and the Cher. They met with Louis l'Helgouach of team Hugh at Le Blanc and received a briefing on the disposition of German forces and the routes they were using to cross the Indre, and then located Lt Colin of team Ivor, who told them the situation in the Cher, before returning to Guéret in order to await the arrival of Hubert and his men. Ellipse had arrived in Guéret by this time, and it soon became clear that although Hubert's group possessed the necessary offensive spirit for the sort of hit-and-run operation proposed, it lacked the equipment. Maj Revez was due to return briefly to London some days later, and it was decided that Singlaub and Le Bel should accompany him to obtain the material required for the operation.

There is a complete disjunction in events at this point, and one which the James report singularly fails to explain. Singlaub and Le Bel left Le

Blanc aboard an RAF Hudson on 10 September, and reported to Col Carleton-Smith the following day, but somewhere along the way they seem to have undergone a metamorphosis of purpose, for in the report of his meeting with the Jedburghs' commanding officer we find Singlaub discussing 'the possibilities of selecting a new mission some- where else' and no mention of equipping the flying column. Nowhere in James' report is this explained, and we have to go to Singlaub's auto- biography to learn more about what was, by any standard, a surreal situation.

It transpires that Hubert's group, when it arrived in Guéret, included 'Coriolan', whom Singlaub names as Lt François Sarre-Demichel and describes as 'an anti-Nazi Austrian who had been active in central France for several years, working under commercial cover and traveling widely through occupied Europe [though in quite what capacity, and on whose behalf, he fails to explain] ... [with the] sharp intellect and the requisite shrewdness and audacity to be a first-class clandestine opera- tive.' Coriolan had first appeared to Singlaub in Égletons, where he had been working as Patrick's intelligence officer. Without apparently spec- ifying how, he said he was in contact with large numbers of French *résistants* who had escaped forced labour in Germany and found refuge in the Austrian Tyrol, and 'proposed forming a new Jed team (or teams) to drop into these mountains and organise the unarmed Frenchmen into the type of Maquis we'd developed in the Corrèze', which proposal Singlaub put before Carleton-Smith.

Leaving aside the question of whether this scheme had any merit at all, it is a tribute to the Jedburgh programme that a very junior officer could reasonably expect to take such a radical suggestion to his com- manding officer and receive a fair hearing; but Singlaub did, and clearly got a positive response. A week later he was on his way back to Le Blanc in the company of Maj Adrian Wise – recently returned from Brittany, newly promoted and at a loose end since Frederick had been stood down – who had been recruited to oversee the new venture, both to recover radio operator Tony Denneau and James' kit, and to 'pick up several men that were to be used on the new mission'. By 20 September Singlaub was back in the Corrèze, contacted 'the necessary parties' and made arrangements for them to travel to Paris, where Le Bel was even then working on plans for the new assignment.

Singlaub and Wise never did get to work in Austria, because the pro- jected operation ran foul of inter-Allied bureaucracy, though we may speculate that the germ of Coriolan's plan perhaps found its way into elements of Operation Iron Cross, the mission in which Capt Aaron

Bank was to be involved on his return from working in the Lozère with team Packard at the end of September. Instead, Wise and Singlaub teamed up for a brief reconnaissance mission to Brittany, to assess the chances of the German garrison in Lorient breaking out of the enclave.

Alexander

The last Jedburgh team to be dropped into the Limousin, Alexander, was composed of Capt René de la Tousche, who called himself Richard Thouville ('Leix'), Capt Stewart J Alsop ('Rona') and T/Sgt Norman R Franklin ('Cork'). Alexander's orders were to accompany a troop of French SAS soldiers who were engaged on Operation Snelgrove, and to assist the Inter-Allied Mission, Bergamotte, which had been in place since 27 June, to organise the Resistance in the Creuse. Of their departure, on the night of 12 August, Alsop, who wrote Alexander's report, said:

> Team Alexander arrived at an SAS airfield with two other Jed Teams [Alan, which was dropped into the Saône Valley, and the ill-fated Jacob, destined for the Vosges]. Arrived at the airfield it became apparent that no one had the faintest notion who we were or what to do with us, and that furthermore, no one was particularly interested. We located the Lancaster [sic; aircraft of this type were not used to drop parachutists] at the last moment …

Matters did not improve. The despatcher was either inexperienced or incompetent; he changed the exit procedure of his own volition, and this resulted in the three Jedburghs, who were the first to jump, leaving the aircraft too soon and landing some way away from the DZ, Alsop in a wood, de la Tousche hung up on high-tension electricity cables and Franklin in a cemetery. Their aircraft had become separated from those carrying the rest of the Snelgrove party, and the beacons on to which they jumped were in the Forêt de St Gilles in the Haute-Vienne, sixty kilometres away from their true destination. Happily, however, they were only five kilometres from Hamlet's base at La Croisille-sur-Briance, and were taken there by the reception party at the DZ, which had been expecting only *matériel*.

Alsop – a cousin of US President Franklin Delano Roosevelt – was to become a journalist of some note; he never achieved the acclaim awarded his brother Joseph, but he was an astute observer, and the brief analysis of the situation in France in August 1944 which he included in Alexander's report is worth repeating:

> At this time, and in the weeks that followed, the Germans were never in real and complete control over any of the departments of central and western France. In general, they held the main roads ... and the large and medium sized towns. On the small roads, and in the villages the maquis was, by and large, free to do almost as it wanted. It was always wise to get up-to-date information on where the Boche were before going anywhere, and crossing a *Route Nationale* was for some weeks a pretty nervy business, but even early in August it was possible with a little luck and a great deal of circumspection, to go almost anywhere in France, except of course into the towns. Large areas of every department were completely under the control of the FFI. The Germans could, of course, if they were willing to devote considerable forces to the task and to suffer considerable casualties, have retaken any of these areas, but they found by bitter experience ... that the game was rarely worth the candle.

Alexander and the SAS troopers were taken to their final destination, fifteen kilometres east of Bourganeuf, on the night of 14 August, travelling in a *gazogène*-powered lorry; there were no alarms along the way, and they made contact with Bergamotte (which, 'we had been given to understand in London ... might conceivably turn out to be the *Gestapo* in sheep's clothing') without delay. In fact, the Mission, under Maj Revez, had managed to impose a unified command structure on the very diverse Resistance groups to be found in the area; they too had benefited from Operation Cadillac as well as other massive supply drops, and as a result the Resistance in the Creuse was as well armed as it was organised. The *maquisards* did not have things their own way, however, for on 15 July *Kampfgruppe* Jesser, composed of two mechanised battalions specially trained for counter-terrorist operations, arrived in the area. It immediately began a most effective series of *ratissages*, attacking and dispersing the Mission Bergamotte command post on 17 July. It remained in the Creuse for almost a month, mounting sixteen separate raids and causing serious disruption to Resistance operations, before moving on into the *département* of Puy-de-Dôme the day before Alexander arrived. Its achievements were short-lived, however, and as soon as it left, the partisans reassembled; their weapons stocks were not seriously depleted and they were soon again in effective control of much of the Creuse.

On 18 August Alexander contacted Ellipse, who agreed that there was very little work for the team in the Creuse, and ordered it to move to the northern Dordogne instead, specifically, it seems, to attempt to reconcile two effective but mutually antagonistic Resistance groups – one Communist and one most emphatically not. The team could not take a direct route, but instead was passed by way of the Corrèze, arriving at Égletons just as the battle between the German forces beseiged in the school and the FTP, supported by the SAS party and Jedburgh team James, had reached its conclusion. Alexander spent one night at Égletons, moved to Thiviers, a Resistance stronghold in the northern Dordogne, and then on to Périgueux to find 'the whole town in a delirium, with dancing in the streets and spontaneous public demonstrations in every direction. We ourselves were very nearly killed with kindness'. Later the team moved to Rouffignac-St-Cernin-de-Reilhac, where the FTP group was based, and met with its leader, 'Louis' (Cmdt Parouty) and also the chief of the rightist band, the *Régiment* RAC, Lt-Col Rodolphe Cézard. French sources tell us that the two disliked each other intensely for ideological reasons, and Alsop was to say that while Louis was always friendly to the Jeds, 'he remained secretive and suspicious of us; de la Tousche was from St-Cyr [the French officers' school] and therefore an enemy in the class struggle, and I, myself, an American, would never be anything but a dirty capitalist'.

To begin with, they had very little success in convincing the two ideologically opposed groups to co-operate, but since there was a strong German presence in Ribérac and Mussidan, twenty-five kilometres apart, to the west of Périgueux, and the two could be allocated one each as an objective, this presented no particular problem. Over the next week, partisan forces slowly drove the Germans westward, towards Angoulême, which was the main Axis rallying point on the way north towards Poitiers and the long march across central France towards the Belfort Gap. On 27 August, preparations for the attack on Angoulême began. The city was ringed with Resistance forces, the 2,000-plus-strong Communist contingent taking up positions on the east of the city, while the similar-sized Gaullist force occupied the southern sector. As other partisan groups from the Charente, the Vienne and the Haute-Vienne joined the siege, the differences between the rivals from the Dordogne, according to Alsop, began to evaporate:

'Departmental jealousy is amazingly strong in this region of France, and the arrival of these 'foreigners' had a cohesive effect on the two Nord Dordogne maquis. For the first time [the two leaders] began to tu-toi [sic; *tutoyer* means to employ the familiar, second-person singular instead of the formal second-person plural] each other and to have some liaison. A meeting was also held with the Vienne and Haute-Vienne leaders, and plans were laid to create a general command and active liaison between all units. The meeting broke up with many expressions of good will and much shaking of hands, and the plans were immediately forgotten by all concerned.

In the meantime, organization of resistance within the town was going forward. 50 men who knew the town well were sent in through the sewers. The curé of Torsac [a village to the south], a marvellous character, provided the chief means of providing arms to the resistance movement within the town. Looking extremely solemn, and chanting Latin incantations, he would lead a mournful funeral procession into the cemetery in Angoulême, where the coffin would be interred with much loud weeping. The coffin, of course, contained arms, and would be disinterred during the night by the resistants.

The attack on Angoulême began at around 1700 on 31 August. It was a noisy affair, but very little of the fire on either side was effective. At 2000 a note was sent in, calling on the German commander to surrender, but he declined, and against Alexander's advice Cézard – a career army officer, who had been captured in 1940 and later escaped – launched a renewed attack as darkness fell. Alexander's pessimism was shown to be unfounded. Soon the only thought in most German heads was flight, and by midnight the *tricolore* was flying over the Hôtel de Ville; there were still pockets of resistance to be overcome, and sporadic fighting continued for some days, but by the morning of 1 September, Angoulême was in French hands once more. Again, Alexander's report makes no mention of other Jedburgh teams' presence in the area save a passing reference to meeting up with Capt Lucien Conein of team Mark, who arrived in the Royan area later with the *Demi-Brigade d'Armagnac* from further south.

After the liberation of Angoulême, the *Régiment* RAC continued its westward progress, liberating Cognac and Saintes (firing hardly a shot) along the way, and finally arrived at the enclave of Royan, where it joined the blockade on about 7 September; Alexander accompanied it, and remained in the area, vainly trying to attract London's attention – something it had singularly failed to do with any effect – to request drops of much-needed petrol and arms and ammunition. Until then, partisan forces had been able to rely on captured German *matériel*, but now that the situation had become static, there was far less opportunity to augment its stocks; many men were still unarmed, and ammunition was low. Alexander had managed to obtain 100,000 rounds of .303in ammunition from a dump near Angoulême maintained by an agent of SOE, but this, of course, was only useful in Lee-Enfield rifles and Brens, and the *Régiment* RAC had few of either. There was no reply from London, and eventually, during the last week of September, Alsop set off in search of supplies, travelling as far as Rennes, Le Mans and finally Paris. He managed to obtain 5,000 gallons (about 20,000 litres) of petrol, which was collected from Rennes by a convoy of nineteen *gazogène*-powered trucks. In the matter of arms he was less successful, however, and encountered the same complete lack of co-operation other Jedburgh teams were to experience; SHAEF had ordered that no captured weapons or ammunition – thousands of tons of which had been recovered from the Normandy battlefield – were to be released to Resistance groups, and only very rarely was that order rescinded or ignored.

Alsop returned to Royan in the first week of October, just after the arrival there of the *Demi-Brigade d'Armagnac* together with Jedburgh team Mark. Since the *Régiment* RAC, which was the only formation confronting the eight to ten thousand Germans in the enclave, numbered no more than 3,800 armed men, the reinforcement was welcome, although there seems to have been considerable friction between the two commanders, at least at first. The increase in the size of the force also put still greater pressure on the supply situation, and as Alexander set off for Paris once more Alsop tried to persuade OSS HQ to intervene. He was no more successful this time, but obtained orders allowing him to return briefly to London, where finally he was able to obtain consent for seven plane-loads of weapons and ammunition to be delivered to the partisans blockading the Royan enclave.

Alexander returned to the Royan sector in time to supervise the distribution of the weapons from London, but three weeks later all Jedburgh teams in the area were recalled at the request of General de Larminat, whom General Koenig had appointed to command the entire Atlantic coast south of the Loire. René de la Tousche remained in France, and rejoined his original regiment, while Alsop and Sgt Franklin returned to the United Kingdom. Alsop summed up the team's experiences:

> Our hegira from Thiviers to the sea had been as much fun as war can ever be – always on the move, doing the Germans some serious damage, with plenty of *piquage* (the maquis word for loot) it had been exciting and exhilarating.

George

Team George was originally destined for the Morbihan in southern Brittany, to operate under the orders of the commander of 4 (French) SAS's Operation Dingson, Cmdt Pierre Bourgoin. It was was led by a Frenchman, Captain Philippe Ragueneau, who called himself Érard ('Save'; he had been one of the conspirators who assassinated the Pétainist Admiral François Darlan in Algiers in December 1942), with an American, Captain Paul Cyr ('Wigton'), as his deputy and S/Lt Christian Gay, who took the *nom de guerre* Lejeune ('Rupee'), as radio operator. The team was briefed simultaneously with Frederick and left Fairford aboard a Stirling just before midnight on 9 June with elements of the Dingson party, to be dropped to a ground named Baleine near the village of St-Marcel in the narrow strip of upland heath known as the Landes de Lanvaux. The ground was a good one, and had been in occasional use since February 1943. The insertion was satisfactory, but one radio was smashed, the other damaged; Gay managed to repair it, but it was never completely reliable thereafter.

The team was to report near-hysterical crowds at the DZ and at the nearby farm where the FFI Departmental Commander, 'Col Morice' (Maurice Chenailler), had established his headquarters, even though there was a sizeable detachment of German troops no more than four kilometres away at Malestroit. Chenailler had ordered the mobilisation of the Resistance battalions of Ploërmel-Josselin, Vannes, Auray and Guéméné-sur-Scorf, a total of 3,500 men, the previous day; these men were encamped in an area which ran to 500 hectares (*c.*1,200 acres), and the situation was fast getting out of hand in a number of senses. Bourgoin was deeply moved by the exultant spirit of the people but he quickly realised that the *kermesse*, as he described it (the word can be translated as 'fair' or 'fête', but according to other observers that hardly went far enough) was an open invitation to an assault by Axis troops who certainly knew of the *parachutages*.

Over the next eight nights further drops were made to Baleine, sometimes by as many as thirty aircraft, and a large dump of weapons was established. The arrival of four armed jeeps on the night of 17 June (the same night that the Bulbasket SAS party received its jeeps; these were the first combat parachute drops of the vehicles) was perhaps the last straw, for at dawn the next day, Sunday 18 June, two cars from a *Feldgendarmerie* detachment arrived to investigate. One was destroyed by a PIAT anti-tank bomb fired by an SAS trooper, the other escaped but was later destroyed by machine-gun fire. Four Germans were killed and three were captured, but the eighth escaped, and succeeded in reaching the *Wehrmacht* garrison at nearby Malestroit. By 0830 the base had come under attack by perhaps 200 infantrymen, and by early afternoon the assault force probably numbered 3,000. Bourgoin called in the Allied Tactical Air Force, and between 1530 and 1630 a squadron of P-47 Thunderbolts bombarded the attackers, but with limited results, due to the enemy infantry and supporting armoured cars taking cover in woodland. By 1900, Bourgoin and Morice had concluded that dispersal was the only valid option, and gave orders accordingly, the *résistants*' retreat being covered by the SAS. The pull-out started at 2200, as darkness fell; by morning, the would-be guerrillas and the parachutists had gone, taking only such *matériel* as they could carry.

Almost all the accounts of pitched battles between partisans and Axis forces include casualty figures which are hard to credit because they are so heavily unbalanced, and St-Marcel is no exception. By apparently reliable French sources we are told that forty-two Frenchmen died there, including six SAS parachutists (SAS sources put the figure at eight); around sixty were wounded and fifteen (including three recently arrived SAS troopers who had escaped the Samwest débâcle) were captured and later killed, while a report by a *Wehrmacht* inquiry put the Axis dead (many were Georgian or Ukrainian 'cossacks') at over three hundred, with more than a thousand wounded. For the next three weeks, German patrols scoured the countryside, arresting and later shooting, or simply killing on the spot, anyone of whom they were at all suspicious. The Resistance claimed St-Marcel as a great victory in consequence of the casualty figures, but it is hard to justify that by more rational standards, for not only were the *maquisards* – and the SAS party – scattered to the winds, but most of the ammunition and explosives they had received, together with some 5,000 weapons of various sorts which had still to be distributed, had been irretrievably lost or destroyed, most of them when the supply dump was blown up to prevent its falling into enemy hands.

By the night of June 17, Jedburgh team George had concluded that it could not improve the situation in the Morbihan in any material way. The Resistance groups had a unified command structure; all were well-armed, and the SAS, in conjunction with a considerable number of experienced soldiers among the ranks of the *maquisards*, could be relied upon to set up a weapons and tactics training programme. They agreed with Bourgoin, Morice and 'Hauteur' ('Cmdt Villecourt', whose true name was perhaps Barthélemy, the COMAC *délégué*, who had been in the area for some time) and 'Fonction' ('Cmdt Martel'; Maj Alex Willk of SOE, who had parachuted in just days before) that they would shift their operation to the Loire-Inférieur (now the Loire-Atlantique), to the south-east, and planned to make the move the next day. A signal to that effect was sent to London. Team Gregory, which was to have jumped into Baleine the following night and proceed from there to the Loire-Inférieur, was stood down, and George took over its mission.

The German attack disrupted that plan but only delayed George's departure by twenty-four hours. The team set off on 19 June, accompanied by Hauteur and Fonction, who had orders to operate jointly as DMR with responsibility for the Loire-Inférieure and the surrounding *départements*. So heavy was Axis activity in the area that they had only reached Questembert, barely fifteen kilometres from St-Marcel, by 26 June, and still had over eighty kilometres to go to their objective, a partisan base near the village of Saffré, forty kilometres due north of Nantes, where 'Kinley', a *chef divisionaire* of the FFI, was believed to be located. Hauteur, dressed in civilian clothes, went into Questembert, and by chance encountered Jean-Pierre, one of his liaison agents. He obtained the use of a truck, and by early the following afternoon they arrived at Saffré, to a tumultuous welcome from an enthusiastic but largely unarmed band, about 200 strong. Kinley was not there, but was due to arrive the following morning.

Shortly after dawn, the sound of vehicles could be heard from all directions. Minutes later, George was on the run again. It proved impossible to break through the German cordon, and instead the Jedburghs were forced to go to ground in the dense undergrowth, remaining there all day. As darkness fell, George, together with Hauteur, crept away; of Fonction there was no sign, but they met up with him and Jean-Pierre later.

They reached the village of Puceul that night, and stayed near there for two days while the situation stabilised. Jean-Pierre, meanwhile, set off on a bicycle for Ancenis, on the River Loire, fifty kilometres to the south-east, where his parents lived. Surprisingly, the Jedburghs had managed to hang on to much of their kit, including their radio, but by now its performance had deteriorated to the point where Christian Gay was sure that his transmissions were not getting through to London, and he ceased trying until he could obtain new batteries.

On 4 July, by now established in a safe house near Ancenis, the joint DMRs suggested that Ragueneau should accept the responsibilities of *Délégué Militaire* for the Loire-Inférieure. This, it was pointed out, would allow Hauteur and Fonction to address wider issues, and Ragueneau agreed, allbeit reluctantly, realising that the role would be both thankless and difficult. The task facing team George was enormous, for it had only dispersed elements with which to work, most of whose leaders were only interested in establishing a power base which could be exploited post-liberation. The Loire-Inférieure had long been riddled with effective *Sipo*-SD agents; they had crushed resistance there by means of a series of brutal *actions*, and seen to it that any would-be partisan group was broken up as soon as it showed signs of becoming active. In consequence, there was a pervasive atmosphere of mutual mistrust throughout the *département* which was being exploited whole-heartedly by a number of individuals, each with his own agenda and ambitions. Ragueneau wrote:

> The political situation was a nightmare. However, with some difficulty we succeeded to distinguish four categories:
>
> a. The political groups interested in resistance.
> b. The resistance groups interested in politics.
> c. The political groups pretending to be interested in the resistance but only really interested in politics
> d. The resistance groups not interested in politics (these being the angels).
>
> Each category included a good many independent groups, each one naturally suspecting the other. The leaders issued daily orders 'to kill the traitors', in other words, the other leaders.

George remained in the area, first at La Roche-Blanche and then near the small town of Varades, until the end of the month. Ragueneau eventually made contact with an important *résistant*, the leader of the Liberation-Nord group in the *département*, who had been arrested, had escaped and was now on the run from the *Gestapo*. This man 'Daries', Ragueneau decided, was to liaise between him and other groups, and his lieutenant, 'Chassaing', was to organise the best-placed of them to receive a *parachutage*, both to begin the process of arming the guerrillas but also – and this was perhaps of greater importance – to establish George's *bona fides*.

On 13 July George made more progress when Ragueneau met one of Kinley's liaison agents, and then, the next day, the *chef divisionaire* himself. There was a temporary difficulty – Kinley 'hated Daries like poison' – but their differences were resolved through Ragueneau's diplomacy. The same day a courier who had been despatched to Bourgoin's base in the Morbihan to obtain new batteries for the radio returned, and a message was transmitted to London – the first the team had been able to send since it arrived at Puceul, fifteen days earlier – asking for a supply drop to be laid on for 18, 19 or 20 July.

There was no reply, but Ragueneau, hoping for the best, arrived at a safe house near the DZ during the afternoon of 18 July, and met with the reception committee Daries had recruited. As darkness fell they made their way to the ground, and Ragueneau was appalled to find that it was made up of small fields, criss-crossed by hedges, and totally unsuitable for the purpose. None the less, they laid beacon fires and settled down to wait. No aircraft came, and at 0300 they gave up and dispersed. They repeated the exercise the following night, with similar results, and then the Jedburgh leader, who had still received no confirmation that the *parachutage* had been arranged in the first place, called off the operation.

Despite the lack of a supply drop, George made considerable progress in identifying local Resistance they could trust and eventually set up a sort of 'round-robin' conference, with individual *maquisards* placed in secure locations, close enough so that Ragueneau and Cyr could pedal from one to another on their bicycles. By this means, even though it was still deemed inadvisable to bring all the group leaders together, an outline table of organisation and a rough plan for concerted action was devised. The Jedburgh team had also embarked on a very basic programme of sabotage and demolition, using old and unstable explosives and some material stolen from the Germans. It managed to cut the railway line which followed the river between Nantes and Angers and the line which ran southwards towards La Rochelle; disabled two locks on the canal which linked Nantes with Brest; blew up a small petrol dump, and ambushed a convoy after blocking the road by felling trees across it.

For the remainder of July, George attempted to contact London, sending request after request for supply drops to grounds which were proving very difficult to locate in an area where small farms – with small fields – were the norm, and where there were very few open, uncultivated spaces. The Germans, too, were no less persistent in their efforts to catch the Jedburghs; on more than one occasion, the reception party arrived at a DZ to find it ringed with troops and *miliciens*. Radio locator trucks were proving very troublesome, as were two sophisticated static listening posts, one at Beaucouze, west of Angers, the other at Ingrandes, east of Varades. Gay had to travel considerable distances on his bicycle to find a suitable place from which to transmit, keeping the message as short as possible. Because he often left out essential corroborative phrases, SFHQ became increasingly convinced that George had been captured, and that its codes had passed into the hands of the *Gestapo* – a suspicion which had its roots in the fifteen-day period when the team had been off the air entirely. London made no effort to discover the truth of the matter – and could have done so by simply consulting Hauteur, with whom both SFHQ and team George were in contact; this, it later emerged, was the reason why George's requests for resupply were not being even acknowledged.

While there had been no German activity around the Varedes safe house since it had moved in, the team's presence in the locality was widely known, and Ragueneau became increasingly uneasy about remaining there. During the last week of July George moved again, eight or nine kilometres north, to the village of St-Sigismond, where it was to remain until it was overrun by the advancing American 3rd Army. By now, Ragueneau and Cyr had become frustrated to the point of despair by their continuing inability to attract London's attention:

We had one constant preoccupation which was becoming a real nightmare; arms, arms, arms and money. The reorganization of the department was going very well owing to constant contacts, inspections and meetings with leaders and men, but they were all begging for weapons, ammunition and money. We foresaw the moment coming when the famous message would ring out *'Le chapeau de Napoléon, est-il toujours à Perros-Guirrec?'* ['Is Napoléon's hat still at Perros-Guirrec?', the signal for general guerilla war.] We would never understand why the planes never arrived nor why we did not even get clear replies to our messages ...

When we received the message giving us the order to attack [it was broadcast on the evening of 2 August], as we were about to be overrun without having received the armament for the 4,000 men we had at that time organized and for the 5,000 who would very soon be ready, we cried like kids considering our useless [radio] set, our useless work and all the dangers the patriots of Loire-Inférieure had gone through to get to that point, remembering how many guys in prison or under the earth had paid for the trouble they had looking for useless grounds and organizing useless reception committees for planes which never came.

Then, just days after the mobilisation signal was received, with no warning and no introduction, a man known as 'Col Félix' (Vaudel) arrived and announced that he was the Departmental military chief, sent by EMFFI. He knew all the correct recognition phrases, and insisted that Fonction would vouch for him. Ragueneau was understandably suspicious, but sent a messenger to Fonction and received back information which allowed him to validate the newcomer's identity. The authority Vaudel brought enabled him and Ragueneau to cut away much of the dead wood and actually realise the theoretical Resistance organisation George had so painstakingly created over the previous month. But the problem of how to arm the partisans was to remain unresolved for some time, and even as late as the second week of August they were reliant on weapons stolen or captured from German troops. But then, Cyr and Félix met an American unit and were taken to VIII Corps HQ; they passed detailed information on the deployment of Axis forces along the north bank of the Loire, and were able to set up a supply operation to bring arms to the partisans of the lower Loire.

During the next week, the partisans' primary task was to be intelligence-gathering along the line-of-march the Americans would follow, up the right bank of the Loire towards Angers and Tours. They also took on the role of flank guards, preventing the retreating German forces to the south of the river from crossing it. Not all the German forces in the region were intent on escape, however, and when the flood had passed, the FFI units George had helped to organise, stiffened by parties from 3 SAS (3 French Para), which had mounted independent operations further south, concentrated on containing the large number of Germans who had withdrawn into St-Nazaire and the neck of land across the Loire Estuary between the towns of Paimboeuf and Pornic. In all, this force amounted to perhaps 18,000 men. At first they were somewhat undetermined, but soon fresh officers and senior NCOs were brought in to stiffen their resolve. They were resupplied by air, both by parachute and to the airfield at La Baule, and by submarine, and became an effective fighting force which held out until the war's end.

From mid-August, team George's function became largely administrative, concerned with establishing both civilian and military organisations which could take over the running of the region until a central government could be put in place. On 21 August it was ordered to withdraw, and arrived in the United Kingdom two days later. There followed a rather acrimonious exchange which centred on what the team saw as SFHQ's complete abdication of its responsibility to support them, and what SFHQ regarded as the team's failure to remain in contact during an essential period. George's report concluded:

Our mission was done and had succeeded by miracle. We had been running all the time along a precipice and these results had been heavily paid for by hundreds of arrests and murders. Besides, we were feeling very depressed, considering what could have been done if we had received the arms and money we were begging for at the time. In that case we can guarantee that on 5 August 10,000 men could have been armed. Not a single Jerry would have escaped and damage done to the enemy would have been incredible.

It followed that with a long, sometimes reasoned and sometimes rather irrational, rambling discourse on who had done, or not done, what, and to whom, but finished on a pertinent note with a plea to establish a more effective system for checking the authenticity of communications:

But if this experience resolves a tricky point and helps to build a more perfect checking system of Jedburgh's authenticity for the next war and even this one, we'll think that this was a useful confusion and our only regret will be that team George had to be the one to bring the question out.

George II

The team was duly stood down, but if Ragueneau, Cyr and Gay thought they would have a decent period of rest and relaxation before being assigned to other duties, they were mistaken, for on 30 August they were reactivated, to be reinserted into the area south of the Loire at the request of Hauteur and Fonction, who had been reassigned to lead an Inter-Allied Mission, Shinoile. Shinoile was tasked with establishing a transitional administration covering a large area, roughly between the Loire and the Gironde Estuaries, but this included German-held enclaves, and in addition, there were still substantial numbers of German troops in the region trying to make their way eastward. George's new mission would be to assemble mobile columns to pursue and contain the pockets of Germans across the region, as well as liaising with the American forces north of the Loire.

The team was reinserted by the USAAF on the night of 7 September into the northern Vienne; this time all the team's kit and weapons were destroyed and Ragueneau broke his right leg on landing. This incapacitated him for some time and placed the entire responsibility for initiating the mission on Cyr while the Frenchman fretted in a bed in a hospital in Loudun which lacked even plaster-of-paris to make a cast. Although able to leave the hospital on 12 September, he was severely hampered by a lack of mobility, and could only function in an administrative role.

The situation George found in the north of the Vienne in early September was most unsatisfactory. While discipline within the ranks of the *résistants* was good and their morale high, they were unarmed and unpaid, ill-led and ill-fed, and in some cases barefoot. This is in complete contrast to what teams Hugh and Julian reported; we may speculate that what Cyr in fact found was the rump of a Resistance organisation, the most effective units of which had already left the area in pursuit of the German troops fleeing eastward, and that is borne out by reports from other sources. The Vienne was actually clear of Germans by the time George arrived, and it refocused on assisting in the containment of German troops in the coastal enclave between Pornic and Paimboeuf, south of the Loire, rather than establishing *groupements mobiles*. It took some time to organise the move, but it was finally accomplished on 17 September and a command post was established at St-Philbert-de-Grand-Lieu, within striking distance of the coast, that evening.

It soon became clear that reports of the strength and determination of the German troops in the Pornic–Paimboeuf pocket – an area of perhaps 250 square kilometres – had been underestimated; while morale may not have been universally high, the garrison was well supplied with heavy weaponry including artillery, and maintained links with St-Nazaire, across the Loire estuary and with La Rochelle, down the coast. It also had thousands of French men, women and children as hostages (though their release was subsequently negotiated). All efforts by Cyr and Ragueneau to convince the American forces occupying the right bank of the Loire to intervene fell on deaf ears, and it was left to the partisans, with a stiffening of French SAS troops from operations mounted further south, to establish and maintain a cordon around the area and with it the stalemate which had developed. By the end of first week of October, Cyr estimated the strength of the Resistance forces at almost 3,000; while all were armed, the overall supply situation had not improved dramatically, and in particular the men were very short of the warm clothing they would need to see them through the winter.

The stand-off around the Pornic–Paimboeuf pocket, which was to continue until the very end of the war in Europe, was reminiscent of an earlier era: a static affair, with long periods of inaction punctuated by short offensives – little more than raids – mounted by both sides. With their backs to the sea, ringed by substantial numbers of partisans, and with a thousand kilometres of hostile territory between them and the Reich, there was no likelihood of the German defenders breaking out; but equally, with no heavier weapons than 2cm and 3.7cm anti-tank guns at their disposal, there was no prospect of the FFI being able to break in.

In the last days of September, Col Félix, with whom the team had worked so closely during the latter part of its first mission, was given responsibility for the entire Loire-Inférieure; badly in need of experienced senior staff, he co-opted both Mission Shinoile and the Jedburgh team, Hauteur becoming his Chief of Staff and Fonction his GSO 3 while Cyr took on the task of liaising between the FFI and the American forces, and Ragueneau, still incapacitated by his broken leg, became his chief administrator. Between early October and mid-November the Jedburghs played an important role in the transition to French control, but all concerned recognised that this was a waste of their talents and training, and on 17 November they were stood down.

Harold

Of the other two Jedburgh teams already in the area immediately south of the Loire when George II arrived, Harold, which was inserted on 16 July along with a French SAS party which was to carry out Operation Dickens, fared dismally, though whether that was due to poor performance or sheer bad luck is open to debate. It had some initial difficulties, largely thanks to its radios and much of its kit being destroyed during its insertion, when it missed the DZ completely. The team leader, Maj Valentine Whitty of the Royal Armoured Corps ('Ross'), actually landed on the roof of a bakery in a village, and Lt Pierre Jolliet, who called himself Rimbaut ('Tyrone') and Sgt Harry Verlander ('Sligo') did only marginally better. The team was out of contact with London until 7 August, when it received a replacement radio via the SAS party. It received its first *parachutage* shortly thereafter, on 11 August, but that was an abortive affair; due, presumably, to some sort of administrative error at the packing station, it consisted largely of gas capes, and that did little to improve the team's credibility with the partisans. Sadly, the next *parachutage*, on 27 August, also consisted largely of irrelevancies – bandages, webbing, haversacks and socks, although there was some ammunition – to the frustration of a large reception party that been assembled to handle the four plane-loads. Whitty was furious at what he saw at best as total incompetence, and signalled to London:

> Have just received message from Chief of Department that work of your organisation is useless. Reason as follows – I asked you for arms. First you ignore my requests, then you send me four planes full of medical supplies and bullets but not a single gun of any sort. Operation fixed for tonight has been cancelled. You have endangered all our lives and made me a fool. Name 'Jedburgh' mud. Do you think we fight with bandages?

It was not until mid-September that Harold, by now based in the city of Niort, actually received any weapons, from a large consignment shipped by Royal Navy destroyer to Les Sables-d'Olonne, and obtained more from the same source two weeks later; but by that time there were few, if any, Germans left in the Deux-Sèvres. Whitty was clearly exasperated by his failure to achieve anything meaningful, and perhaps as a result quarrelled with almost everyone he met; he was derogatory in his comments on the performance of the SAS party with which he had been inserted (the contempt was mutual), and SOE's agents, including Samuel, who was widely held in high esteem, were by no means immune from his criticism. SFHQ threatened to withdraw the team as early as 12 October after it had misappropriated a *parachutage* destined elsewhere. Although Harold actually remained in the field until mid-November, by that time it had become marginalised and was largely redundant, and the men it had armed and helped to organise had joined the siege of the Pornic–Paimboeuf pocket.

Tony

A second team, Tony – Maj Robert E Montgomery ('Dollar'), with Lt Lucien Paris, who called himself Marc Devailly ('Écu') and T/Sgt John E McGowan ('Quarter') of the USAAF – was sent to assist Harold during the third week of August, but Whitty insisted that there was no work for it in the Deux-Sèvres, and it moved into the Vendée instead. Tony's personnel had originally been briefed on 17 June as team Gregory, to jump into the Dingson base and carry out the mission which took George into the Loire-Inférieure, and later, as team Patrick, to operate under the orders of Colonel Eon and the Aloès Mission (q.v.), but that was cancelled too. Now it was to be sent south of the Loire, and was dropped on 18 August to a 'rather unsuitable' ground Harold had chosen, south-east of Parthenay, landing safely but shaken, having jumped from a height of barely seventy metres which hardly gave the men's parachutes time to open. (They lost much of their 'luggage' in the process. This was the second time they had lost their kit in a week, it having earlier been mistakenly loaded aboard a flight bound for the Haute-Vienne and dropped with team Lee.)

Tony moved into the Vendée after four days in Harold's company, to find the Resistance there virtually non-existent. The three groups it managed to contact numbered no more than fifty men in all, although that had not prevented the FTP leader, 'Col La Roche', from entering into a spirited dispute with the leader of the Gaullist faction, 'Col David'. The dispute was never entirely settled, though Tony made it clear to La Roche that if he did not 'play ball' he would get no arms. He apparently submitted, though with no good grace, and in fact the FTP received 'only enough to keep them quiet' as a result. This decision was to have repercussions later, when London stopped sending supplies and Tony became dependent in part on the FFI regional headquarters in Poitiers, where the commander had Communist leanings.

Notwithstanding the meagre number of *résistants*, Tony immediately identified a DZ and called for a *parachutage*, which duly arrived on the night of 25 August. The supply drop was much smaller than the team had requested, but the speed with which it came impressed the partisans enormously, and word spread quickly across the *département*; as a result, by 28 August some 1,200 new volunteers had come forward. The following day the Jedburghs received word that the German garrison in the port of Les Sables-d'Olonne had begun to evacuate, and that the situation in the town was unstable and rapidly worsening, with rival factions engaged in a power struggle. Montgomery decided that restoring order and securing the port took precedence over setting up some sort of training programme, and next day the Jedburghs moved into Les Sables with forty men. They were none too soon, for a day later, German troops tried to reoccupy the town. A convoy of five trucks attempted to force a roadblock and was engaged by a Bren gun team; the first vehicle was set ablaze, and seconds later it exploded, setting off sympathetic explosions in the others. Another attempt the next day was also blocked. By 3 September the Germans had given up any notion of re-establishing a presence there, and Les Sables-d'Olonne was firmly in Allied hands. Nine days later, two Royal Navy destroyers landed forty-

four tons of arms and ammunition, half of which, Tony said, was immediately sent, as per instructions from London, to Harold (Whitty
complained that its share of the consignment was meagre).

Tony's share was enough to arm around 800 men, and the weapons
were distributed to the *maquisards* on a *pro rata* basis, according to the
groups' numerical strengths. Now, with the equivalent of approximately
two battalions under arms, it became possible to mount offensive operations against the small German enclaves which were dotted around the
département. Much of the fighting was house-to-house in the small
towns; armour would have made short work of the defensive positions,
but since the American forces refused to cross the Loire, the FFI had to
take on the task instead, losing considerable numbers of men in the
process. As more weapons were obtained, the strength of the fighting
units rose, and by the time Tony left the region it stood at more than
3,000 men, all of whom were by then concentrated around the
Pornic–Paimboeuf pocket or around La Rochelle in the Charente-Maritime.

A further shipment of arms arrived at Les Sables near the month's
end, to be shared with Harold, and also with Shinoile. Four additional
Jedburgh teams which were to work in the area – Frank, Quentin,
Raymond and Simon – arrived by the same transport, but with it came a
signal from London that Tony could expect no more supplies. From
then on, much of the team's time and energy was taken up with trying to
obtain stores and weapons from the American military administration
in Nantes and from stockpiles FFI had established there and in Poitiers.
Montgomery had little success in obtaining even captured German
arms and equipment (and the other teams in the area were to tell the
same story), but eventually he managed to extract 1,200 rifles and two
2cm cannon from a dump near Rennes. Even clothing was difficult to
obtain, and as summer turned to autumn, this became increasingly
important. As late as mid-October he was still complaining that many of
the volunteers in the Vendée had worn-out shoes and no coats or caps,
but his requests for uniforms went unheeded even though he personally
visited FFI headquarters in Paris in an attempt to expedite them.

The American members of team Tony were ordered to Paris on 13
November, and Sgt McGowan returned to London within a week. Maj
Montgomery reported to the US 6th Army Group HQ at Vittel, and
was debriefed there, and returned to London on 24 November. Lt Paris
remained in France.

Frank

Of the teams landed by ship at Les Sables on 28 September, it had been intended that Frank and Quentin would operate to the north, in the Loire-Inférieure. Frank reported to Fonction the following day at Ste-Pazanne, where Shinoile had its headquarters, and was to remain with the Mission until 12 October without, as far as can be determined, ever finding any useful function. It was despatched to Saintes, from where the containment of La Rochelle was being conducted, busied itself for ten days 'obtaining accurate maps and information of the sector' and then returned to Shinoile's HQ and reported to Fonction once more. After a further week of idleness it was ordered south again, to Niort, where Harold was based, to supervise airborne resupply operations. The team was stood down on 15 November when its leader, Capt Idris Isaac ('Westmoreland'), was hospitalised due to illness, and its French officer, Lt Alexandre Martelli, who called himself Massoni ('Dumbarton'), and the team's W/T operator, Sgt Thomas Henney ('Cheshire') preceded him to the United Kingdom.

Quentin

Quentin had previously been briefed for a mission to the Vienne, and later for another to the Vosges, to operate alongside the ill-fated team Jacob in support of SAS Operation Loyton. It, too, reported to Shinoile on 29 September, but was perhaps more proactive than Frank, for after a conference with Hauteur and Fonction, its leader, Capt Ronald Fenton, of the Sherwood Foresters ('Cornwall') sought permission to operate with Col Félix, who had just been given responsibility for the whole of the Loire-Inférieur; while awaiting Félix's agreement, he put Quentin at the disposal of the commander of a small American reconnaissance unit, and operated for five days in the no-man's-land surrounding St-Nazaire. On 5 October Quentin met Félix, who appointed the team's French officer, Lt Jean Raux, using the name Lasserre ('Wicklow'), to command an FFI battalion, while Fenton acted as Liaison Officer between FFI and the American 376th Infantry Regiment, and the team's radio operator, Sgt David Rawson ('Merioneth'), took on responsibility for W/T training.

On 8 October, Raux's battalion took over the defence of the left flank of the sector surrounding St-Nazaire to the east, over a four-kilometre-wide front between the Loire and the main road from Nantes into Brittany, between Savenay, which was in German hands, and St-Étienne-de-Montluc. It was a marshy area, unsuited to permanent defensive positions, and the French had to rely on machine-guns – for which there was never enough ammunition – sited on higher ground, and night-time patrolling. Their baptism of fire came on the third night, when a strong German contingent attempted to penetrate the sector, and was driven off after a fire-fight lasting some hours, during which ammunition stocks got perilously low; that set a pattern which was to be repeated regularly over the next six weeks. Fenton based himself with Raux's battalion, politics demanding that he act as second-in-command to his 2i/c, taking part in general activities and running a training programme. He also mounted sabotage operations, laid a minefield which discouraged German patrolling and managed to obtain light artillery from the Americans, which imposed a further check both on enemy patrols and a gunboat which on most nights shelled French positions from the river.

When Raux's battalion was pulled back out of the line in mid-November, all three of Quentin's members switched over to the organisation of a programme of training in weapons handling, basic infantry tactics and small-unit leadership based in Orvault, a suburb of Nantes; later, this evolved into a special forces school in miniature, with additional instruction in sabotage, infiltration and silent killing. Quentin was supplemented by three additional French officers who had been specifically trained at SOE's STS-41 at Gumley Hall to infiltrate sabotage teams into the St-Nazaire enclave, where there were suitable targets aplenty. So successful were they that the team remained with the school until late January, when, after a lengthy wait at the airfield at Rennes, the two Britons returned to the United Kingdom, and Lt Raux was reassigned to other duties.

Raymond

The other teams which landed at Les Sables, Raymond and Simon, had – like Quentin – been briefed to work in eastern France, but those operations were cancelled and they were re-assigned. When they arrived in France, Team Raymond – which had two French officers, Capt R de Hosses, known as Waguet ('Waterford') and Lt HHL Cadilhac, who took the name Chaulais ('Gloucester') and a British radio operator, Sgt Walter Adams ('Kincardine') – was despatched to Niort and attached to the French 114th Regiment, newly formed from volunteers and in need of much organisation and training. The team assumed these tasks forthwith, and was thus occupied throughout its time in France. When Harold was withdrawn in mid-November, Raymond left as well.

Simon

Team Simon comprised Capt Maurice Fouère, who used Fontaine as his *nom de guerre* ('Fernard'), Capt Anthony Coomber ('Coustard') and Sgt Claud Somers of the RAF ('Stephane'). It had left airfields in the United Kingdom no less than six times to attempt to parachute into the Vosges; each time it returned to base. When its mission was finally cancelled, it was rebriefed and embarked aboard a destroyer to join Tony at La Roche-sur-Yon in the Vendée, with the intention of establishing a training programme. The FFI in the region were so short of arms that it was decided instead that the team should concentrate on procurement, which meant, in effect, going cap-in-hand to American and British supply officers in eastern Brittany and even as far as Normandy, where there were substantial stocks of captured weapons and ammunition. In Normandy, Coomber and Tony's leader, Maj Montgomery, failed to persuade the British No. 1 Battlefield Clearance Group to release any material at all from the enormous dumps it controlled, and resorted to stealing a few rifles while a sentry was distracted. The exercise was repeated with American forces in Rennes and Nantes with similar results, although the pair did extract an empty, palliative promise that supplies would become available once all the FFI units north of the Loire – an area clear of Germans since late August – had been armed.

Montgomery and Coomber returned to La Roche-sur-Yon on 5 October, in time to separate the feuding leaders of the FTP and rightist factions, La Roche and David, who were locked in dispute once more, and to take part in a set-piece battle between a reinforced German battalion and FFI forces which had been raised, trained and equipped by the SAS before the embargo on sending weapons directly from London to western France came into effect. The fighting lasted all day, and saw significant German losses inflicted at very little cost, although the Germans did gain some ground, using flame-throwers to force the French to give up two advanced defensive positions. The following day

Montgomery and Coomber, this time accompanied by Lt Paris of Tony, left La Roche-sur-Yon to drive to Paris, leaving the two teams' W/T operators with orders to contact them should the situation around La Rochelle change dramatically. The trip was a complete waste of time and energy. SHAEF representatives made it clear that the pockets of German resistance on the west coast were no real threat to anyone and, in their opinion, could be contained by the forces already in place with such weapons as they possessed, while EMFFI issued a meaningless and, it turned out, worthless, order allowing the French team-members to withdraw material from French stores if they could find them and per-suade their custodians to comply. They did not. Capt Fouère went south to Toulouse on the same mission, and he, too, returned empty-handed.

Back in the Vendée on 18 October, largely disillusioned, Simon and Tony returned to more purely martial affairs, the former finally initiat-ing a basic training programme for FFI units. German artillery occasionally reached out to strike at the French advanced headquarters, and there was still sporadic fighting around the La Rochelle perimeter, defenders making hit-and-run raids across the remaining bridges which spanned the canal system ringing the port in the northern sector. Coomber resolved to limit that activity by blowing the bridge across a canal at Esnandes; together with *Sergent-Chef* Michel Gervais of 3 SAS, who had already distinguished himself during Operation Dickens and had now attached himself to the Jedburgh team, he succeeded in placing charges beneath the bridge, bringing down its main span. Despite coming under fire three times during the course of the short operation, and having to swim a canal in full kit, Coomber and his small party returned safely.

This was Simon's last warlike act. For the next fortnight, Fouère and Coomber renewed their attempts to procure arms, ammunition and – equally importantly, for winter was fast approaching – warm clothing, successfully obtaining 3,600 uniforms, 2,000 pairs of boots and 2,000 sets of underwear and shirts from EMFFI in Paris. Fouère returned with the consignment to the Vendée, where he continued to operate until January 1945; Capt Coomber and Sgt Somers departed for the United Kingdom to be stood down.

Part Three

BRITTANY

Frederick

The first Jedburgh team to operate in Brittany, Frederick was to work with a large SAS party mounting Operation Samwest, based in the Forêt de Duault between Guingamp and Carhaix-Plouguer, in the Côtes-du-Nord (known today as the Côtes-d'Armor). It was made up of Maj Adrian Wise, of the Royal Warwickshire Regiment ('Kinross'), Capt Paul Bloch-Auroch, who took Aguirec as his *nom de guerre* ('Vire'), and M/Sgt Robert R Kehoe ('Peseta'). Like George, which accompanied the other SAS operation mounted in the region, Dingson, it was placed under the orders of the commanding officer of 4 (French) SAS, Cmdt Pierre Bourgoin, but actually operated independently.

Frederick was inserted on the night of 9 June. The delay in its (and George's) deployment has been attributed to friction between the Jedburghs and the SAS. Correspondence in SAS archives points to two other teams having originally been selected and then stood down after they had argued with Bourgoin, and Frederick and George having been hastily briefed in their place; it is certainly true that Capt Philippe Ragueneau, leader of team George, had previously served with the SAS commander, and that the two were on good terms. By the time Frederick arrived in the Duault forest, the SAS base had become a focal point for every would-be *maquisard* in a wide area, despite there being a strong German garrison just seven kilometres away. The following evening armed partisans (and, some reports say, uniformed SAS men; in any event, security around the base was nothing short of atrocious) were surprised by a German officer at a nearby farmhouse; they shot him, but his driver and escort managed to get him away. The following morning German paratroopers arrived at the farm. They were driven off by the SAS, but returned in strength. The Frenchmen held their own initially, but by mid-afternoon it was clear that they would soon be surrounded, and Capt André Leblond, in command of the operation, gave the order to scatter and make for the Dingson base, some sixty kilometres to the south-west.

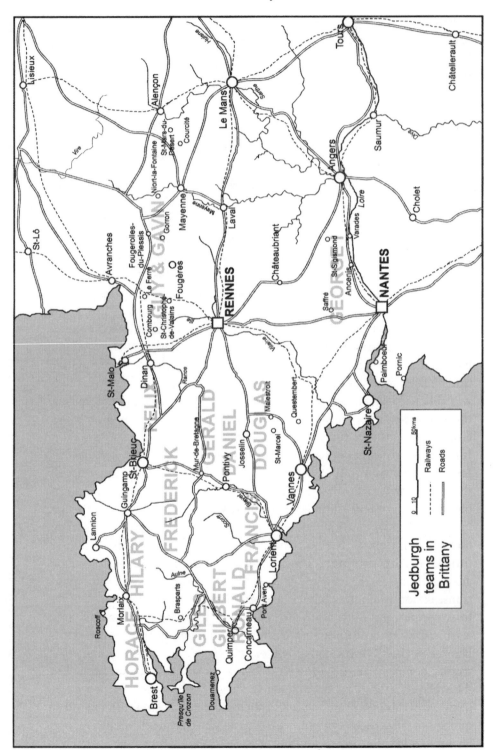

Frederick was forced to abandon much of its kit, and together with S/Ldr PH Smith of the RAF, who led an SAS liaison mission known as Wash, made its way to Peumerit-Quintin, seven or eight kilometres from the Samwest base, where it found a small SAS contingent, all of whom had been wounded in the fight in the forest. Frederick operated for over a fortnight from the vicinity of Peumerit, living in the open in a rough campsite located on a gorse-covered hillside two kilometres from the nearest hard-surfaced road and a kilometre from the deserted farm-house where the SAS wounded were being cared for. Although the weather that June had been almost unremittingly wet, they made no shelter and had no fire, and were always ready to move off at a few minutes' notice. They relied completely on local *résistants* to provide food, and once contact had been established with more distant guerrilla groups, further communications were always carried by couriers on bicycles: five girls in their teens and early twenties, and two gendarmes. When Wise decided that the time had come to shift his base he settled on a site about fifteen kilometres east of Peumerit, near the village of Canihuel, and on 8 July the team moved into a small abandoned cottage.

By this time, Frederick had managed to arrange two *parachutages*, and had used the opportunity to train *maquisards* in the selection and opera-tion of DZs; now that training paid off, and from this point on the team was able to leave to others the task of receiving aircraft and recovering the containers and panniers they dropped. The first *parachutage* the Côtes-du-Nord FFI received unaided took place in the early hours of 9 July. In all, six aircraft dropped not only stores but also an additional Jedburgh team, Felix. The drop was uneventful, though the sheer size of the *parachutage* meant that it took most of the night for the reception committee to collect all the containers.

Frederick had hardly settled into its new base when it was forced to move again, this time very hurriedly indeed and leaving behind what little kit it had managed to salvage from the Samwest base, including the all-important Jedset. Kehoe was actually making a scheduled radio transmission when news came of a battalion of German troops starting to sweep the area. By now Frederick had become accustomed to such alarms, and Wise simply posted a lookout armed with a Bren; minutes later they heard him open fire from close at hand, and saw German troops, some of them on horseback, just a few hundred metres away. The three managed to scramble out through a window, taking only their personal weapons, the all-important crystals which controlled the fre-quency of their radio transmitter, and the code-pads and signals. They lay up in a patch of gorse until nightfall, with enemy troops all around, but their luck held; when the hunters withdrew, the Jedburghs followed. People round about, who knew of the team's presence, were too frightened to shelter them, but did provide food, and Frederick moved off to a patch of woodland to spend an uneasy and uncomfortable night. The loss of the radio was a serious blow, but in the event the team was only out of direct contact for ten days, a replacement set being dropped to team Felix and brought to Frederick by courier.

On 13 July the team moved to a campsite between Plésidy and Étang-Neuf, where three well-armed *maquisard* companies were based. The high level of activity around this site meant that it was certain to be a target, although it was almost two weeks before the attack came. Once again, perimeter security seems to have been somewhat lax, though Wise reported that the single man on sentry duty killed around thirty Axis troops with his Bren before being overrun, giving the rest of the men chance to get into defensive positions. In the seven-hour fire-fight which followed, Wise estimated that *maquis* casualties amounted to twenty-seven, while a staggering 500 Germans were killed or wounded out of an assault force he put at around 1,200. Frederick, which had no remit to become involved in a pitched battle between partisans and Germans, cleared out as soon as the fire-fight started. The next day Wise established a new command post at Kerien, back in the direction of Peumerit.

By 2 August US forces had broken out of Normandy to the west and elements of 1st Army were poised to begin the drive into Brittany. Frederick was instructed to secure the main road between Morlaix and Lamballe, which ran through Guingamp and St-Brieuc, and Wise assembled a strong force of partisans to guard key points. It was also ordered to begin preparations to receive an Inter-Allied Mission, Aloès, which would both control the FFI's role in the liberation of Brittany and oversee the transition to civilian control once the fighting in the region was over. Aloès, which arrived on the night of 4 August (many of its members, some of whom were women, had had no parachute training, and the jump was the first they had ever made) was nominally under the command of Col Eon, but the store de Gaulle set by it may be gauged by the fact that it included André Dewaverin, his head of intelligence.

By now, American combat troops had begun to arrive in the area and Frederick's job was coming to an end, but before the team was stood down there was one last battle to be fought, in the very north of the *département*, where an estimated 3,000 Axis troops had taken up defensive positions with their backs to the sea. Partisans Wise had armed and trained – a total of over 4,000 men, all told – were used in the conven-

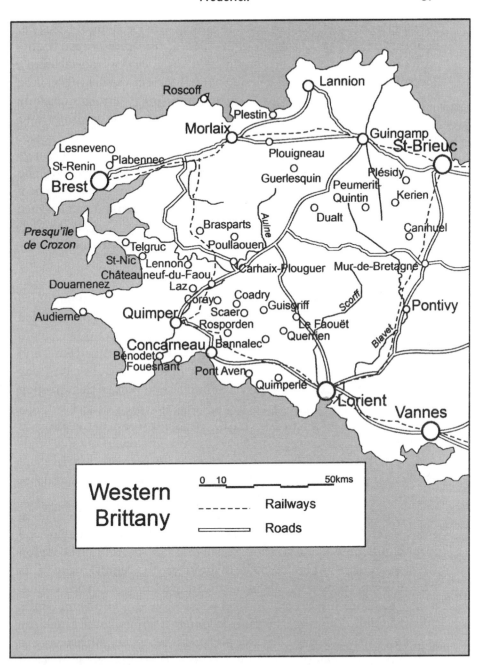

Western
Brittany

0 10   50kms

- - - - - - - Railways

———— Roads

tional infantry role, supported by American armour and self-propelled artillery, and slowly but surely cleared the area of effective resistance in a series of engagements which began on 2 August and were concluded a fortnight later. Wise and Kehoe returned to the United Kingdom on 20 August and were debriefed and stood down; Bloch-Auroch followed a week later. Adrian Wise later returned to Brittany in the company of John Singlaub of team James, to carry out a reconnaissance mission around Lorient.

During the ten weeks the team was active in Brittany, partisans under its direct control killed or wounded around 2,500 Axis troops; cut telephone and telegraph lines around 300 times, and railway lines some 200 times, derailing forty trains in the process; ambushed some fifty convoys and captured over 200 vehicles, and destroyed 50,000 litres of fuel.

Felix

Team Felix, which comprised Capt Jean-Paul Souquet, alias Jean Kernevel ('Carnavon'), Capt John Marchant ('Somerset'), and Sgt Peter Colvin ('Middlesex'), landed on a ground three kilometres north of Jugon-les-Lacs, between Lamballe and Dinan, in the eastern Côtes-du-Nord, in the early hours of 9 July, together with a large quantity of *matériel*. Felix's task was twofold: to organise and equip the local *résistants*, but also to survey the coast to the north with a view to selecting a site where substantial amounts of stores could be landed; the second requirement was soon abandoned.

Before they left Fairford, Souquet and Marchant had decided that the key to security was mobility. Resolved never to remain longer than forty-eight hours in one location, they had equipped themselves accordingly, with a bare minimum of kit. In the event, they hardly paused at all for the rest of the month, staying on the move while they made contact with Resistance leaders and located a selection of grounds for supply drops, finding lodgings and food at isolated farms. They found few cohesive partisan groups, though plenty of volunteers, little organisation and a grave shortage of junior leaders. They never succeeded in making contact with any of the SAS troops in the area.

In their first fifteen days in Brittany, Felix received forty-six aircraftloads of stores, making it possible to arm almost half the estimated 6,000 volunteers in the region. When the signal to begin all-out guerrilla warfare was broadcast by the BBC on the evening of 2 August, the eastern Côtes-du-Nord fielded some thirty companies of armed partisans, in five battalion-sized groups. In the fighting which followed, Jugon was taken and held; coastal defences were overcome at Pléneuf, and the garrison killed or captured, as was that of Plancoët; a radio station, a substantial dump of food and another of ammunition were taken intact around Dinan, and across the entire region, troop and supply convoys were attacked and trains derailed. In all, over 300 German troops were killed, and more than twice that number taken prisoner. FFI losses stood at fifty-eight dead and forty-one wounded, with a further twenty-four civilians killed in reprisals. First contact with advancing American forces was made on 6 August, and within days, effective German resistance in the region had ceased. Team Felix returned to the United Kingdom on 23 August.

Giles

A second Jedburgh team, Giles, was also inserted on the night of 8 July – although it had been briefed as early as 16 June – to a ground near the village of Stang-Kergoulay, fifteen kilometres north of Quimper in Finistère. The team was tri-national, with Capt Bernard Knox ('Kentucky'; British by birth but a naturalised US citizen, a university lecturer who had fought on the Republican side in the Spanish Civil War) in command, accompanied by Lt Paul Grall, who called himself Lebel ('Loire') and Sgt Gordon Tack ('Tickie'). The drop, from a Carpetbaggers' Liberator, was a complete success; the reception committee gathered up the packages, and men and supplies were taken to a camp in woodland near Laz, not far from the small town of Châteauneuf-de-Faou. That evening they were amazed to hear a message on the BBC directing them back to the same DZ, where they received a much heavier drop; they were still loading containers aboard the trucks at daybreak, and the men were exhausted by the time they returned to Laz. In the event, the *parachutage* – which they had thought extremely risky; 'how we got away with it, I'll never know', said Knox – actually saved them an encounter with the Germans, for soon after they had left the campsite half a battalion of paratroopers had arrived, and had combed the area.

The next day they were also able to identify two DZs, the co-ordinates of which were radioed to London. On 11 or 12 July Giles learned that two other teams destined for the *département*, Francis and Gilbert, had been inserted the night after they themselves had arrived, and that the latter had jumped on to one of those two grounds. When a large supply drop was made there on the night of 14 July, Axis troops arrived while the partisans were collecting the cannisters and a prolonged fire-fight ensued; Giles' report says that the mixed force of Germans and Russians suffered heavy losses, but others suggest that the partisans came off worse, that most of the consignment was lost, and that total disaster was only avoided by the timely arrival of partisan reinforcements.

On 15 July, word of an impending German sweep forced Giles and the partisans to move, to St-Thois. Two evenings later they received a message during the regular BBC transmission alerting them to the arrival of nine men at a DZ they had identified near Le Pénity, around thirty kilometres away and close to the original Samwest base in the Forêt de Duault. Team Frederick was actually much closer to this DZ, but Giles, having identified it, had to deal with the reception. Grall was deputed, and the men – teams Hilary and Horace, and three liaison officers from EMFFI – were safely lodged with a local group, awaiting transport to their operational areas, to the north and west. Next night, just as Knox was setting out with two cars to take them on the first leg of their journeys, a suspected *milicien* who had been under interrogation escaped, and they were forced to make a hurried move, to the vicinity of Lennon, three or four kilometres away across the (canalised) River Aulne. The following night, Knox says he brought Horace to Giles' base (Horace's report suggests a different chronology) and the next saw it on its way to the Brest area, where it was to work, while Grall conveyed Hilary part of the way towards Morlaix.

Giles' stay near Lennon was brief; after four days, German activity in the area began to increase, and Knox decided to move once more, but his decision to head further north proved a mistake, and the group which initially numbered about twenty failed to outrun the German cordon and was forced to double back. On the way, more than half the partisans dropped out due to fatigue, and the party was only eight strong when it stumbled into its old campsite at St-Thois.

This was only a temporary haven, for the campsite was too widely known, and Knox and Grall planned to move on to Plessis, west of Laz, but first they turned their attention to a château, the Domaine de Tré-varez, in a dominant position close to Châteauneuf. During the previous week, *Feldgendarmerie* units searching for Giles had moved into the house; Knox called in the Allied Tactical Air Force to bomb and strafe the château, and it was hit by RAF Mosquitoes the next morning,

Sunday 30 July, while the people who lived close by were at church. Giles left undisturbed the following day – the last time the team moved until the area was liberated – and later made a reconnaissance of the château. They found the German garrison in complete disarray, without effective defences, and launched an assault, in the course of which seventeen more German lives were added to the extensive toll taken by the air raid.

On the morning of 2 August, Giles learned that elements of the German 2.*Fallschirmjägerdivision* based in the Châteaulin area to the west were taking the road through Châteauneuf and heading east, to confront the Americans. The paratroopers were on foot and on bicycles, much of their equipment carried in horse-drawn carts. Knox decided that Giles and 'their' partisans, who now numbered around 800, could strike an effective blow since there would be ample scope for ambushes. The all-important activation signal '*Le chapeau de Napoléon, est-il toujours à Perros-Guirrec?*', a phrase proposed by Grall at the request of Gen de Gaulle, was broadcast by the BBC just in time for him to put the plan into effect. In all, seven companies – few of the men properly trained, but all armed – began to attack the German column, blocking the road in many places and forcing the paratroopers to spread out across the countryside, where they took revenge on all and sundry.

By the time the ambushes were sprung, the German divisional commander had already arrived in Carhaix, and in order to separate him and his headquarters from the combat units strung out along the road, Knox ordered the demolition of a bridge across the river at Landeleau, midway between Châteauneuf-de-Faou and Carhaix. Those paratroopers left to the west turned, and began to trek back towards Châteaulin, laying waste to villages as they went.

On 5 August, *maquisards* brought two jeeps from an American reconnaissance unit into the camp at Plessis. These men had become separated from the rest of their company, and their arrival in Châteauneuf had provoked scenes of jubilation. The population hung out French flags, convinced that they had been liberated at last, and nothing Knox could say would persuade them that their celebrations were premature. That night a strong German force arrived in Châteauneuf, heading west. They killed perhaps fifty townspeople and then settled into defensive positions; the next day an American reconnaissance unit approached the town, and was taken completely by surprise, the Germans killing all but a very few and driving off in such vehicles, including light tanks, as remained serviceable.

One wonders why Knox had not warned the approaching Americans of the presence of German combat troops in the town. He tells us he had sent thirty or more of his men to cover the roads east of Châteauneuf for just that purpose, two days earlier, but apparently they proved ineffective, perhaps because of the communications barrier between the French, none of whom spoke any English, and the Americans, none of whom spoke any French. Somewhat naïvely, perhaps, Knox suggested in his report that the Americans should have sought *him* out:

> We would like to state here that London knew the exact location of our HQ and should have informed US advanced units in the area of our whereabouts. If the CO of that reconnaissance column had been able to contact us, he would never have run into that ambush.

Superficially, this is a minor point, but it does have a deeper implication and significance: were the Jedburgh teams sufficiently aware of the full range of the responsibilities on their shoulders? Knox, in particular, older than most and already a veteran (albeit of the Spanish Civil War, no showpiece of tactical discipline) should perhaps have shown a clearer understanding of the wider nature of the task. By encouraging the partisans to disperse the column of German paratroopers on 3 August, when a more prudent solution would have been to have contained them, he failed to foresee the effects and ramifications of what was really no more than a knee-jerk, revenge-driven reaction; and in failing to ensure that the approaching Americans were aware of the local situation, he abdicated an important element of his responsibility to them and allowed them to fall into a death trap.

Over the following days, the Aloès Mission moved into Giles' area; Colonel Eon appropriated Lt Grall, and Knox was given the job of liaising between Aloès and the American 1st Army. By now, orders had been given to all German troops in Finistère to fall back on Brest, Lorient and the Presqu'île de Crozon – a neck of land across the broad Rade de Brest from the port itself. (It is clear that Concarneau, Fouesnant and adjacent Bénodet, as well as Douarnenez and Audierne, on the Cornouaille Peninsula, were also being defended, but see the account of team Gilbert's activities for a fuller analysis.) By 10 August, save for isolated pockets which had been cut off earlier, the interior of western Brittany was now thought to be free of Germans and FFI units under Giles' direction had begun a blockade of the Crozon Peninsula. In fact, those assumptions were premature; the paratroopers who had ambushed the Americans at Châteauneuf were still at large, and on 11

August attacked Brasparts, releasing 130 prisoners held there and laying waste to the village before fighting through to the temporary safety of the Crozon enclave. Their assault had been spearheaded by two light tanks they had taken at Châteauneuf, and perhaps owed its success to the employment of American vehicles.

That *was* the last meaningful encounter with German troops outside the enclaves, however; from then on, fighting was limited to their perimeters, and although it was occasionally both prolonged and intense, there were no successful sorties in strength. During the first week of September Giles received orders to terminate its mission, and all three men arrived back in the United Kingdom on 10 September. Brest and the Crozon Peninsula fell little more than a week later.

Francis

Team Francis was dropped by a B-24 Liberator into the south-eastern corner of the *département* of Finistère, some forty-five kilometres, as the crow flies, from Giles' insertion point, on the night of 9 July, to be met by a group of *résistants* from Quimperlé. The team – Major Colin Ogden-Smith ('Dorset'); Lt Guy Leborgne, who had taken the name le Zachmeur ('Durance'), and Sgt Arthur Dallow ('Groat') – faced a difficult situation, for fully half the *département* was so heavily garrisoned that guerrilla activity was out of the question, and even supply drops were very risky.

The drop missed the DZ by a small margin, and fell instead into a wood. The Jedburghs had problems extricating themselves, their 'luggage' (some of which was never found) and the thirty-six containers of weapons and equipment which accompanied them, from the trees. It was four days before Maj Ogden-Smith joined the others, largely because the fall-back RV on which the team-members had agreed before they left England – the village of St-Fiacre – was adjacent to the small town of Le Faouët, home to a German anti-terrorist unit, and was thus unapproachable. Meanwhile Leborgne took charge, and enlarged the team by the addition of three Frenchmen: two locals, one of whom was a trained radio operator, and an SAS trooper named Maurice Myodon, who had become separated from the Dingson party. He also located both 'Col Berthaud', the FFI chief in the department, and Resistance leaders from the towns of Scaer and Carhaix-Plouguer, and arranged for a *parachutage* for the former to take place on the night of 14

July. This used the ground on to which team Gilbert had been dropped, five nights earlier, and as noted, it was intercepted by Axis troops.

The situation improved the following day when Francis made direct contact with team Giles near Châteauneuf (it was already in touch, via Berthaud, with Gilbert, which had also been inserted on the night of 9 July, and Sgt Dallow was passing messages for it, its own radios having been smashed), and demarcation lines between the three teams' operational areas were established. Francis moved that night to Guisgriff, to the east of Scaer, to contact a *maquis* band led by an SAS officer, Lt de Kerville (French sources name him as Gérard-Gaultier de Carville), who had become separated from his unit during the flight from the Samwest base; the next morning, trucks full of German infantry arrived in the village, and Francis made itself scarce. After three days spent largely in hiding, the team joined up again with de Kerville's group which, in the meantime, had received enough weapons to arm 300 men, to meet a *parachutage* that had failed to materialise. The following night, of 25 July, a drop was made near Pont Aven, to the west. The partisans could do no more than attempt to hide the containers, all of which were discovered by German search teams during the day. This reinforced the view that resupply operations in the coastal zone were unlikely to succeed, although the fact that the aircraft did not arrive until almost dawn did little to help matters. A second operation scheduled that night for a ground near Bannalec was cancelled, by the simple expedient of not lighting the signal fires, when German troops arrived in the area.

As 29 July dawned, it became clear that the team's base had been surrounded by something like a battalion of German troops. Francis managed to escape, but the sheer number of Axis troops in the area made movement very difficult, and the men could do little more than lie up and hope not to be discovered. That evening the team found itself surrounded again, by a *Feldgendarmerie* company, at a farm near the village of Querrien, ten kilometres due north of Quimperlé. When the sound of trucks was heard, at around 2100, the six men were in a ditch some hundred metres from the farm buildings. Dallow set off down the ditch, followed by his French assistant and Ogden-Smith. As he tried to clamber out, he slipped and fell, landing in a tangle of briars; he remained there undiscovered for the next few hours, despite search parties passing close by, and then set off, with nothing but his Colt side-arm, in what he judged to be a northerly direction. The next day he stumbled by lucky chance upon a *maquis* group, and was sheltered until reunited with Lt Leborgne, three days later.

Major Colin Ogden-Smith was less fortunate. By Leborgne's account he was shot as he tried to leave the ditch; wounded in the stomach and unable to move, he was shot again as he lay on the ground. The French radio operator, 'Guyader', though wounded, hid himself in the nearby river for four hours and then managed to walk and crawl to another farm, where he was given shelter. The SAS trooper, Maurice Myodon, was wounded by grenade fragments during the first exchanges; unable to run for it, he kept up covering fire, first with his carbine and then, when his ammunition was exhausted, with his pistol. When that too was empty he shouted to the Germans that they need not worry, he was out of ammunition; he received a burst of submachine-gun fire in response, and was then finished off with a pistol shot to the head. Both he and Ogden-Smith were in uniform. The second of the two French civilians with the party, 'Deneville', was also killed during the course of the fire-fight. Leborgne managed to kill the German captain who led the raid and escaped in the resulting confusion. The farmer, a man of seventy-one, was subsequently bayoneted to death. The four corpses were stripped, and left exposed for forty-eight hours before being roughly buried; they were later exhumed and the two parachutists and the *maquisard* were reinterred together in the Communal Cemetery at Guiscriff.

During the night, Leborgne managed to catch up with de Kerville's group while a *parachutage* was taking place. He took charge of distributing the six plane-loads of weapons, one half to the Carhaix *maquis*, the other to Bannalec. Other drops had been made on previous nights, and he estimated that by now there were some 3,000 armed men in the area. For the moment, at least, he was unable to move, since anti-terrorist activity had redoubled following the killing of the two parachutists, the Germans having recovered Ogden-Smith's map, which had campsites and DZs marked on it. Leborgne did succeed in joining up with Sgt Dallow, and by 2 August, when the signal for open guerrilla warfare was transmitted, they were in a position to assemble a strong force to block the expected German retreat into the city of Lorient by way of the road from Quimper, and to attack such garrisons as remained in smaller towns. Rosporden was the scene of heavy fighting, being liberated and occupied by partisans and then attacked by a strong force of Russians. The local Resistance chief asked Leborgne for assistance in repulsing them, and he sent part of de Kerville's group, about 150 men under the lieutenant's command. The Russians were driven off, but not before the SAS officer was killed.

Leborgne and Dallow made their way to Quimper on 5 August, and joined forces with teams Ronald and Gilbert. On 8 August Quimper fell, and from then on the rump of team Francis, now working closely with the Aloès Mission, turned its attention to infiltrating women and girls into Lorient, to obtain up-to-the-minute information as to the strength of the German garrison and its intentions. In the first week of September they received orders to return to the United Kingdom.

Gilbert

Team Gilbert – Capt Christopher Blathwayt of the King's Royal Rifles ('Surrey'), Capt Paul Carron de la Carrière, who took the name Charron ('Ardèche'), and Sgt Norman Wood of the Royal Armoured Corps ('Doubloon') – was somewhat hurriedly briefed, together with Francis, Hilary and Horace; it left Harrington aboard a Carpetbaggers' B-24 late on 9 July, and dropped to a reception committee on a ground near Coadry, just a few kilometres from the town of Scaer, at around 0100. The drop was poorly executed – the aircraft was flying too fast and too low – and though the men were unhurt, virtually all their equipment was smashed. The reception committee consisted of several hundred men, and discipline was poor; while they were searching the ground for packages, two German trucks appeared, and stopped some hundreds of metres away, and it was all de la Carrière could do to restrain the partisans from attacking them. Eventually the ground was cleared, and Gilbert was led away, but only as far as the nearest ditch, where the team spent its first night in France.

The priority was to obtain replacement radios, and both Giles and Francis were contacted and sent messages to London on Gilbert's behalf; they were received within twenty four hours of each other, and SFHQ, assuming that the teams were co-located, immediately sent what Blathwayt described as 'a pathetic message' telling them to scatter. That may have had some bearing on Blathwayt's decision to move Gilbert to a location on the other side of Quimper, to a château owned by a man the Germans believed to be a collaborator. The team was to remain there for ten days; during that period it achieved little, being out of direct contact with London – it was to be 28 July before it received a replacement radio, and by that time Sgt Wood had succeeded in getting a damaged Jedset to work. Meanwhile Gilbert could only pass messages to London via Francis or Giles, and since it was thus reliant on communications channels it did not control, it received only four *parachutages*, most of the material dropped being lost at that, before the signal for general guerrilla warfare was broadcast, on 2 August.

On 21 July, Blathwayt and de la Carrière decided to relocate to be with an active partisan band, even though doing so would risk their losing touch with Giles and Francis. There was an element of impatience involved; Blathwayt said 'We were sick of being "in an office" and wanted to make sure we had at least one striking force for "D" day', meaning the day the signal for overt guerrilla warfare would be transmitted by the BBC. The following day the team moved to a site occupied by a well-organised partisan group led by 'Capt Mercier', five kilometres north-west of Coray. On the night of 26 July Gilbert received its first *parachutage*. It was 'sold by a traitor. There was a battle but one third [of the material] was saved'. The next night another, on a ground identified by Francis, south-west of Coray, was entirely successful. The following day a replacement Jedset, which, by Gilbert's report, had been dropped to Giles almost a week earlier, was brought by courier.

The earlier lack of a direct communications channel between Gilbert and London meant that when the order to begin overt guerrilla warfare came through, the *maquisard* bands in its area were still only partially armed. These groups soon acquired significant amounts of German weaponry, both by attacking small German forces who were prepared to surrender rather than fight it out, and from arms dumps discovered in towns which the Germans had hurriedly evacuated, which they had neglected to destroy. On one occasion Gilbert even decoyed a *Luftwaffe* Junkers Ju.52 into dropping a load of *panzerfaust* rocket-propelled anti-tank grenade launchers to it, together with a few hundred Iron Crosses, Second Class. Nevertheless, Blathwayt was to complain that even towards the end of the campaign in Finistère, partisan bands made up of trained soldiers were still badly under-equipped:

> Had we received arms in accordance with our requests [i.e. those passed via Francis and Giles] many well-organised, but unarmed companies could have been turned into fighting units at a much earlier date, and could thus have been in a position to carry out actions against the Boche on a greater scale and in the critical early days of fighting.

In the early hours of 5 August a further Jedburgh team, Ronald, was dropped to act as liaison between the Finistère partisans and Mission Aloès, and joined forces with Gilbert. The two teams separated from Mercier's partisans, who were ordered to take and hold Rosporden, and made for Quimper, but even before they got there they were presented with a target too tempting to ignore – a convoy of perhaps fifteen German trucks, heading out of the town on the Rosporden road. 'We killed quite a lot of them with LMG fire at about 800 yards,' said Blathwayt, 'across a little valley … It was like a field firing exercise and morale was very high. The [surviving] Boche got as far as Rosporden, where they were shot to blazes by Capt Mercier's boys.' That night they began to organise the investiture of Quimper; the Germans trapped in the town made a number of attempts to sortie, but all were stopped. An attempt to persuade the garrision to surrender was rebuffed, and for the next few days an uneasy truce prevailed. Col Berthaud was more successful at Douarnenez, which was held by Russians; he managed to convince them to cease fighting, and they soon withdrew to Audierne, 'where they did no further harm', releasing the partisans surrounding Douarnenez to supplement those at Quimper. He met with less success at Concarneau, which was to become the scene of prolonged fighting.

Meanwhile, at Quimper, the FFI were running short of ammunition. Gilbert called for a supply drop that night, along the line of the Quimper–Coray road, but the aircraft carrying out the mission went astray, dropping one load as far away as Carhaix (where it was collected by Giles) and others near Rosporden and Tourch, a little way to the north, where they were collected by Mercier's men. On the evening of 7 August, the Germans in the city sent a message indicating that they might, after all, consider surrender, but when Blathwayt, de la Carrière and Berthaud met with their senior officers, they were told that they had just received orders to break out and join the Brest garrison.

> At 11 o'clock [the next morning, 8 August] out they came, and the battle went on till 7pm, when the Boche were either dead on the road (about 60), or were scattered and having their throats cut in the countryside. The Bretons fought like hell, and skilfully (only 9 killed and 15 wounded). It was an honour to be with them.

German resistance was now centred on Bénodet, Fouesnant and Concarneau; the troops in the first two towns tried to break out, but were prevented from doing so, and suffered heavy losses in the process, while Concarneau came under naval bombardment on 10 August. An armed truce prevailed there for the best part of a week, but on 16 August a small detachment of American armour appeared and gave the defenders a surrender ultimatum; they refused, and the American unit turned and left after lobbing a few rounds into the town. 'Concarneau had hitherto been fairly quiet,' observed Gilbert, 'now it was like a wasp's nest.' A parlay arranged for the next day turned into a shooting match, and that evening the American tanks returned in greater strength, this time launching a frontal assault, with the FFI acting as the infantry screen. Things appeared to be going reasonably well until around 2000, when the vehicles started coming under effective fire from A/T guns and *panzerfaust*, and without warning turned and disappeared once more, leaving their supporting infantry exposed and pin-pointed. The *maquisards* extricated themselves only with considerable difficulty.

The next seven days saw intermittent fighting, as the French slowly gained ground, but there was still little sign of any resolution. Then, on 24 August, Capt Mercier ordered flares to be sent up from all around the perimeter in an attempt to provoke a reaction; quite coincidentally, a lone RAF reconnaissance aircraft appeared and dropped a parachute flare. Other aircraft in the vicinity joined it, and all of a sudden, German troops, who clearly feared that this was the precursor to a major air raid, could be seen flocking out of the town. Concarneau was entirely in French hands by that evening, and it remained only to disarm and dismantle the demolition charges which had been placed on, in or around any object of note, a task in which Gilbert played a leading part.

Two days later the until-then quiescent garrison at Audierne left *en masse*, heading for the north coast of the Cornouaille Peninsula, where boats were waiting to transport it across the Baie de Douarnenez to the Presqu'île de Courzon or to Brest. The FFI waited until they were massed on the beaches, and then began to annihilate them. At least 200 were killed, and the rest taken prisoner. 'Team Gilbert was sorry to miss the battle,' says its report, 'but was taking a day off in the sea.' Now only the Crozon Peninsula remained, and all the FFI assets and the four Jedburgh teams in the area rushed to strengthen the cordon which had been thrown across it from St-Nic on the southern shore to the River Aulne near Trégarvan. American troops in significant numbers, complete with artillery and armour, were also involved in the containment operation, and thanks to their presence, and significant tactical airpower, the siege was soon brought to a conclusion. Each day saw the German defensive positions pushed back, sometimes in response to only very light pressure, and sometimes over considerable distances.

Even at this late stage, weapons were still in short supply. The advance was not without its mishaps, however, and one, which took place two days later, was very serious:

When main forces came up (American and French) patrols pushed forward through Telgruc and after only slight opposition, a line was established on favourable ground, 3 or 4km to the west. [On 3 September] Telgruc was bombarded by US [B-17] Fortresses and [B-26] Marauders. The east end of Telgruc was razed, killing 60 Americans, 25 FFI and 20 civilians.

The ground forces had displayed the correct recognition signals (orange smoke and orange identification panels) but the aircraft ignored them. To make matters worse, 'they' (presumably, in fact, other aircraft) returned an hour later and bombed and strafed again, while ambulances were collecting the wounded.

This 'blue-on-blue' airstrike was a dreadful, costly mistake, but the arrival on the scene of more and more American troops, and a complete lack of any real liaison between them and the FFI, let alone an integrated command and control structure, meant that misunderstandings on the ground were inevitable. In particular, the American practice of pushing out reconnaissance patrols in strength and then drawing back confused the French, who took the American manoeuvre to be an advance, and happily joined in, only to be left high and dry, and usually exposed, when the reconnaissance elements withdrew. The solution was to remove the FFI from the main battle and employ them as 'flank guards'. On 18 September Brest fell, and two days later effective German resistance in Brittany ceased (save, of course, for Lorient and St-Nazaire, which continued to hold out). It was time for Gilbert to stand down, but fate still had one more twist in store for the team. The next day, de la Carrière and Sgt Wood were making their way to Rennes when they were involved in a car accident; the radio operator was only slightly injured, but Capt de La Carrière was to spend the next two months in hospital. Capt Blathwayt collected Neville Wood the following day, and the pair arrived back in London, via Paris, on 28 September.

Hilary

Hilary and Horace, the two teams dropped on the night of 17 July to the ground Giles identified and manned at Le Pénity, were briefed to operate separately in the northern part of the *département* of Finistère, the former around Morlaix, the latter further west, close to Brest. Hilary was led by a Frenchman, Capt Edgar Mautaint, who took Marchant as his *nom de guerre* ('Charente'), assisted by Lt Philip H Chadbourne ('Nevada') and S/Lt Roger Hervouet, who used the name

Pariselle ('Kopek'). The drop was largely successful, even though by Mautaint's account the DZ was not actually suitable for personnel. Forty-five containers and nineteen panniers were dropped with the team, and some, including all of Hilary's equipment, went astray, although most was later found. News of its arrival was passed by Horace, and it was the evening of 19 July before Hervouet himself established contact with London. Chadbourne's report says that even at that comparatively late date, the partisan bands in the area had very few weapons and only minimal organisation. Their principal occupation seems to have been mutual recrimination, the FTP accusing the FFI of timidity, the FFI reproving the Communists for their over-enthusiasm.

Hilary moved the short distance to Poullaouen on 20 July, driven by a local doctor in a car which was little more than a motorised chassis. It established itself with the leader of a group from Liberation, and set about the task of locating dropping grounds and potential landing sites for gliders, and contacting other local leaders. Within days their presence was known throughout a wide area, and prudence dictated another move; the intention was to relocate to Scrignac, but word came of a strong German force near there, so Hilary moved instead to Guerlesquin, where the team found lodgings with an FTP band. *Actions* by the Germans and the *Milice* forced a further move four nights later, to another FTP group at a campsite between Plouigneau and the small town of Plestin-les-Grèves, near the coast, fifteen kilometres east of Morlaix. Here Hilary remained until the area was liberated.

Hilary's reports (both Chadbourne and Mautaint wrote their own) are unsatisfactory; the American's is full of inconsequential detail, while the Frenchman's has virtually nothing to say of the team's activities in the all-important period before the arrival of American forces in the first week of August, and thereafter concentrates on the difficulties of maintaining law and order. Neither gives us any information as to how the partisan bands were armed and organised, nor how the '4 battalions of 3/4,000 men each' (Mautaint's extraordinary estimate; the third zero may have been a slip of the pen) who made them up were involved in the liberation of northern Finistère and the heavy fighting which led to the eventual capitulation of Brest. Neither makes any mention of the presence of a detachment of men from 3 SAS (Operation Derry) or the OSS Operational Group Donald in the area, nor of the 'anti-scorch' operations which we know were undertaken to preserve important railway viaducts. Hilary was withdrawn to Paris 'after two months in the bushes', according to Chadbourne, although its report's header sheet says it returned to the United Kingdom on 6 September.

Horace

The report submitted by team Horace is both more comprehensive and much clearer than Hilary's, and consists of a detailed chronology and a sensible analysis of the situation in the area and the way events unfolded. Horace, with two American members – its leader, Maj John Summers ('Wyoming') and its radio operator, T/Sgt William Zielske ('Dime') – and Lt Georges Leclercq, who took the name Levalois as his *nom de guerre* ('Somme'), was briefed to operate in the region around Brest. It was inserted by a Tempsford-based Halifax in the early hours of 18 July, and its drop went entirely according to plan; no one was injured, and all the team's equipment was located intact. Paul Grall from team Giles had been on the spot to meet them, and he drove them to a *maquisard* camp to the north of Châteauneuf-du-Faou. Sgt Zielske was able to establish contact with London at the first attempt.

Things did not go so well over the next three days, however; Bernard Knox of team Giles was supposed to have arranged transportation to Brest for them, as well as contacts there, but he himself could not be reached, and by the evening of 19 July, the team's presence in the area – though not their whereabouts – was known, and 'wanted' posters offering a substantial reward for their capture had appeared. Clearly it was necessary to leave the area, but with no further contacts and no transportation, Summers was at a loss to know what to do. Then, in the early hours of 20 July, Knox arrived to conduct the team to a group based some way to the north, but was forced to return with them to his own base when no trace of it could be found. The group's leader turned up the next night, however, and after a somewhat stressful car journey they arrived at his base; but it soon transpired that he had no useful contacts in the Brest area. In fact, so many of the significant members of the Resistance movement in north-western Finistère had been arrested or killed since 6 June that it would be no easy matter for Horace to establish itself with such partisan elements as remained. For two days more Summers sent out messengers to try to locate key figures, but met with no success. By 24 July he had decided, against all advice, to make the move into Brest anyway, unaccompanied if need be.

The following evening, two complete strangers arrived unannounced at the campsite, saying they had orders, from another man whose name meant nothing to anyone, to transport the team to Brest. They would be hidden in three of the barrels – the rest contained wine, and were to be delivered to the Brest garrison – in their *gazogène*-powered truck, but time was of the essence, because it was now 1830, it was a two-hour journey, and their travel permit expired at 2100 ... Summers immediately decided to trust them, and the team hastily assembled its packs and weapons. Summers noted:

> The 40 mile trip was made in two and a half hours, during which time we were completely miserable in mind and body. If the unknown Frenchmen were not collaborators, then probably some German patrol would find us, and if neither of the two happened, then surely we would suffocate inside the barrels.

In fact, the two men were envoys from one of the surviving leaders in Brest, a lawyer, Maître Garion, who used the *nom de guerre* Somm-Py. He had received word of the team's predicament from Col Berthaud, whose assistance had been solicited by Bernard Knox. The truck was stopped twice, but evidently the papers were in order, for Horace arrived at its destination, a large area of woodland eight kilometres east of the city, without further mishap, and bedded down for the night in a ditch.

Summers and his men had finally made it into their operational area, after a delay of over a week, but even now they were to be frustrated. When Somm-Py met them the following day, he said he could do little more until delivery was made of an attache case containing details of DZs and the deployment of the remaining local *résistants*. That afternoon the wine truck returned, they were packed into their barrels again, and set off for a safe house near Lesneven, fifteen kilometres to the north.

Another couple of days were passed in idleness, for the courier bringing the attache case was arrested by the *Sipo* – to be released, presumably for lack of damning evidence – and did not turn up until late on 29 July. The next day the team moved following increased German patrolling in the neighbourhood, and then again after only twenty-four hours. By this time, they had informed London of perhaps half-a-dozen DZs, and now learned that all had been refused by the RAF by reason of their proximity to anti-aircraft batteries. They sent details of more DZs, with little hope of them being accepted, but were then delighted to learn, by way of messages transmitted by the BBC along with that which released the partisans to wage open warfare, that their first *parachutages* would be made that night.

The situation over the next days was very confused. Horace was receiving supply drops on several grounds most nights now, and almost unbelievably all seem to have been recovered safely. As quickly as arms were received they were distributed – chiefly, it seems, to FFI groups, which contained large numbers of men with military training – and for the first time the *maquisards* were able to go on to the offensive, albeit in a limited sense. On 5 August, Summers judged that it was safe for the team to work openly, with a perimeter guard, rather than continue to keep itself hidden, but that decision proved premature, for the next day they were surprised by a German cavalry patrol and had to run for it, having hastily hidden their kit and the radio. Then, shortly after dawn, the sound of heavy diesel-powered vehicles indicated the arrival of American armour, and Horace's situation changed yet again.

Now the Jedburghs took on the role of liaising between the American troops and the FFI, as well as continuing to help direct the latter's activities, and seem to have met with a rather more co-operative attitude on the part of the US Army than some of the other teams in Brittany. Horace found it expedient to split up, and Lt Leclercq remained with FFI headquarters, located at Plabennec, while Summers and Sgt Zielske stayed with the US 6th Armored Division. The initial objective was to contain the Axis troops in and around Brest, and if possible prevent the troops flooding in from the surrounding areas from gaining the comparative, though temporary, safety of the enclave; but within days reports started coming in of small pockets of Germans who seemed willing to surrender, and more and more of Summers' time was occupied with checking them out.

By mid-August, despite all the Allies' best efforts, the German garrison in Brest had grown to perhaps 30,000, far outnumbering the American and French forces surrounding it. There was a serious danger that a break-out, while it would certainly be contained in the long run, would result in very heavy casualties, particularly among the lightly armed and poorly trained French. The situation became graver still when, on 14 August, the US 6th Armored Division was withdrawn, leaving the containment of Brest to two battalions of infantry and two of artillery in addition to the FFI, which by this time numbered perhaps 4,000 effectives. A superhuman effort on the part of John Summers and the newly installed French military commander, Cmdt Louis Faucher, established an effective counter-reconnaissance screen in a matter of hours, and although there was fierce fighting in many quarters, no German ever managed to penetrate it and return with news of just how thin the Allies were on the ground. Not until 22 August was the containing force brought up to a realistic level, with the arrival of the US VIII Corps.

That signalled renewed activity to take the enclave, which was now reduced to the city itself and the area to the west, around to the Pointe de Corsen and then inland along a line running through St-Renan and Guilers. This area contained large numbers of heavy coastal batteries, some of which could be trained on the Allied positions, and they, plus field artillery, set up a prolonged barrage which was answered in kind. The artillery duel continued for almost three weeks. The American component of Horace was by this time working alongside the US 2nd Ranger Battalion, acting as its link to a similarly sized unit of the most experienced FFI troops in what was to be the team's final contribution to the liberation of Brittany. By 9 September they had taken the German positions on the west coast, including the 'Graf Spee' battery of four 28cm guns, which had remained in action to the very last. This, however, was pure battlefield infantry combat, and hardly an effective use of the Jedburghs' special skills. The team was reunited on 10 September, returned to an assembly area, and by 15 September was back in the United Kingdom, where Operation Horace was stood down.

Gerald

Gerald was led by an American, Capt Stephen Knerly ('Suffolk'), assisted by Lt Claude l'Herbette, calling himself Jean-Luc Beaumont ('Norfolk'), who had lived in the United States for some years, and with another American, T/Sgt Berent Friele ('Selkirk') as radio operator. They boarded a Stirling at RAF Harwell on the night of 17 July, but the mission was cancelled as the aircraft was taxiing to the runway. They tried again the next night with more success – although Knerly, the last man out of the aircraft, got tangled first in the despatcher's safety line and then in his parachute shrouds, and landed heavily on a road, badly spraining an ankle – and were met on the ground by men of 4 SAS. Four panniers of kit and equipment dropped with them were recovered the next day, which was fortunate since one of them contained six million francs, additional operational funds for the SAS.

Cmdt Bourgoin's Dingson party had by now been distributed in small groups across the entire southern part of the Morbihan, with a small fixed logistical base known as Grog, near Pontivy. Unlike Frederick and George, there was no suggestion that Gerald was to be under Bourgoin's command. Instead, the Jedburghs were to operate independently, in an area where there were few SAS troopers. Next morning the team was handed over into the safekeeping of a dozen *maquisard* bodyguards

from a band known as 'Surcouf', which was led by an SAS sergeant, travelled with them to the borders of the Morbihan and the Côtes-du-Nord
and established themselves close to Mur-de-Bretagne, where the Aloès
Mission would later be based. The Jedburghs' opinion of the SAS was
low, particularly after l'Herbette put himself at some risk travelling sixty
kilometres to meet Bourgoin only to have the SAS officer fail to turn up.
Like team Frederick, Gerald was critical of the SAS's hands-on
approach to organising the Resistance groups:

> The stories which we heard of the SAS led us to believe that the work
> they had been doing was contrary to all aid which should have been
> given to the resistance. It seems that in action they actually took
> command of resistance in the area, whereas the mission of the Jed-
> burghs was merely to advise, and take over the leadership only in
> instances where it was needed.

That betrays a lack of understanding of the real situation and typifies
the mindset of many Jedburghs. In fact, Bourgoin's 4 SAS, which had
many Bretons in its ranks, was specifically chosen by HQ Airborne
Forces to carry out the Brigade's operations in Brittany. Despite the
very considerable influence exerted by certain individuals who had
agendas of their own, the battalion succeeded admirably both in
restraining the excesses of over-excited partisans who believed their
arrival to have been the signal for a nationwide armed uprising (which it
most certainly was not) and containing the very substantial German
garrisons in the Morbihan. In the months which followed, and especially after the fall of Paris on 25 August, 4 SAS, its ranks swollen by
many Breton partisans, was to prove itself to be arguably the most effective Special Forces unit in the entire European theatre of operations.
We should perhaps place Knerly's comments in context, however, for it
is clear from his written report that his views on the SAS were formed at
the team's briefing, long before the two bodies met, and were actually a
product of deep-seated prejudice in SFHQ. It is clear from many
sources that SFHQ and the SAS Brigade co-existed in an atmosphere of
mutual distrust.

Like Felix, Gerald had decided on a policy of mobility, and the team
changed location frequently, ensuring that only a bare minimum of
liaison agents knew its whereabouts. Through them, Knerly and l'Herbette met the leaders of local Resistance groups over the last two weeks
of July, promising to arm them before the signal for all-out guerrilla
warfare was broadcast. In fact, Gerald seems to have made little effort to

obtain supplies of weapons from London, and the requests it did make were nullified by inexplicable errors in aircraft loading. The team called up just two *parachutages*; both brought not weapons but clothing (including one pannier of 'women's undergarments, silk [sic] stockings and shoes. We cannot explain how this came about. In fact, all the containers sent to us contained material that we had not ordered'), although there was one consignment of sixty World War One-pattern bayonets. As a result, the partisans were reliant on weapons which had been furnished to them in June by the SAS. In consequence, in the three weeks during which it was operational before American forces arrived in the area, Gerald was able to carry out only minor acts of sabotage using the stocks of explosive, detonators and igniters it had itself brought from London, requests for replenishment of these small stocks having gone unanswered. Its report skips rapidly over such operations without even trying to enumerate them ('Our personal actions against the Germans consisted of small attacks on roads and against vehicles, and then running away...'), and one may conclude that they were neither numerous nor spectacularly successful.

Gerald's report suggests that the BBC broadcast which contained the phrase '*Le chapeau de Napoléon, est-il toujours à Perros-Guirrec?*' was twenty-four hours late in coming, and that the team received it on 3 August, by which time it had heard rumours of American forces advancing into Brittany and had issued 'restricted orders to start attacking convoys and generally harassing the Germans' off its own bat. The team led one of those attacks itself, using explosives to fell a tree in the path of two trucks filled with soldiers and then spraying the vehicles with fire from its two Brens, killing thirty and wounding fifteen more, and destroying both the vehicles. There were no casualties among the members of the small partisan force. The next day, 4 August, Gerald linked up with reconnaissance elements of the US 6th Armored Division advancing down the main road from Rennes towards Brest, and remained with the Americans from then on, taking part in the liberation of Pontivy and remaining there until 18 August, when it retired to Rennes and thence to Coutances, where it boarded an aircraft bound for London.

Gavin and Guy

Two more teams were briefed in mid-July, to operate in the *département* of Ille-et-Vilaine: Gavin – which consisted of Cmdt Joseph Cabucca, using the name Daniel Jeanclaude ('Shilling'), Capt William Dreux ('Sixpence') and S/Lt Paul Valentini, who took Masson as his *nom-de-guerre* ('Halfpenny') – to the north of Rennes, the regional capital; and Guy – Capt André Duron, calling himself Dhomas ('Dronne'), Capt Aubrey 'Troff' Trofimov ('Gironde') and S/Lt Georges Groult, who used the name Deschamps ('Dordogne') – to the south of the city. Gavin and Guy were actually to operate as one unit, allbeit with some members detached from time to time, and it will be convenient to consider them as such.

The teams were briefed together on 8–9 July, and warned to expect very little organised resistance in the Ille-et-Vilaine, all contact with partisans there having been lost in March 1944. They left Harrington in two separate aircraft on the evening of 11 July and were dropped three hours later near the village of Courcité in the very east of the Mayenne, 125 kilometres away from the areas in which they were to operate. The delay in reaching their operational area, combined with the failure to furnish them with Resistance contacts, effectively prevented Gavin and Guy from carrying out their missions as briefed.

A significant amount of material was dropped with the teams – thirty-six containers in all, says the after-action report's header sheet – but some of the Jedburghs' own kit was destroyed in the process, including Guy's radio and Gavin's carbines, and Groult's rucksack was never found. The reception committee was headed by 'Barbier', the departmental representative for the *Bureau d'Opérations Aériennes* (BOA) set up by EMFFI to oversee the distribution of weapons and supplies from the United Kingdom. Barbier was to become an influential figure, and largely succeeded, at least initially, in determining which of the Resistance factions' representatives should have access to the Jedburghs. The teams were provided with three *maquisards*, Émile, Louis and Marcel, to act as their bodyguards and to generally assist them, spent the rest of the night at a nearby farm and were then taken off to safe houses in the village, where they remained for two days before transferring to a farm near St-Thomas-de-Courceriers, a few kilometres away. Joseph Cabucca, dressed in civilian clothes but without identity papers of any kind, and mounted on a bicycle, now tried to contact local leaders, and over the course of a week located 'Col Michelin', 'Gen Rodolph' and 'Col Laboureur'; during a second meeting with the latter, on 23 July, he met 'Col Fonction' (Maj Alex Willk of SOE), the joint DMR of the adjoining region which included the *département* of Ille-et-Vilaine. Fonction, who had arrived from London on 15 or 16 June, and who was in intermittent contact with team George, told him that he had had no success in locating Resistance leaders north of Rennes, but did have some contacts in the area where Guy was to have operated; so it was decided that it would transfer there while Gavin remained in the Mayenne.

The following day, the Jedburghs made contact with one of the men from whom Barbier had been shielding them – 'Dennis' the head of an FTP group based at St-Mars-du-Désert (who may also have been an SOE agent). Dennis immediately put them in touch with 'Tanguy', the leader of the FTP in a wide area which included part of Normandy and some of the neighbouring regions of Brittany, including the Ille-et-Vilaine. Gavin and Guy learned from Dennis that they could have been dropped directly into the Ille-et-Vilaine, and that there were active Resistance cells there, including at least two in the area where Gavin was to have operated. All thoughts of Gavin remaining where it was were abandoned, and the two teams immediately began to prepare to move westward.

The nine men set off from St-Thomas on foot (their 'luggage' had preceded them, in a local doctor's car) as soon as it was dark on 25 July, and arrived in Niort-la-Fontaine, about thirty kilometres away, on the morning of 27 July. Tanguy was waiting for them, with bicycles he had procured for himself and Capts Cabucca and Duron, and they were to go on ahead, leaving the others to follow on foot. They moved off that night, and reached the outskirts of Gorron by the next morning; here they were to have been met by a guide sent from Fougerolles-du-Plessis to lead them there, but of him there was no sign. Louis was sent off to find a bicycle and return to Niort, to try to re-establish contact, but before he returned one of the other boys located a *résistant* named 'Rossignol', who told them that the Germans were very active just to the west of the town.

Rossignol found them safe lodgings for the night, and introduced them to two *gendarmes*, Plassart and Leray. The next day, 28 July, they received word that Tanguy was sending them a guide to bring them to Le Ferré in the Ille-et-Vilaine. Thus far, in three nights of travelling, the Jedburghs had covered little more than a quarter of their journey, and would be hard pressed to reach their operational area before the advancing Americans arrived. It was decided to try to buy a car of some sort, and the *gendarmes* found a serviceable vehicle which could be had for 10,000 francs (about £50 at 1940 values). The deal was done that evening, just outside the town, but as the Jedburghs were preparing to push-start it, a German half-track appeared, and in a moment eight soldiers surrounded them. Said Dreux in his report:

The others had seen the German vehicle at the last second and had been able to escape and hide in a nearby hedge but Lt Masson, Marcel and I, who were in uniform, were unable to get out of the car before the Germans were on top of us. This was a rather ticklish situation inasmuch as the Germans had their weapons in their hands and we had not. We got out of the car and got our weapons out and I was about to fire on the Germans when I suddenly realised that they were quite confused and did not grasp the situation very well and therefore, that it might be possible to slip away without having to fire. The leader of the patrol kept asking me questions in German to which I replied by OK and various uncomplimentary English expressions all of which evidently puzzled him very much ... I told Marcel to slip away and this we did. I still do not know how we bluffed our way out of that one ...

The Germans contented themselves with pushing the car to the side of the road, and went on their way; Dreux, Valentini, Groult and Marcel climbed out of the hedge, but of Trofimov and Louis there was no sign. The Englishman rejoined the rest of the group at Combourg, twenty-five kilometres east of Dinan, on 7 August, having spent much of the intervening period operating in civilian clothes, assisted by the two *gendarmes*, gathering intelligence in Gorron, where the retreating German forces soon began to set up defensive positions, and then communicating it to American units he was able to contact. He mapped out a poorly defended route by which they could enter the town, and led a reconnaissance squadron into Gorron with hardly a shot being fired despite there being perhaps 400 German troops in the town. They immediately began pulling out, and the Americans were not in sufficient strength to stop them; few prisoners were taken, but Trofimov's activities saved the town from the damage a frontal assault with tanks and artillery would have caused, not to mention the casualties.

The remaining three Jedburghs recovered the car, got it started, located the guide and set off for Le Ferré, arriving there the following morning and meeting Carbucca and Duron, who had already begun to contact Resistance leaders – almost all of them FTP, as identified by Tanguy – and locating suitable dropping grounds. The following day, the two team leaders travelled to Jugon to confer with team Felix, and on the next Gavin and Guy relocated to St-Christophe-de-Valains, roughly midway between Combourg and Fougères; they subsequently pushed on to Combourg, where they arrived on 1 August. The following day, much to their surprise, the advance guard of the US 6th Armored Division reached them.

The arrival of the Americans did not, however, mean that Gavin and Guy were completely redundant, for the tanks and their supporting infantry were eager to press on towards Rennes and into Brittany, soliciting the help of the Resistance in rounding up groups of sometimes dispirited, sometimes combative, Germans who were still to be found right across the area. Gavin and Guy organised groups in all the larger towns across an area which stretched right across the northern Ille-et-Vilaine, and over the next weeks took some 1,400 prisoners. Their final act was to establish a screening force to the south of St-Malo, where German troops were still holding out in the citadel. On 17 August the two teams reported to British 2nd Army HQ near Vire, and were returned to the United Kingdom the following day on board a landing craft.

Daniel

Three additional Jedburgh teams were dropped into Brittany on the night of 4 August, specifically to liaise between Mission Aloès and the *maquisards* in the Côtes-du-Nord, Morbihan and Finistère *départements* respectively, and not to operate according to the basic Jedburgh plan. Team Daniel comprised Capt Kemys 'Ed' Bennett of the Royal Armoured Corps ('Apôtre'), Lt Pierre de Schonen, who, almost alone among the French Jedburghs, took no alias ('Argentier'), and Sgt Ron Brierley of the Royal Armoured Corps ('Florin'). The team was intended to be Aloès' link with the *maquisards* of the Côtes-du-Nord. It left Fairford together with the Mission, but in a separate aircraft, on the night of 4 August. Its pilot was deceived by signal fires lit by a band of a hundred or so teenage would-be partisans when they heard an aircraft approaching. They hoped that he would mistake their beacon for the one for which he was searching, and drop them a consignment of arms – a very common stratagem – and were astonished to receive a Jedburgh team instead. Daniel was escorted to Peumerit-Quintin and thence to Frederick's base at Kerien, where they linked up with the Aloès Mission. They soon discovered that there was little or nothing for them to do, save participate in a number of unsuccessful attempts to persuade small pockets of Germans to surrender. On 7 August they received a signal from London recalling them. They made a move to Mur-de-Bretagne, whence Colonel Eon had moved his headquarters, on 8 August, being briefly held captive by elements of 3rd American Army on the way; by teatime on 11 August, after less than a week in France, the team was back in London. The men were rebriefed to carry out a mission in the Allier, which was cancelled, and were subsequently redeployed as team Gregory, to carry out a mission in the Vosges mountains.

Douglas

A second liaison team, Douglas – Capt Dick Rubenstein of the Royal Artillery ('Augure'), Lt Jean Roblot, who called himself Ronglou ('Anachorère') and Sgt John Raven of the Royal Armoured Corps ('Half Crown') – which was to have provided Aloès' liaison with the Resistance in the Morbihan, left Fairford on the night of 5 August. It, too, failed to find its allotted DZ; this time, however, the pilot refused to allow the team to jump, and took them back to base. The following night they departed from Keevil, together with a fifteen-strong group of SAS troopers destined to join Cmdt Bourgoin's Dingson party, which was now scattered all over the *département*. The Stirling was hit by anti-aircraft fire as it was running in to the DZ, and the pilot took violent evasive action, with potentially disastrous effects on the parachutists, who were by then standing, waiting to make their way to the 'joe hole'; amazingly, all managed to stay on their feet, no one was hurt, and the jump subsequently went according to plan despite all the static lines being tangled.

Unusually, and at the last minute, the team was supplemented by an additional radio operator, S/Lt Poignot, whose job it would be to communicate with Aloès; this point-to-point radio contact in the field was not attempted elsewhere. Poignot took with him a completely unrealistic load – three B2 transceivers, each of which weighed almost 50 lbs and was packed in two metal cases, plus eight extra accumulators and three hand-cranked generators – which was far more than the four men could ever have hoped to have carried. In consequence, while moving away from the DZ towards the RV with Cmdt Bourgoin they were forced to make caches of equipment and then commute between them, which not only slowed their progress to snail's pace but did nothing to improve security already threatened by inquisitive locals. Happily that was not much of an issue after the first few days, since the German forces in the area were all retreating on Lorient.

Douglas spent some days at the Dingson party's base near Pontivy, while Poignot tried to make contact with Mission Aloès and largely failed, but it was obvious from the start that it was actually redundant. Housed at a small oyster farm on a tidal inlet east of Lorient, Douglas busied itself gathering information about the disposition of German troops around the city and along the coast towards the estuary of the River Villaine, to the east, and then, on 16 August, moved to Vannes, to co-locate with the local FFI chief. The team followed Daniel to Mur-de-Bretagne on 16 August, only to discover that Colonel Eon and his party had already left, and returned to London on 24 August, to await reassignment. It too was redeployed to eastern France.

Ronald

Team Ronald, composed of a French officer, Lt Georges Deseilligny, who called himself Dartigues ('Boutton'), as team leader, together with Lt Shirley Ray Trumps ('Boursier') and T/Sgt Elmer B Esch ('Pound'), was also tasked with liaising between Mission Aloès and the departmental FFI commander, this time in the Finistère. Ronald, too, dropped to the wrong DZ in the early hours of 5 August, although this time the cause was simple pilot error, and not optimistic subterfuge on the part of *maquisards*, but was soon united with team Gilbert, and remained co-located with it thereafter. As was the case with Douglas, an additional radio operator, S/Lt Dumas, accompanied the team, his job being to set up and maintain communications with Aloès. Dumas failed completely to contact Aloès, and messages between the Mission and the Jedburghs in the Finistère were passed by courier instead. With no radio traffic to handle he reverted to being an infantry platoon commander. He was later hospitalised, having lost two fingers from his left hand when he was hit by machine-gun fire during the battle to take Concarneau.

Ronald's after-action report is impossible to reconcile both with the accepted chronology and with the much more comprehensive account compiled by team Gilbert, and in the interests of clarity the latter's report is preferred. On 7 September Ronald withdrew to Paris, and a week later Trumps – who had taken some mortar fragments in the face during the fighting at Concarneau – and Sgt Esch returned to the United Kingdom to be stood down, while Lt Deseilligny remained in France.

Part Four
THE SOUTH WEST

Quinine

The first teams to be sent into south-western France, Quinine and Ammonia, left Blida aboard a pair of Halifaxes late on the evening of 5 June; both aircraft returned to Algeria with the teams still aboard. Quinine tried again on the night of 8 June, and this time the pilot identified the ground, 'Chénier', on the Luzettes plateau south of Aurillac in the *département* of Cantal. The team was dropped to a reception party composed of 'a dozen, ragged ill-armed men' under the mayor of nearby Le Rouget, who had never heard of 'Droite', the DMR (Col Schlumberger), to whom the Jeds were supposed to report, and seemingly had no contact with either of the SOE F Section circuits which were active in the region. Quinine was under the leadership of Maj Tommy Macpherson of the Queen's Own Cameron Highlanders ('Anselme'), who dropped wearing his kilt. According to one report, the leader of the reception committee first encountered the French member of the team, Asp Michel de Bourbon-Parme, who used the name Maurice Bourdon ('Aristide': Bourbon-Parme was a nephew of the pretender to the French throne, and at eighteen was the youngest of the Jedburghs), and on seeing Macpherson exclaimed 'Look! The French officer's brought his wife with him!' The team's radio operator was Arthur Brown ('Felicien'). Macpherson makes no mention of the arrival of the fifteen-strong Operational Group Emily on the same DZ that same night, nor does he refer to Emily at all in his report, even though it was to operate extensively in the area – destroying amongst other things three important railway viaducts and twenty-eight locomotives.

Quinine's task was to operate in the neighbouring Lot *département*, against enemy lines of communication between Montauban and Brive. The Montauban district was temporary home to 2. SS-Panzer Division *Das Reich*, and the Jedburghs' chief target was to be the railway it would take to Normandy, via Limoges and Châteauroux or Poitiers. In fact, saboteurs recruited around Montauban by SOE F Section's 'Alphonse'

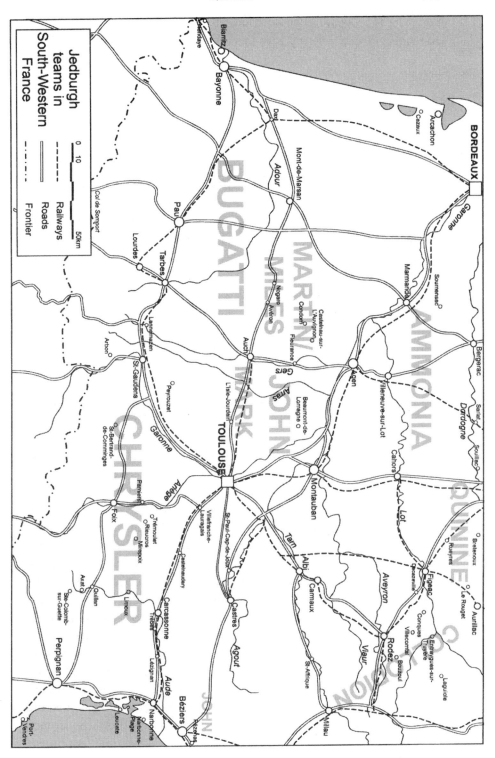

Jedburgh teams in South-Western France

Railways
Roads
Frontier

0 10   50km

(Tony Brooks, organiser of the Pimento circuit) had done a superlative job of disabling the heavy low-loader freight wagons upon which the *Das Reich* Division's tanks were to have ridden (they added abrasive carborundum powder to the axle boxes and the bearings seized up after just a few kilometres). The Division was thus forced to take to the road; not only was its progress delayed, as a result, but the move probably cost Germany well over 500,000 litres of petrol.

Quinine first operated in the south of the Corrèze, arming a small *maquisard* group from the containers of weapons dropped with it, and leading them in a brief campaign of sabotage and ambuscade. Although intended more as encouragement and example than as a serious attempt at disruption, this included a bridge blown at Bretenoux, and an ill-judged ambush mounted on a company-strength patrol from one of the *Das Reich* Division's Panzer Grenadier regiments, which cost many *résistants'* lives.

Moving south and further west, Quinine concentrated on the N20, the main north–south road which runs through Montauban, Cahors, Brive and Limoges, and the stretch of the railway between Cahors and Souillac. Macpherson tells us in his rather terse report (it runs to only slightly more than one close-typed foolscap page) that they entirely eliminated traffic in that sector by 1 July, before switching their attention to co-ordinating the activities of the large number of small partisan bands spread out over the area, many of which were armed from Operation Cadillac.

By early in August, Koenig had appointed Pierre Bertaux to lead the Resistance movement in the south-west of France, and Col Schneider to act as his military commander. Enemy forces were largely restricted to the main towns and cities, and only ventured out in strength, although encounters between them and the partisans were often very bloody affairs, with relatively large numbers of casualties on both sides. Quinine was by now helping to form a powerful mobile column, the *Groupement Mobile du Sud-Ouest*, which would, under Schneider's command, move across the southern Massif Central in the direction of Clermont-Ferrand and the valley of the Allier and then continue north, offering protection to the left flank of the French *Armée B*. Macpherson is vague about the team's movements after it left the Lot; all he tells us of Quinine's activities after early August is that 'we extended to the Vosges our very widespread intelligence net'. Asp Bourbon-Parme returned to the United Kingdom on 9 October, and Macpherson and Brown volunteered for a Jedburgh-style mission in Italy.

Ammonia

After returning to base on the morning of D-Day, team Ammonia –
Capt Benton 'Mac' Austin ('Gaspard'); Lt Raymond Le Compte, who
used the name Conte ('Ludovic') and Sgt Jacob B Berlin ('Marcial')
went out again the following night. This time the pilot found the DZ
but did not accept the recognition letter, and once again the team
returned to Blida. A third attempt put them on to the ground near Sarlat
in the Dordogne at around 02 30 on the morning of 10 June; the deployment went smoothly, the men landed safely and all the containers
dropped with them, save for one package containing batteries and radio
spares, were recovered.

Ammonia was to have reported to the organiser of SOE F Section's
Wheelwright circuit, 'Hilaire' (Lt-Col George Starr), but his base was
far away, at Castelnau-sur-l'Auvignon, between Auch and Condom, in
the Gers, and it was his deputy, 'Claude' (Arnault), with whom they
liaised. Like Quinine their primary task was to attack enemy lines of
communication between Montauban and Brive, but their objective was
switched instead to the Montauban–Bordeaux axis, and the team moved
to Soumensac in the north-western corner of the Lot-et-Garonne.
Here they were put in touch with 'Col Beck' and 'Col Main Noir', two
resistance chiefs whose *bona fides* were suspect (Hilaire and Claude
believed them to be little more than criminals) but who were said to
have a strong grip on the partisans of the *département*. They received the
Jedburghs amiably enough, but it soon became apparent that they were
simply flattering to deceive, and before long Austin broke off all contact
with them. He relied instead on leaders of smaller groups, who were
nominally under the orders of Main Noir but had become disillusioned
by his failure to act. These men were willing but completely untrained,
and by the time Austin and Le Compte had succeeded in getting them
even partially effective the Allies had landed on the Côte-d'Azur and
German troops in the area had begun to withdraw down the Garonne
Valley in the direction of Bordeaux. Ammonia and their partisans followed, and joined in the cordon which had been thrown around the
southern and south-eastern sectors of the city to keep the Germans
penned there.

When the garrison withdrew, some to try to fight their way through
to Poitiers and from there into the Loire Valley, others to the Pointe de
Grave, at the mouth of the Gironde, where they were to hold out almost
until the end of the war, Austin tried to find other work for the team. He

tells us that the DMR, 'Triangle', chose it to represent him in four *départements* – Charente, Charente-Maritime, Vendée and Deux-Sèvres – but soon found that that did not amount to much.

Clearly, Austin was frustrated by his inability to carry out a meaningful mission, and that spilled over into the conclusion to his after-action report, in which he lambasts almost every aspect of its management. His comments on the poor quality of his briefing, the timing of the team's deployment and the unreliability of resupply operations were echoed by other teams, but Ammonia seems to have had particular difficulty with its radio communications. Sgt Berlin was blamed (by Algiers) for this, and another operator – S/Lt Jean Verneuil ('Marcellin') – was sent to join the team; his report makes it clear that it was the base-station operators, and not Berlin, who were deficient.

Capt Austin and Sgt Berlin returned to the United Kingdom on 26 October, and Lt Le Compte followed a fortnight later; it is unclear when or if Verneuil was withdrawn.

Bugatti

It was the night of 28 June before another team was inserted from Algiers, the long hiatus being caused by impossible weather conditions. Team Bugatti consisted of Maj Horace Fuller ('Kansul'), Lt Guy de la Roche du Rouzet, using the name Rocher ('Hopei'), and S/Lt Martial Sigaud, who took Guillemot as his *nom de guerre* ('Chekiang'). Like Ammonia, it was to report to Hilaire on arrival, and work within the framework established by his Wheelwright circuit.

The team left Blida at 2030, arrived at a DZ midway between St-Gaudens and Lannemezan, in the Hautes-Pyrénées, were met by a reception committee which included Hilaire's courier 'Colette' (Anne-Marie Walters) and were taken to a farm. The next day, Colette drove Fuller, in civilian clothes, to meet Hilaire, who had moved to Condom, a hundred kilometres away, after his base at Castelnau had come under concerted attack on 21 June. He remained with Hilaire for three days and in his absence the farm where de la Roche and Sigaud were hiding was surrounded by Germans searching for them; they escaped through a window. When Fuller returned they moved south, into the mountains, to a *maquisard* camp near Arbon, only fifteen kilometres from the Spanish border, and organised the destruction of four pylons carrying power lines. The weapons, material and spare radio dropped with the team had been cached in Lannemezan; communications with Algiers via the set the team had with them were extremely poor, and by the second week of July it had become essential to recover the spare. In the meantime Lannemezan had become home to two battalions of German troops, but de la Roche and four *maquisards* managed to spirit the consignment away under their noses, and a request for a supply drop was, for once, answered promptly. It was most timely, too, for the next evening, 17 July, Bugatti got word that a battalion of mountain troops had left their barracks to rout them out from the isolated farm to which they and the partisans had moved. The troops arrived in Arbon early the following morning, but heavy fog had come down, and they elected to wait until it had cleared. Fuller had withdrawn the partisans to a position overlooking the farm, and when the Germans arrived, at about 1730, the partisans were able to kill sixteen and wound a score more before withdrawing into the woods and making good their escape. The move this time took them to a camp in the mountains above St-Bertrand-de-Comminges.

The *parachutage* Bugatti received on 16 July was enough to arm about a hundred men, and Fuller gave the weapons to a group led by M. La Chaux, the manager of the oil refinery at Peyrouzet, near St-Gaudens, which was established further up the valley. This group constantly harried the traffic using the road there, which leads into Spain, until its campsite was attacked by a strong detachment of SS and mountain troops, and forced to scatter, leaving behind many dead and wounded. Fuller and de la Roche, meanwhile, had decided to split up, the former to work with the partisans in the mountains and as far east as St-Gaudens, to mount a campaign of ambush and sabotage, the latter to direct the FFI from their headquarters at Tarbes. Both were to be hampered by a shortage of arms, ammunition and explosives, for despite almost daily requests for further resupply, they received no more *parachutages*, and their credibility was much reduced by their inability to produce weapons for the *maquisards*. Such small supplies of explosives as they had were used sparingly against rail targets, particularly the line which runs across the Col du Somport into Spain, which was in use, even at this late stage, to bring in iron ore. The line was cut in the first week of August, blocking 50,000 tons of ore at the frontier. The refinery at Peyrouzet had been a priority target for the team, but after consultations with La Chaux it became clear that it could be disabled rather than destroyed, simply by cutting off its water supply. Two days after the Germans left, Fuller tells us, the refinery was in operation again.

On the evening of 14 August, the BBC broadcast the message which signalled all-out guerrilla activity against the Germans in the south-west of France, and two days later Fuller moved his men down into a position to control the Garonne Valley, and cut the road there. Over the next week, the German garrisons in the mountain towns close to the Spanish border began to move northward, and despite a shortage of ammunition, the *maquisards* managed to account for many of them. The regional headquarters at Tarbes evacuated the city on 18 August, but not before a strong partisan force got itself into position to ambush it. 'Result: 20 Boche killed, 45 wounded and rest taken prisoner. The maquis suffered 3 dead and 6 wounded.' In three days of fighting, Fuller records, they took 600 prisoners, twenty of whom were officers, including a general and four colonels, and captured large quantities of much-needed material.

Bugatti, now reunited once more, moved into the Hotel Moderne at Tarbes on 23 August. Within five days, a column, a thousand strong, had been organised, and Fuller and a local commander, 'Col Soule', led it north-west towards Bordeaux, fighting an engagement at Mont-de-Marsan along the way (Fuller makes no mention of the presence there of teams Martin and Miles, nor of the death of Martin's leader, Capt Thomas Mellows) and arriving on 29 August, by which time the German garrison there was in full retreat. Meanwhile, de la Roche had begun to assemble a small air force from planes captured intact on the many airfields in the region. He had ten working before the team was withdrawn, using them for reconnaissance flights and, after fuses for captured bombs had been located at Biarritz, for occasional airstrikes on the Pointe de Grave enclave from their base at Cazau, near Arcachon, to the west of Bordeaux.

Bugatti received the order to cease operations in mid-September. Horace Fuller returned to the United Kingdom, via Lons-le-Saunier, where he was debriefed by Neil Marten, and Paris, on 9 October, and Guy de la Roche rejoined him a week later. Martial Sigaud remained in France, and there are reports that he was later killed in action.

Collodion

A tripartite team, sometimes confusingly referred to as 'Loch', Collodion was made up of Capt Harold Hall from the 27th Lancers ('Augustine'), Lt Henri Marsaudon, who called himself Morgan ('Benoît') and Sgt Theodore Baumgold ('Jules'). Its orders were to join

Tommy Macpherson's team Quinine, which had by this time begun its move eastward, in the Aveyron *département*. Collodion was dropped – on the third attempt – to the Chénier DZ in the Cantal, which Quinine had used two months earlier, in the early hours of 7 August, and from there, guided by Michel de Bourbon-Parme, moved south to Decazeville in the Aveyron. Here it met 'Marc', the leader of an FTP group, and then moved on to Pommiers, near Conques, ten kilometres away, where 'Col Benoît' (not to be confused with Col Bertrand from the Cher, who also used that name), who is described as the chief of *Maquis* in the north of the Aveyron, had his HQ. Hall tells us that there was 'little work in this area', and two days later the team returned to the north of Decazeville, just in time to witness a raid on the town by Germans from Rodez, the principal city of the *département*.

The following night Collodion demonstrated that it was not only FTP bands who appropriated *parachutages*, for it did so itself (Hall does not tell us from whom), and distributed the arms to a group named Fred which was based near Entraygues-sur-Truyère, to the north. Two nights later it repeated the process, this time to the benefit of *Maquis* Jules from Laguiole. Fred put its newly acquired weaponry to good use when, on 17 August, a German column left Rodez, heading north-east towards Bozouls. The partisans mined the road just a few kilometres north of the city, and forced the enemy troops to detour towards Entraygues by way of a minor road. Running into an ambush, the Germans dispersed, machine-gunning and burning a small hamlet before concentrating on the village of Villecomtal. Here, Hall had prepared demolition charges at a key bridge, the destruction of which would have prevented the Germans from entering the village, but 'unfortunately owing to red tape encountered in getting permission to do this [from whom he does not tell us], it was too late, and the Germans entered'; Hall was lucky to escape after being cornered in the post office. Later that day, now joined by team Quinine, Collodion oversaw the preparations for an attack on a power station at Rueyres on the River Truyère, where a strong anti-air-craft battery was installed. Roads and bridges were blown, and the battery completely isolated; its 140 men surrendered four days later, presenting the partisans with twelve AA guns, a direction-finding station and all their transport.

The following day, before dawn, the Rodez garrison began to with-draw south, towards Millau and Montpellier. By 22 August, after falling foul of a series of damaging ambushes, it had reached Larzac, where there was an airfield used by the *Luftwaffe*; there they came under attack by two American P-38 Lightning fighters, and managed to shoot one down with light AA fire. They had a further success that night when a partisan ambush party, moving into position ahead of the column, stumbled upon one of its security elements and was wiped out. (French sources say that the party's purpose was sabotage, and after it had successfully carried that out it attacked the German vanguard, and was annihilated in the fighting which followed.) Over the next two days, partisan forces continued to pick away at the Axis column; by late on 24 August the main road had been mined in so many places, and the column itself subjected to so many ambushes, that it had become fragmented. With unified command lost and all hope gone of reaching Montpellier as an effective fighting force, the survivors began to turn eastward across the open plateau which covers much of the northern Hérault, aiming for the Rhône Valley. Many of them were hunted down and killed along the way.

The Jedburghs continued on down the N9 to Lodève, where they met the members of a Mission known as Choeur, under the command of a British captain named Stansfield ('Hubert'). Here they were joined by a five-man support team from the French Army, parachuted in, together with a substantial amount of arms and equipment, from Algiers. The following day, 26 August, they began to hear rumours of a strong Axis column approaching from the west – these were troops who had been based near Toulouse and had opted to take the arduous but more direct route eastward, via Albi and St-Affrique, rather than the long detour through the Carcassonne Gap to the coast at Narbonne – and began to distribute the weapons from the *parachutage* to the 300 and more partisans gathered at Lodève. In the event, although the team moved around the whole area, Hall reported seeing no enemy whatsoever, and came to the conclusion that the reports were a fabrication designed to ensure the distribution of arms to partisan bands which had no need of them, but simply wished to stockpile them against the day they would be needed for the civil war against the Communists. He was able to recover some of the weapons.

On 28 August, Collodion left Lodève accompanied by a team of about thirty partisans to move towards Le Vigan, fifty kilometres to the north-east, in the general direction of Alès. Around fifty German troops were stationed there, operating and guarding a telephone exchange which served the trunk lines for the whole of central southern France, from Toulouse to Marseilles. The installation was well guarded, with two 15cm mortars, 3.7cm anti-tank guns and well-sited machine-guns, and surrounded by a stone wall ten feet high and an electrified barbed-wire fence. The partisans took up their positions before dawn on 29

August, and prepared for what would perhaps have been a very costly and prolonged fire-fight, but as day broke the garrison surrendered.

The following day, 30 August, Collodion moved to Nîmes, and thence to Alès; the next day advance elements of the French *Armée B* arrived, and the team made its way to Brignolles in the Var, to 4 SFU's base, where it was debriefed and directed to Grenoble to rest before returning to London.

Chrysler

Team Chrysler left Blida on the evening of 13 August, but the pilot failed to find the DZ, and returned to Algeria with the team – Capt Cyril Sell of the Royal Artillery ('Elie'); Capt Paul Aussaresses of the Foreign Legion, who took the name Soual ('Bazin') and Sgt Ron Chatten of the Royal Armoured Corps ('Artus') – still aboard.

The team's principal objective was the lines of communication in the Carcassonne Gap, between the Montagne Noire – the Black Mountain – to the north and the Corbières, foothills of the Pyrénées, to the south, through which run the main road, canal and railway linking the Atlantic coast with the Mediterranean by way of Toulouse, Castelnaudary, Carcassonne and Narbonne. (Aussaresses was no stranger to this region, having been born and brought up in the village of St-Paul-Cap-de-Joux, some fifty kilometres north of Castelnaudary.) Chrysler was also to target 11. Panzer Division, although its exact whereabouts at that moment were unclear. In fact, the bulk of the division had pulled out of Chrysler's operational area on 12 August, before the team arrived there. Chrysler was also to attempt to prevent Axis forces from crossing into Spain.

The team left Blida again on the evening of 16 August. It was one of five teams dropped in the area immediately north of the Pyrénées that night. Chrysler boarded a B-24 Liberator at around 2030 and were over the dropping zone – Pamplemousse, near the village of Rieucros, between Pamiers and Mirepoix, fifty kilometres south-west of Carcassonne – just before midnight. They were treated, if Sell's account is to be believed, to one of the most incompetent insertion operations yet, being dropped from a height of around 1,500m and with no attempt made at throttling back to slow the aircraft. The speed at which it was travelling caused the men to somersault as they fell. The team members and their containers were strewn across a wide area and the reception committee was not even aware that a *parachutage* had taken place until Capt Sell managed to make his way to the DZ. After an hour's searching, Aussaresses was located. Sgt Chatten was found, the following morning, in a village where he had taken refuge. By the time the containers had been retrieved all had been opened, and much material was missing.

The Chrysler reception party was composed of Spaniards from a 250-strong band calling itself the *Reconquista de España* battalion – anarchists who had come over the border hoping to build to sufficient strength to one day march on Madrid and do what their name proclaimed. They were led by 'Cmdt Royo' (Ramón Rubio). Two weeks earlier, these Spanish *guerrilleros* had received an Allied Mission known, from the code name of its French co-leader, Cmdt Bigeard, as 'Aube', and under its guidance had taken over from the local SAP agent, 'Richard', the reception of material from SPOC. On the night in question, Aube's co-commander, a British major named Bill Probert ('Crypt'), had been in charge of the reception committee at Pamplemousse. While searching for Chatten, Probert heard reports of parachutists being sheltered near Trémoulet, seven kilometres to the north-west. When he went to investigate, he discovered the three members of Jedburgh team John, plus S/Lt Verneuil, the quite unnecessary replacement radio operator for team Ammonia, who had been dropped from a different aircraft to that which had brought Chrysler, some hundred and fifty kilometres or more away from their intended destination in the Tarn-et-Garonne.

Apparently Richard's wife had somehow heard of the imminent arrival of Chrysler and, unaware of the change of plan, and in the absence of her husband, had decided to take matters into her own hands. She had mobilised local farmers to man a ground near Trémoulet which her husband had selected to replace Pamplemousse – which he believed to be too close to a main road – but which he, or his chief, 'Pasha', had neglected to identify to Algiers. All that was necessary to complete the farce were an incompetent Flying Fortress crew, which located a DZ 150 kilometres away from the one to which they had been directed but decided it was the correct one anyway; a reception committee leader with a shaky hand on the signal lamp, and the unhappy near-coincidence of the recognition code for Pamplemousse (J; '.--.') and that for John's intended DZ (P; '.---'). The pilot took the J flashed from the ground for a P, and without more ado dropped his load; the result was seven more-or-less mystified Jedburghs, all of them on the ground some distance from their intended operational zones (though only fifty kilometres in Chrysler's case) and – thanks to the absence of Richard, the damage caused to Chrysler's radio sets during the insertion, and John's operator having been given the wrong frequencies – no immediate liaison with anyone save a group of disgruntled Spaniards and a few farmers.

There we shall leave John, and return to them in due course. The following day, Maj Probert arranged for Chrysler to move to Ste-Colombe-sur-Guette, to contact 'Albert', seemingly with a view to his helping them move towards Carcassonne. The move to Albert's HQ took most of the day, due to the intensity of German patrol activity on the roads.

Early on 19 August Chrysler met with *maquis* chiefs at Ste-Colombe to make a plan of action. It was decided that their first target should be a nearby electricity sub-station which controlled distribution through much of the Aude and the neighbouring Pyrénées-Orientales; that steps should be taken to block the roads leading to the Spanish border; that ambush activity should be stepped up, and that the Jedburghs would request *parachutages* of weapons and stores. One of the *maquisards* present was from Quillan, which was a step closer to the Carcassonne Gap, and Sell and Aussaresses returned with him, continuing on to Limoux that afternoon. At Quillan they first crossed the tracks of OG Peg, which had been inserted (with orders almost identical to Chrysler's own) near Axat, south of there, on 12 August. Peg had been in action in the Aude Valley between Quillan and Limoux for almost a week by this time, and had lost one of its officers, Lt Swank, (there is no indication as to whether or not he was related to Lawrence Swank of team Ephedrine) in a fire-fight two days earlier when a team placing demolition charges to block the road near Alet-les-Bains was surprised by a German patrol. Swank remained to give covering fire while the others withdrew, and was killed.

In Limoux, the Jedburghs met 'Cmdt Georges', the local FTP leader who was also the Departmental FFI chief, and Lt Weeks, Peg's leader, who was eager to join forces with them. Together they continued towards Carcassonne, and began to operate against the railway which links Toulouse with Narbonne, cutting it in several places to the west of Carcassonne, and then working up a plan to demolish a short tunnel near Trèbes, to the east of the city. In the event, the tunnel was too well guarded, and they contented themselves with blowing up the permanent way near it, but with satisfactory results: no more trains used the line until after the liberation. Returning to Limoux, the subject of the occupation of Carcassonne came up. The citizens were extremely nervous following a German proclamation that, in that event, the city would be put to the torch. Cmdt Georges was opposed to any such plan, but more junior FFI leaders, 'Talon' and 'David', argued that control of the city would allow them to dominate the through routes, and in the end they prevailed.

As it happened, although reinforcements were expected at any moment, the German presence in Carcassonne was light. Aussaresses took charge of the situation, deposed the Vichy-ite Prefect, secured the co-operation of the *Gendarmerie* and revitalised the dormant Committee of Liberation, then set about preparing defensive positions. Rumours that there were 5,000 Allied parachutists in the city soon reached German ears, and the expected force coming down from Toulouse via Castelnaudary skirted Carcassonne to the north, and continued eastward. Meanwhile, Sell set out to clear German skirmishers from the hills surrounding Limoux, and later that day proceeded to Carcassonne. On 23 August the Jedburghs began sending out reconnaissance patrols in the direction of Lézignan-Corbières and Narbonne; there were few Axis troops left in the area, and fighting was sporadic. Over the next days Sell and Aussaresses ranged as far as Perpignan and the Spanish frontier, using both the easier route via Narbonne and the coast road (where Aussaresses reconnoitred the beaches between Narbonne-Plage and Leucate), and the more difficult direct route through Quillan. Any pockets of German resistance were suppressed. News of a new column coming from the west brought them back to Carcassonne, and a series of ambushes were mounted; these troops, too, skirted the city to the north, but were attacked there as well by elements of the *Corps Franc de la Montaigne Noire*. At the end of the month, Chrysler shifted the focus of its operations to Perpignan, where it received two drops of arms and ammunition. It soon became clear that the weapons were actually surplus to requirements in the eastern Pyrénées-Orientales, and after Sell visited Toulouse to confer with Hilaire and the leaders of other Jedburgh teams, the arms, together with four instructors who had dropped with them, were moved there and distributed to the men who were making up the *Groupement Mobile du Sud-Ouest* which team Quinine would accompany as it moved northward.

By now, Aussaresses had met Gen Cochet, Gen Koenig's representative in the area from the Rhône to the Spanish border, and had begun to work more closely with him. He accompanied him to Nîmes on 5 September, and then on to Marseilles, while Sell returned to Perpignan briefly, and then travelled northward himself on 7 September. The following day Chrysler was reunited in Marseilles, and travelled north to Avignon, to report the completion of its mission to 4 SFU. Paul Aussaresses was to remain in the army for many years, reaching the rank of general. He was instrumental in the creation of France's Special Forces, and co-operated closely with American special forces at the time of the Vietnam War, being seconded to Fort Benning and Fort Bragg for some of that period.

John

We left team John asleep in a safe house near Trémoulet, having been dropped just before midnight on 16 August to a ground at least 150 kilometres from their true destination, a DZ known as Pinocchio, south of Cahors. In addition to the three men of the team – Capt David Stern, of the Lancashire Fusiliers and more recently of SOE ('Beau'); S/Lt Maurice de Galbert, who called himself Le Rocher ('Lucide') and Sgt Donald Gibbs of the Royal Armoured Corps ('Silence') – the group included the replacement radio operator for team Ammonia, S/Lt Jean Verneuil ('Marcellin'). John had been briefed to operate in the Tarn-et-Garonne, reporting to 'Alphonse' (Tony Brooks) of the Pimento circuit; in fact, they discovered that they were being sent in response to a request Alphonse had made in June 1943, for sabotage instructors to operate in civilian clothes, and later that Alphonse, whose circuit covered two operational areas, one in the south-west, the other in east-central France, was then operating around Lyon. They spent much of their time searching for him, to no avail.

John waited for two days at Trémoulet for Bill Probert of Mission Aube to make good a vague promise to help them on their way northward, and on the return of 'Richard', the local SAP agent, enlisted his aid. He passed them to an associate, 'Jean-Pierre', who agreed to have them taken to Fleurance, in the northern Gers, where 'Pasha', the regional SAP chief, had his base. This was at least a move in the right direction, and the team left, by car, on or about 21 August. Pasha had no idea of Alphonse's whereabouts, but he did know where Ammonia was located, and passed Jean Verneuil on to them. As for John, the best he could suggest was that they contact a *maquisard* chief at Beaumont-de-Lomagne, which at least had the virtue of being in the right *département*. They had no better luck with 'Bourcier', another local leader, but were impressed by his fighting spirit, and promised to call up a *parachutage* for him; then they moved on, first to Montauban and later to Toulouse, in search of the elusive Alphonse.

In Toulouse, on 25 August, John met Hilaire, and teams Mark, Martin and Miles, all of which had been dropped into the area the same night they had arrived. There were partisans of all colours and shades of colours in Toulouse by this time, but the group which most impressed David Stern was the *Demi-Brigade d'Armagnac*, which was about to set off in pursuit of the Axis column which had bypassed Carcassonne on 22–23 August, and was now believed to be near Béziers. They accompanied it when it gave chase, but were too far behind ever to have caught up; by the time they got to Pézenas, on the coast, the Germans had long taken to the railway, and had, in fact, been largely wiped out by a series of airstrikes.

John returned to Toulouse, and at last, on 1 September made contact with Alphonse's lieutenant in the city, 'Gilbert', who simply said that there was no work for them, and requested them to stay well away from the battalion he was trying to form from the Resistance faction to which he was allied, for fear that the rival FTP would brand his men as mercenaries, working for a foreign power.

John now became involved – though only marginally – in Hilaire's plan to set up some form of regional government in Toulouse. Other Jedburghs, see below, were to be scathing in their criticism of Hilaire in this respect, and suggested it was for this scheme that de Gaulle ordered him out of the country within forty-eight hours when he visited Toulouse a fortnight later. They were wrong; the General ordered *every* non-French Resistance fighter he met out of the country, so desperate was he to maintain the illusion that at least that part of France where American and British armies had not ventured, south of the Loire and west of the Rhône/Saône, had been liberated by Frenchmen alone. John helped arrange for the repatriation to the United Kingdom of Allied sick and wounded, and the team was also instrumental in the recovery intact of a Heinkel He.177 *Grief*, a heavy bomber which had entered limited squadron service in July 1942, used to deploy advanced weapons systems such as the 'Fritz-X' and Henschel Hs.293 radio-guided bombs, which had already showed themselves most effective against even capital ships.

This kind of activity could clearly not last; de Galbert soon found a reason to go to Paris, returned briefly to Toulouse and then left for London on 4 October. Stern and Gibbs, by now installed in a Toulouse hotel, stuck it out somewhat longer, but they, too, were back in the United Kingdom on 16 October.

Mark

Team Mark also left Blida aboard a B-24 Liberator at around 2030 on 16 August, and was dropped to a well-marked ground known as Buffalo Bill, the location of which cannot be deduced. The team was composed of two Americans and a Frenchman – Lt Lucien Conein ('Intrepide'), French by birth but brought up in the USA, Lt Johanes Thévenet, who called himself de Thévenet ('Sympathique') and Sgt James Carpenter ('Lester'). Mark was detailed to work for Hilaire, whose Wheelwright circuit extended right across the south-western extremity of France, but who was increasingly concentrating his activities in and around Toulouse, in the Haute-Garonne.

The drop was, once again, poorly executed, the pilot flying downwind towards the DZ at too great an altitude and failing to slow the aircraft; the containers were dropped first, then the packages, then the men, and in consequence the team landed six kilometres from the DZ, 'Lulu' Conein with a sprained ankle thanks to his rigging lines having twisted, degrading his control over the canopy. The three men hid in the field where they had landed for the rest of the night, and next day walked until they met a farm worker, who led them to a group of wounded *maquisards*. They were thus put into contact with Hilaire, who told them it would be impossible to work in the Tarn-et-Garonne due to the uncertain military situation there. Later that day they met 'Cmdt Ravanel' (a twenty-five-year-old former lieutenant, Serge Asher or Ascher, who was also known, according to Conein, as 'Hexagon' and 'Verdun'); there are question marks hanging over Ravanel's motives, and another Jedburgh team leader was to be highly critical of him; see the report of team Miles, below. He had been appointed as Regional Commander by COMAC, which was Communist dominated, on 4 June, having previously been a member of EMFFI's *Troisième Bureau*, but was in dispute with the man Gen de Gaulle had named to the post of *Commissaire de la République* for the city, Pierre Bertaux. Also present was 'Rosette', representing 'Droite' (the DMR, Col Schlumberger) and other assorted 'colonels', who were by now appearing from all over the place. Ravanel tried to stamp his authority on the meeting, insisting that all orders to *maquisard* combat units should be issued by him, but Hilaire, using a device also employed elsewhere to good effect, pointed out that the Jedburghs represented Gen Koenig, and through him the Supreme Commander, Gen Eisenhower, and thus outranked him. The stratagem worked, at least temporarily.

The immediate danger was the German garrison at Auch, which was preparing to pull out of the town, almost certainly in the direction of Toulouse, directly to the east. Conein says he 'called in' (a trifle presumptuous, perhaps, for a lieutenant) the commanders of the partisan brigades – the *Demi-Brigade d'Armagnac*, led by Cmdt Parisot, and the *Corps Franc* from the Gers led by Cmdt Cellerier, a regular officer who had commanded a regiment of *Chasseurs Alpins* in 1939–40, as well as a Spanish group led by 'Cmdt Camillio' – and outlined a plan to blockade the N124 between Auch and Toulouse, as well as the secondary roads (which assertion does not quite square with the account of team Miles; the two are often at odds). The force set out the following morning, 19 August, but did not arrive at L'Isle-Jourdain, about twenty-five kilometres due west of Toulouse, until six hours later.

The first contact, says Conein, was made at around 1730, and the fire-fight lasted until around 0100, when both sides seem to have decided to break it off simultaneously, each feeling that they were getting the worse of the encounter. At a council of war later, it was decided to 'try to make an armistice', which seems somewhat bizarre. Conein tells us that Mark strongly opposed this but 'due to the higher rank and greater number of the French leaders, we were over-ruled', which hardly seems to gell with the notion that they had been able to prevail over Ravanel earlier. Conein goes on:

> At 0500 next morning with Capt Parisot and Cmdt Cellerier we advanced down the road where we encountered all the Germans lined up in columns of four in the middle of the road. Capt Parisot advanced and began negotiations … After fifteen minutes the Oberst said the Germans would continue fighting. A five minute armistice was agreed on and the Germans dispersed to take up battle positions. If this armistice had not been made we could have mowed down all of them in five minutes as we were now superior in numbers; their force numbering only slightly over 300.

That afternoon a messenger arrived bringing news that the Spanish column under Camillio was coming up on the German right flank, and should arrive about 1730. Conein sent orders to Camillio that he should attack the house the Germans were using as a command post at 1840, intending that the existing forces would simultaneously hit them from the other side. 'This worked very well,' he said, 'except that Camillio never arrived, for he was celebrating in Auch and looting the tobacco store.' In any event, things had already started to go the partisans' way, and by 2000 the battle was effectively over. Total German losses were reckoned at sixty-two dead and forty-six wounded at a cost of nineteen French dead and over forty wounded 'and how many [Germans] got away, I still don't know'.

Well-authenticated French sources give a very different view of the combat at L'Isle-Jourdain (which occupies a place of honour in the annals of the Resistance in this area). By those accounts, the Auch garrison, which numbered 300 and was made up largely of *Feldgendarmerie* and infantry units, under the command of Col Priepke, started from the city at around 1530 on 19 August, and reached the vicinity of L'Isle-Jourdain just as night was falling. Here it was stopped, at the bridge over the River Save to the west of the town centre, by elements of the *Corps Franc Pommiès* (CFP), who were soon reinforced by units of the Armagnac battalion. The German column made no further progress that night, but the fire-fight was renewed at daybreak. There was stalemate throughout the day despite the French numerical superiority, and it was only the arrival of the CFP's *Brigade Le Magny* in the late afternoon which swung the affair in favour of the French. By 1915 they had gone over to the attack, and by 2030 the battle was effectively over, with large numbers of exhausted Germans capitulating. The German casualty toll was put at sixty-two dead, and 192 were made prisoner; French losses amounted to ten dead and twenty-eight wounded. No mention is made of the non-appearance of a Spanish column – nor of any attempt at truce-making – and there is an irreconcilable disparity in the chronology of the two accounts. Almost certainly the French account is the more accurate.

By now, the situation in Toulouse was critical; the German garrison had begun pulling out on 20 August, and had set fire to many of the public buildings. There was no gas, electricity or water, and virtually no food, 'but rival leaders still quarrelled and tried to arrest or oust each other', as one observer put it (according to one eminent historian of the Resistance, there were no less than thirty-seven self-appointed leaders and commanders in the city, each with his own 'secret service'). By the next day the bulk of the city's garrison had left, though there were still isolated pockets holding out, and also many *miliciens* who knew that surrender probably meant death at the hands of the mob. Hilaire duly asked Conein to go to Toulouse to negotiate with Ravanel to allow the Armagnac Brigade into the city:

> The FTP ... [were] waiting to make their entry after having let all the Germans escape from Toulouse. Ravanel received me very coldly and

finally agreed on the entry of the Brigade of Armagnac. On my way out of town one motorcycle of my escort broke down and I was left in the middle of town. When the Milice saw the American flag flying from the car they began firing at me from the roof tops. The civilian population began to mob the car and I had to draw a gun to keep them away. I then made my first public speech. I announced in public that the American troops [which, of course, were no nearer than either the east bank of the Rhône or the north bank of the Loire] were 10 kilometres from Toulouse, that I was the advance guard, and that we would enter the next day. At that moment I did not realise the proportions a false rumour would make. For three weeks the people were sewing American and British flags, and standing on the roads expecting the phantom column.

At this point, Hilaire started using Jed Team Mark for political-military work. Many secret meetings were held at which I was not present, and I was sent on missions for Hilaire of which I did not have full knowledge althought Lt Thevenet was fully acquainted with all the details.

Two days later Conein baulked at the situation, and told Thévenet that from then on, he would attend all 'secret' meetings, that he was responsible for the team and that no 'telegrams' (i.e. radio messages) were to be sent without his knowledge or permission 'as had been done in the past', enforcing this with a reminder that the W/T operator was American, and could thus be expected to obey his orders over those of his French colleague.

The overall situation was deteriorating rapidly. On 30 August, Mark went to 'Besier' (Béziers) where there was considerable civil unrest, with armed factions fighting each other openly. The house where the Jedburghs were staying was, Conein tells us, 'attacked twice [in six days] by the French. Inasmuch as I had no power to disarm the civilian population I returned to Toulouse to inform Ravanel of the situation and request his co-operation. Ravanel said he would have to call a meeting of the council [of Liberation, which he had packed with his supporters, most of whom were FTP]'.

Mark's next excursion was to the border with Spain (the location is not specified, but Conein's report talks of 'French officers going to and from St Sebastian' by way of a bridge, which implies it was somewhere like Hendaye, on the Atlantic coast). 'During the week, over 800 Spaniards had come from Spain to France and over 1,200 Germans had gone to Spain, where they were cheered and received by the Fascists.'

Conein next went to Marseilles to see Gen Cochet and give him a situation report (typically, he makes no mention of another Jedburgh, Paul Aussaresses, in the general's entourage, but rather implies that he alone was able to furnish an accurate sitrep) and returned to Toulouse with orders from Cochet that Pierre Bertaux, nominally in command of all Resistance forces in the area, was to stand down as of 12 September.

On his return to the south-west, Conein learned that Thévenet had left for Paris, and he and Sgt Carpenter teamed up with 'Capt Raymond' (Lt Georges Redonnet) of team Martin, moving first to Bordeaux and then to Royan, where they 'organised a group of agents'. The arrival in the sector of Gen de Larminat and his headquarters, in late October, finally convinced Conein that he was surplus to requirements, and on 13 November he left for Paris. Several days later, along with another redundant Jedburgh – Maj Robert Montgomery of team Tony – he travelled to Vittel, to US 6th Army Group HQ, to deliver another situation report. He returned to Paris on 19 November, the day after Sgt Carpenter had left to return to London, and joined him there on 24 November.

Martin and Miles

The last Jedburgh teams to be deployed in Gascony, Martin and Miles, went into the field together, dropped from another Blida-based B-24 Liberator, on the night of 16 August. Martin consisted of Capt Thomas Mellows of the Royal Armoured Corps (Blasé), Lt Georges Redonnet, alias Rémond ('Substantif') and Sgt Neville Carey ('Placide'); Miles was made up of Capt Everett T Allen ('Libre'), Lt René Éstève, who took the name Pierre Fourcade ('Lumineux') and T/Sgt Arthur Gruen ('Fidèle'). Due to the death of Mellows on 21 August, team Martin never made a formal report, and we have to rely on that of Miles, plus occasional insights from other sources, to chart its activities.

The teams' insertion, to a DZ near Avéron, south-east of Nogaro, in the Gers, fifty kilometres west of Auch, was uneventful, although – once again – the pilot flew across the lights, instead of along their line; this time, however, the ground was wide enough to accommodate the six parachutists, though Mellows landed heavily and was not fully mobile thereafter as a result. The reception committee included Hilaire and men of the Armagnac battalion, which had its origins in this area.

On 17 and 18 August the teams found their feet and distributed the weapons and stores they had brought with them, and the following day set off for the *Demi-Brigade d'Armagnac*'s camp, south of Auch. They arrived at noon, and immediately became involved in the planning for an assault on Auch. The battalion moved up in preparation for an attack, but it soon became clear that the German garrison was itself on the point of departing. It pulled out the following morning, 20 August, with the *maquisards* in pursuit, towards L'Isle-Jourdain. Allen says Martin and Miles 'participated in this fight and then left for Mont-de-Marsan … Arrived outside of Mont-de-Marsan [which is around 150 kilometres from L'Isle-Jourdain] at 1800 that night'.

The German garrison in the city – which was under the command of *Generalmajor* Botho Elster – was already destroying the stores it would not be able to take with it, in preparation for its departure during the night of 20 August. By the following morning the city was empty of German troops, and the *maquisards*, led by 'Col Carnot' (Jean de Milleret, chief of the *Corps Franc Pommiès*' western group, which had been engaged in open guerrilla warfare against the Germans of the Pau and Mont-de-Marsan garrisons since late June) entered. Celebrations were to be short-lived:

> While dining [actually, lunching] at the Prefecture Carnot was handed a report that between 40 and 50 German lorries were advancing towards Mont-de-Marsan from the direction of Dax and Bayonne [i.e., from the west]. Between 1500 and 1600 hours that day made a reccy of defence installations guarding town – found none in existence so took military commandment of town. At approximately 1730 while inspecting one of the abates [sic] on the Dax road along with Lt Four-cade and Capt Mellows, the German column, previously reported, appeared and opened fire spraying the road with machine-gun and anti-tank fire. Myself and the other two officers immediately took to the woods. The car in which we had placed all our equipment was captured by the Germans. The manner in which Capt Mellows met his death was as follows.
>
> During the initial burst of fire he was undoubtedly hit and due to his bad ankle – injured in the jump – he was unable to get away. Although I never saw Capt Mellows again I talked with the Maquis who found him the next day and the Doctor who inspected the body. The following statements may be made:
> 1. That Capt Mellows was hit by machine-gun fire in the chest and stomach and unable to get away.
> 2. That Capt Mellows received four .45 cal. bullets in his temple fired by the Germans from his own weapon.

3. That although this looks as if it might have been a case of deliberate assasination [sic] on the part of the Germans such a statement may not definitely be made due to the lack of facts.
4. Capt Mellows body now lies in the cemetery at Mont-de-Marsan.

The fighting west of Mont-de-Marsan lasted five hours; the partisans lost three men killed and fifteen were wounded, but German dead amounted to forty to fifty (once again, there is no clear explanation for such an enormous discrepancy; in an ambuscade situation, whith the French enjoying the advantage of surprise, one might understand it, but here, where by Allen's account it was he and his companions who were surprised, it is inexplicable).

Miles (and, presumably, the now-leaderless Martin) withdrew to Auch the following day and there received instructions from Hilaire to join him in Toulouse (which does not quite square with Conein's account). They found the city 'in pretty bad shape', Allen says, and the barracks where they were quartered came under attack by the *Milice* that night; they were driven off without difficulty, but 'this type of sporadic firing was prevalent in Toulouse for the first three weeks of the occupation'. Other accounts talk of *Milice* and even German troops riding around in vehicles armed with machine-guns for some considerable time after the city was 'liberated'.

The Jedburghs now readied themselves for a pursuit of the Toulouse garrison, together with unnamed Resistance factions. They paused at 'Villepouch' (unidentifiable, but by deduction Villefranche-de-Laura-gais) and rounded up *miliciens* and collaborators who had taken to the hills, as well as 'small groups of Algériennes' (which sounds a little unlikely) before continuing for Narbonne, and thence to Pézenas, where they abandoned the chase, Axis forces having left the area two days before they got there on 26 August. From there they turned back, and continued towards Perpignan, to gauge the situation there and at nearby Port-Vendres, with its deep-water harbour. By 31 August they were back in Toulouse, where they remained until 23 September. On 24 September they reached 4 SFU's Avignon base, and set off by road for Paris the following day. After a five-day stop in the French capital, Allen and Sgt Gruen returned to London on 4 October, having been preceded by Sgt Carey from team Martin, who arrived back on 28 September. Lt Éstève joined them on 18 October, but Lt Redonnet remained in France until the following January.

Everett Allen made thumbnail sketches of the principal figures the teams encountered. Of Monet he said: '… a fine leader, entirely dependable with one aim in view, the complete liberation and rehabilitation of France', but there his good opinions were exhausted. Of the DMR he observed: 'Droite was a man who could never make up his mind and if he did it was usually along the wrong lines. His presence in Toulouse will only serve to confuse and endanger the already dangerous situation that prevailed there when we left.' Carnot was 'absolutely incompetent as a soldier. Lacks force and his only interest lies in the fulfilment of vain personal ambitions'. Of Ravanel he said: 'The sooner Toulouse is rid of this incompetent upstart, the sooner this city [the sixth largest in France, we should perhaps note] will assume its rightful role in the inhabilitation [sic] of a new France.'

Allen was scathing in his opinion of Lt-Col George Starr, 'Hilaire' – one of SOE's most effective organisers (though 'not an easy man', according to the official historian of the Executive, Prof William Mackenzie) and one universally praised by his peers, who was awarded the Distinguished Service Order and the Military Cross, the American Medal of Freedom and, despite his very public row with Charles de Gaulle, the Croix de Guerre avec Palme (he was also admitted to the Légion d'Honneur) in recognition of his work in south-western France between November 1942 and September 1944). Allen said:

> 'Fortunately the officers in the Maquis brigade to which he was attached[sic; it was almost entirely through Starr's efforts that the unit in question was formed] had sufficient knowledge of military tactics to enable this brigade – the 'Demi-Brigade Armagnac' to do a fine job in helping drive the Germans from the south-west. Hilaire was defi- nitely not a military man [that much at least was accurate; he was actually a mining engineer] and credit for the operations carried out by this Maquis is due to the officers and men of the Brigade and not Hilaire. Upon our arrival in Toulouse Hilaire commenced to play the dangerous game of politics, a thing about which he knew little and into which he had no direct right to intervene – thus endangering the status of the Jed teams in Toulouse to the extent that on the arrival of General De Gaulle all Allied missions were ordered out of Toulouse by him.'

This is entirely fanciful. As noted elsewhere, de Gaulle's overriding wish – and a pillar of his agenda – was to ensure that the liberation of 'unoc- cupied' France was seen as a French achievement, and during the course of a whirlwind tour of the region he ordered *every* non-French Resis- tance worker he found out of the country within forty-eight hours, under pain of arrest. Starr actually defied him, with London's approval, and remained for nine more days to finish the essential work he had started, especially the reconciliation of leftist and rightist factions. His final words to the 'sepulchrally abusive' general, and the straw which broke the camel's back, during their spectacular public row of 18 September, are worth repeating:

> Mon Général, je vous connais comme chef du Comité Français de la Liberation Nationale, et même comme Président du Gouvernement Provisoire de la République, mais pas comme un officier supérieur, et je vous emmerde. [General, I recognise you as chief of the CFLN, and also as President of the GPR, but not as [my] superior officer, and I shit on you].

De Gaulle eventually shook him by the hand, saying: 'Il y a une chose vrai dans ce qu'ils m'ont dit de vous ... que vous êtes sans peur et que vous savez dire "merde".' ('There's one thing true in what they tell me about you – that you're fearless and you know how to say "shit".'.) One is left wondering whether Allen's condemnation would have been perhaps less forceful had he known that Starr's father was American.

Part Five
THE RHÔNE VALLEY

Veganin/Dodge

The second team to be deployed from Algiers, Veganin, was made up of Major Neil Marten of the Northamptonshire Yeomanry ('Cuthbert'), Capt Claude Vuchot, who took the name Noir ('Derek') and Sgt Dennis 'Jesse' Gardner of the Royal Armoured Corps ('Ernest'). It was to operate in the Drôme and Isère departments east of the Rhône in support of SOE F Section's Jockey circuit, run by 'Roger' (Lt-Col Francis Cammaerts), and by the time it was inserted, on the night of 8 June, the *maquisards* of an adjacent area, the Vercors Plateau, had risen up against the Germans. The Germans were somewhat slow to react, and it was 13 June before they struck, moving into the village of St-Nizier-du-Moucherotte on the north-east shoulder of the Vercors massif. This toe-hold on the plateau allowed them to control much of its northern end, but surprisingly no further offensive ensued until mid-July, and by that time two massive *parachutages*, part of Operations Zebra and Cadillac, had ensured that all the partisans on the Plateau, who by now numbered perhaps 4,000, were armed.

Jedburgh team Veganin was inserted at Roger's request 'to assist resistance movement and to stimulate guerilla [sic] action in the area of main lines of communication east bank of the Rhône between Avignon and Vienne'. Marten's report adds that the plan was for the team to recruit, arm and train teams of partisans to carry out *coup-de-main* operations in the Rhône Valley on the day the Allies landed in the south of France.

The aircraft located the DZ, 'Tarsis', west of the village of Beaurepaire, and Marten, then Vuchot, then Gardner jumped from a height of about 600 metres. Marten and the Frenchman landed safely and soon met up, but there was no sign of Sgt Gardner. The containers and packages dropped with the men were spread over a wide area and it took some time to locate them; some, including those containing both radio sets, were smashed. In the course of the search Vuchot came upon Sgt

Clermont-Ferrand

LYON
St-Genis-Laval

JUDE

Loire

Rhône

Allier

St-Chamond

Vienne

St-Étienne

Beaurepaire

MASQUE/
SCION

St-Rambert

Annonay
Vanosc

St-Uze

St-Marcellin
St-Vallier

Grenoble

Chantemerle-les-Blés

St-Donat-

VEGANIN/
DODGE

St-Nizier

St-Flour

Le Chambon-
s-Lignon

St-Agrève

Tain

Herbasse

Isère

Le Puy-
en-Velay

Beaumont-
Monteux

Romans

La Chapelle-
en-Vercors

JEREMY

Devesset

Valence

WILLYS

Le Cheylard

Chabeuil

Vassieux

Combovin

Privas

Rhône

CHLOROFORM

Vals-les-Bains

Aubenas

Montélimar

Dieulefit

Serres

Mende

Les Vans

Ardèche

MONOCLE

Florac

Cèze

Buis-les-Baronnies

Millau

Barre-des-
Cevennes

Aygues

Le Collet-
de-Dèze

Le Vigan

Nant

Vallerauge

Alès

Orange

Sault

Carpentras

St-Christol

La Cavalerie

PACKARD

Uzès

Avignon

CITROËN

MINARET

Larzac

Ganges

Gard

Cavaillon

Apt

Manosque

Lodève

Hérault

Nîmes

Salon-de-
Provence

Durance

Bédarieux

Montpellier

Lunel

Arles

Aix-en-Provence

Clermont-
L'Hérault

Béziers

Sète

MARSEILLE

Aubagne

Jedburgh
teams in the
Rhône
Valley

0   10   50km

- - - - - - -   Railways

————————   Roads

Gardner's body. His parachute had failed to open due to the static line not being hooked up correctly (there was no provision for manual release with this type of chute), and he was killed on impact.

The team's briefing had said they would be met by Roger, and they waited for him at Beaurepaire for four days, eventually leaving only after they had been put in contact with his radio operator. On 12 June they began to move southward in the direction of St-Donat-sur-Herbasse and meet other *maquisard* leaders in the region, notably 'Capt René', who commanded the Northern Battalion of the *Régiment du Drôme*. This, he claimed, ran to nine companies, and more manpower was available, but since he lacked weapons, it was only barely effective. Marten coded a message, to be sent by Roger's radio operator, asking for arms for these men, but it was seemingly never sent. In fact, it soon became obvious that there was very considerable unrest within the so-called battalion – which actually numbered less than 200 men at this time – due to friction between leftist and rightist factions, men of both persuasions having been mustered together under 'officers' from the *Armée Secrète* chosen for their political motivation rather than for their leadership abilities or military experience.

The situation had been steadily deteriorating long before D-Day, but came to a head when, after the Resistance leaders in the area gave the signal for a general rising, two companies attacked the German garrison at St-Rambert. The Germans responded by attacking St-Donat in strength, taking many hostages and burning their houses, and then repeated the exercise in villages and farms across the region. Far from offering resistance, the partisan groups began to fall apart, the FTP faction blaming the AS for showing poor leadership, while the population at large blamed the *maquisards* as a group for first stirring up the Germans, and then being able to do nothing to contain them.

By this time Vuchot seems to have assumed the leadership of Veganin. Arthur Brown, in his *Brief History of the Jedburghs*, says that Marten was badly affected by Gardner's death, and was prematurely withdrawn from the field in consequence; he was certainly withdrawn prematurely, but whether his grief or the official explanation – that he was required to convince the planners of Operation Anvil/Dragoon of the viability of the *Route Napoléon* – was the reason is unclear. Vuchot decided the only solution was to separate the two factions, and give FTP supporters the chance to constitute themselves into separate groups. He achieved this by about 20 June, by which time total active membership of the AS groups stood at around 180 and that of the FTP at around a hundred. There was a temporary improvement in morale as a result, but

Built by Humphry Repton for the second Earl Fitzwilliam in 1791, and subsequently extended, Milton Hall stands in a 600-acre park at Longthorpe, near Peterborough in Cambridgeshire. It was taken over by SOE late in 1943 to become the Jedburgh Training School, and known as 'ME-65' to the British, Area D to the Americans. The Jedburghs moved in during the first week of February 1944. (*All photographs are from the author's collection, unless otherwise credited.*)

Great emphasis was placed on training for close-quarters fighting, and both pistol shooting and hand-to-hand combat were an important part of the curriculum at Milton Hall, part of the thirty-acre formal garden being taken over as a pistol range.

Radio operators, seen here at a practical class, were expected not just to work their sets, but also to repair them by any means available should they fail or be damaged during insertion – a depressingly regular event.

Basic training was given in vital skills; this class was being instructed in explosive devices. In the front row, hands clasped, is Sgt Ken Seymour, of team Isaac, one of only two Jedburghs to survive capture.

Communications between Special Force's HQ in London and the teams in the field were vital, and the 'Portable Transmitting and Receiving Equipment, Type B. Mk. II', known as the B2 set, developed by SOE's Major John Brown, was the radio transceiver most commonly used in the field. It came packed in two steel cases weighing a total of 47lbs (21kg). A third case (on the left), weighing a further 12 1/2 lbs (5kg), contained a battery and power supply.

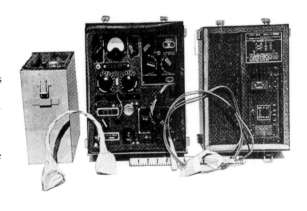

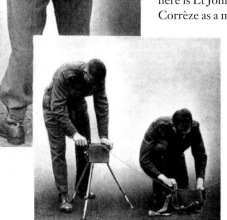

As a back-up to the B2, Jedburghs were also issued with the Jedset (Model 46/1) or the improved Nicholls Set (Type 48/1). These were packed into a total of five webbing satchels which could be linked into a back-pack weighing 44lbs (20kg). Two men were required to operate the set, the second cranking the generator which powered the transmitter stage.

The Jedburghs' standard combat dress was the British Dennison Smock, as issued to parachutists, and 1942-Pattern webbing, comprising a belt and braces, to which pouches of various types and a pistol holster could be attached. The helmet was for protection during parachuting, and was discarded on landing. Photographed here is Lt John Singlaub, USA, who operated in the Corrèze as a member of team James.

The majority of Jedburghs opted to carry the US Army's standard sidearm, the Colt M1911, in .45in calibre. The semi-automatic, blowback-operated pistol's main drawback was its limited magazine capacity – just seven rounds – but it was popular with the men, who believed that its 16g bullet would stop any assailant in his tracks.

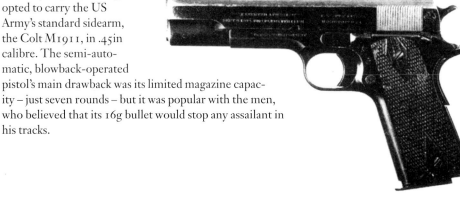

The Browning GP35, in 9mm Parabellum calibre, was a popular option, though many believed it lacked the stopping power of the Colt. Its action was a little more complicated – but no less reliable – than the M1911, and the choice of a round with a smaller, lighter (7.5g) projectile gave it a thirteen-shot capacity. 9mm ammunition was much easier to come by than .45in, in the field.

The American Carbine, calibre .30, M1A1, with its folding metal stock, was the Jedburghs' principal weapon. With an action similar to that of the heavier M1 'Garand' rifle, it was a reliable gas-operated semi-automatic. The choice of a smaller, lighter 'intermediate' .30in round – it weighed half as much as the Garand's M1906 or the British .303in – allowed a man to carry much more ammunition. If the Winchester-developed carbine had a drawback, it was its limited stopping power.

The bolt-action .303 Rifle, Short, Magazine, Lee-Enfield Mk III was first issued to British troops in 1907, and was the most widely used of many models of 'SMLE'. When it was superseded by the simplified Lee-Enfield No. 4 rifle in 1939 huge numbers were taken into storage, and over 35,000 were later distributed to partisans. It was a superb weapon, accurate to over 1000m in the hands of a competent man, and with few foibles. An expert could get off more than thirty aimed shots per minute with it.

The Sten sub-machine gun, adopted by the British Army in mid-1941, was a simple blowback design, firing from an open bolt, intended to be produced in a basic machine shop. Though poorly finished, it actually had few failings not seen in any of its counterparts, chief among them being a tendency for the lips of its single-column magazine (copied from the German MP38) to deform, preventing a round from feeding. It could discharge its 32 rounds in a single devastating three-second burst, but it required strength and training to keep it on target, and was not really effective at more than a few metres range as a result.

In contrast to the Sten, the German MP38 – often called the Schmeisser, though in fact the doyen of German SMG designers actually had nothing to do with it – was manufactured along traditional lines, with all its components machined from the solid. It was a stylish weapon, with none of the rough-and-readiness of the Sten, but it shared all the latter's shortcomings, and was a kilogramme heavier. Nonetheless, it was very popular with Jedburghs and others, but probably more as a symbol of status than due to any superiority in performance.

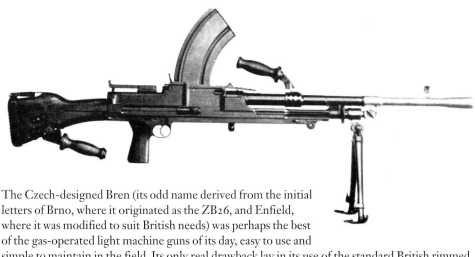

The Czech-designed Bren (its odd name derived from the initial
letters of Brno, where it originated as the ZB26, and Enfield,
where it was modified to suit British needs) was perhaps the best
of the gas-operated light machine guns of its day, easy to use and
simple to maintain in the field. Its only real drawback lay in its use of the standard British rimmed
.303in calibre round, with its inherent problems: if the rounds were not properly loaded into the
magazine, with the rim of each ahead of that before it, the gun would fail to feed. Almost 7,500
Brens were dropped to partisans in Europe during WWII.

Chambered, like the Colt M1911
pistol, for the heavy .45in ACP
round, the Thompson was
perhaps the most popular of all
the WWII-vintage sub-machine guns, thanks both to its utter reliability and its
association with Chicago gangsters. The M1A1, shown here, was a wartime re-vamp of the
original, with the annular finned barrel, forward pistol-grip and drum magazine replaced by more
functional alternatives. It was not intrinsically more effective than any other weapon of the genre.
Jedburghs trained with the Thompson, but few, if any, chose to take it into action.

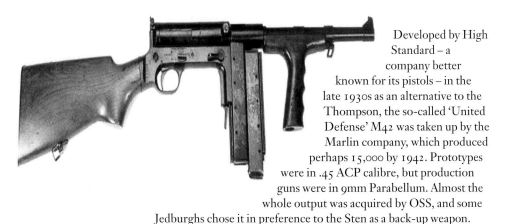

Developed by High
Standard – a
company better
known for its pistols – in the
late 1930s as an alternative to the
Thompson, the so-called 'United
Defense' M42 was taken up by the
Marlin company, which produced
perhaps 15,000 by 1942. Prototypes
were in .45 ACP calibre, but production
guns were in 9mm Parabellum. Almost the
whole output was acquired by OSS, and some
Jedburghs chose it in preference to the Sten as a back-up weapon.

Jedburghs (and other parachutists) were provided with so-called 'jump smocks' to be worn over their equipment. Their purpose was to reduce the risk of a man's equipment snagging on the aircraft as he exited it, and in this they were most effective. They were discarded on landing. The rucksack was often packed into a valise, initially strapped to the leg, but later carried on the chest, which was freed while the man was in the air to hang on the end of a twenty-foot cord, so that it hit the ground before the parachutist.

Right Jedburgh teams arriving at RAF Tempsford, Bedfordshire, the SOE's point of despatch. The kit they brought would be packed into containers to be dropped with them. *Below* Recovery of material dropped by parachute was the responsibility of *maquisards*, and often fraught with danger. Even a standard Jedburgh load of twelve containers required as many men, plus at least a pair of horse-drawn carts.

The Consolidated B-24 'Liberator' – a name given it by the RAF – was the most numerous of the many heavy bombers put into service (from March 1941) with Allied air forces in WWII. The J variant shown here was adapted for many other purposes, among them the transportation of parachutists and supplies, and was used to insert Jedburgh teams from Harrington airfield in Northamptonshire, as well as from fields in Algeria. It cruised at 210mph (335km/h) and had a maximum range of 2,100 miles with a five-ton payload.

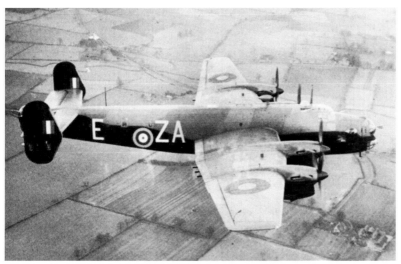

The Handley-Page Halifax, *centre*, also entered squadron service with RAF Bomber Command in March 1941. The B Mk. II shown here was one of a number of variants, and was the model most widely used for Special Forces operations including inserting Jedburghs and others from RAF Tempsford. It cruised at 215mph (345km/h) and had a maximum range of 1,030 miles (1,660km) with a five-ton payload.

The Short Stirling, *above*, certainly the least effective of the RAF's long-range bomber aircraft, entered squadron service in August 1940 and was withdrawn from the front line by late 1943, when it was switched over to transport and glider tug duties. The B Mk. III variant, shown here, was often used to carry parachutists. It cruised at 190mph (305km/h) and had a maximum range of 600 miles (1,000km) with a six-ton payload.

320 Boeing B-17 'Flying Fortresses' of the 8th USAAF's 3rd Bombardment Division – which were not normally used for such duties – carried out the mass daylight re-supply operation known as Cadillac on 14 July 1944. Operation Cadillac saw a total of 3,791 containers delivered to seven areas in France. It was one of four massive supply missions flown during this period.

Many Jedburgh teams spent large amounts of money from their operational funds on cars. This one, a V8 Ford, was actually used by an SOE agent, 'Samuel' (Capt Amédée Mainguard), and is shown here manned by a downed USAAF flyer, Lt Flamm Harper (with carbine), and three SAS troopers from the party which mounted Operation Bulbasket. Note the Vickers Type K machine gun mounted for use by the front seat passenger. Jedburgh team Ian worked with Samuel, and equipped itself with a similar vehicle.

Lt-Col Richard Musgrave, shown here on the left, was the second commander of the Jedburgh Training School, in succession to Lt-Col Frank Spooner. He was a pre-war big-game hunter of some note. The three Jedburghs – who may not have constituted a team; some photographs such as this are known to have been taken for publicity purposes, for use later – are not identified.

Team Ronald – Lt Shirley Ray Trumps (left), Lt Georges Deseilligny, who called himself Dartigues (centre), and T/Sgt Elmer Esch (right, with his back to camera) – was dropped into the Finistère *département* of Brittany on 6 August to operate alongside the French *Mission* Aloès.

Maj Duncan Guthrie, of team Harry, an outstanding Jedburgh. He volunteered for the Finnish Army in October 1939. At the end of the Winter War he made his way first to New York and later to Canada, where he enlisted in the Royal Canadian Artillery. He transferred to the Duke of Cornwall's Light Infantry in 1943, and subsequently volunteered for the Jedburgh programme. After serving in France he was parachuted into Burma, operating behind Japanese lines despite having broken his leg on landing. He is perhaps best remembered for the foundation of a charity for research into poliomyelitis, which later broadened its objectives and became Action Medical Research.

The tri-national team Ivor was led by Capt John Cox of the Royal Artillery (centre), with Lt Robert Colin, who called himself Yves Dantec, of the Foreign Legion (right) and T/Sgt Lewis F Goddard of the Signals Corps (left). Tragically, Sgt Goddard was killed during the team's insertion in the western Cher on 7 August, when his parachute malfunctioned. He was replaced by Sgt Glyn Loosmore of team Andy, whose officers had themselves suffered grave injuries during insertion and had to be evacuated.

Team Frederick was one of the first Jedburgh teams to be inserted, on 10 June, in the Côtes-du-Nord *département* of Brittany. It too was tri-national, and was led by Major Adrian Wise of the Royal Warwicks and the Parachute Regiment (right) with Capt Paul Bloch-Auroch, who was known as Aguirec (left) and M/Sgt Robert R Kehoe of the Signals Corps (centre).

Capt Amedée Maingard, on the left, a native of Mauritius, volunteered for the 60th Rifles on the outbreak of war. He was soon recruited by SOE and parachuted into western France in April, 1943, to assist 'Hector', S/Ldr Maurice Southgate. On Southgate's capture in May 1944, he and Pearl Witherington ('Pauline') assumed responsibility for the Indre and Vienne *départements*. On the right is Capt John Tonkin, commander of the ill-fated SAS Operation Bulbasket. (*Courtesy of Albert Dupont, via Paul McCue.*)

Team Alan comprised Capt Stanley Cannicott (third from the left) and Lt Robert Toussaint, who called himself André Gairaud (bareheaded, third from the right), with S/Lt Robert Clause, who was known as Francis de Heysen (absent from this picture) as its radio operator. It was inserted into the Saône valley on 13 August, and fought with French troops through to the Jura, where Cannicott was wounded six weeks later.

Jedburgh team Aubrey – Capt Godfrey Marchant of the Intelligence Corps (left), Lt Adrien Chaigneau, who called himself Telmon (right), and Sgt Ivor Hooker of the Royal Armoured Corps (centre) – was inserted to the east of Paris on 12 August in civilian clothes (the first Jedburgh team to go into the field so dressed). Lt Chaigneau was to die in action against vastly superior German forces fifteen days later.

Few photographs exist of *maquisards* save those taken at liberation celebrations; this one, however, though undoubtedly posed, purports to give a taste of the partisans' life in the forests of France. Whether the cleaning of weapons was quite such a popular activity is questionable! The machine gun (left) appears to be a rare example of Louis Schmeisser's WWI-vintage Bergmann MG15nA, with an unorthodox anti-aircraft foresight.

The deal US Maj-Gen Robert C Macon did with *Generalmajor* Botho Elster allowed almost 20,000 Nazi troops to escape across the Loire into American-occupied territory with their weaponry intact. They crossed the Cher and the Loir-et-Cher *départements* in three columns, under the eyes of impotent *résistants* who were enjoined from even recovering stolen vehicles, carts and draught animals, many of which were later sold back to them by GIs. This photograph shows one of the columns crossing the river at Beaugency.

Inset Again undoubtedly posed, this photograph at least gives a notion of how charges would be laid to destroy railway tracks, and hopefully derail a locomotive and rolling stock in the process. A relatively small amount of plastic explosive, made up into a series of linked charges, was all that was necessary.

Above At a well-chosen spot, a derailed train could plough up the track for a considerable distance and take days to clear. Training saboteurs, providing material and organising attacks on enemy lines-of-communication were primary tasks of the Jedburgh teams, and it could be argued that such operations were their greatest achievements.

The Jedburgh programme had joint American and Britsh commanding officers. The American Office of Strategic Services' representative was Lt-Col Henry B Coxe, seen here on the left, while SOE's appointee was Lt-Col DLG Carleton-Smith. Smith replaced Maj Henry Coombe-Tennant, who joined the training programme and led team Andrew when it dropped into the Ardennes.

Two of the most effective Resistance leaders in Central France, *Colonels* Bertrand and Colomb. The two were from very different backgrounds, Bertrand (left, who was known as Benôit in the Cher and Dupin in the Morvan) was a career officer and had commanded the *Premier Régiment de France*, while Colomb (centre) was an aristocrat, the Comte de Vogüé.

Generalmajor Botho Elster commanded occupation forces in south-western France from November 1942, but came into his own during the German retreat in 1944.

'Pauline', known as Christine Granville, but actually Krystyna Giżycka, assistant to Lt-Col Francis Cammaerts.

Below Joseph Darnand (left), the founder of the *Milice Française*, with *SS-Oberstgruppenführer* Oberg.

André Dewaverin was in his early twenties in 1940, when he came to Gen de Gaulle's attention. As 'Col Passy' he became head of the French intelligence service, *Bureau Central de Renseignements et d'Action*.

Below Georges Guingouin, the *'Préfét de la Résistance'*, leader of the Communist FTP in the Limousin.

Capt Victor Gough of team Jacob, captured and executed. (*Photograph by kind permission of Mrs M L Burbidge, née Gough.*)

Maj-Gen Sir Colin Gubbins,
head of SOE and the instigator
of the Jedburgh programme.

Lt-Col Francis Cammaerts,
'Roger', who ran the SOE's Jockey
circuit in South-Eastern France.

Lt-Col George Starr, 'Hilaire',
who ran the SOE's Wheelwright
circuit in South-Western France

William 'Wild Bill' Donovan,
who set up and headed the Office
of Strategic Services.

it soon became apparent that the situation was out of hand; no permanent resolution was achieved, and the groups in question were never entirely reliable during the eight weeks before the area was liberated. Vuchot later came to believe that the picture which had been painted for Veganin on their arrival, which portrayed the *maquisards* in the area as well led, keen and eager, was completely illusory. He said of the AS bands:

> Most of them came to the maquis to escape compulsory work in Germany, above all to lead a better and larger life than in their family; what attracted them was the requisitioning expeditions for rations, scrounging in certain places with submachine guns ready. I have rarely experienced anything so painful, as when I saw the astonishing joy on their faces, when the maquis chief announced an expedition for supplies, and, on their return, when we unpacked the jars of jam and barrels of pork. They had the souls of looters and constantly they would go and see the chief to tell him of another victim, saying that he was a war profiteer or collaborator or sympathising milicien, but actually, most of the time, it was some enemy of their family or themselves … In the FTP the same characteristics were found, but exaggerated even more by the lack of leaders.

On 19 June Marten left Vuchot, and made his way on foot to Combovin on the edge of the Vercors, where 'Hermine' (Cmdt Druout, commander of the *Régiment du Drôme*) had his headquarters. Two days later Hermine ordered René to join him, with all his men, but Vuchot countermanded the order. On 24 June, he says, he was joined by Capt Cyrus Manierre ('Rupert') and Sgt LT Durocher, of the Royal Canadian Corps of Signals, ('Oswald') who made up team Dodge, which had been inserted on to the same ground Veganin had used, but without mishap. This was one of only two cases of a Jedburgh team being sent into France without a French liaison officer; under the circumstances, it seems possible that SPOC had already decided to withdraw Neil Marten and consolidate Manierre, Vuchot and Durocher into a single team.

The following day Marten sent word for Vuchot to join him at La Chapelle-en-Vercors, and he and Dodge set off on foot on 26 June, arriving two days later. Manierre states that they were fired on by *maquis* sentries and had some problems identifying themselves, but were eventually taken to meet Marten, Roger, 'Col Joseph' (Henri Zeller), Hermine and 'Hervieux' (Cmdt François Huet, leader of the Vercors *maquisards*).

It soon became clear that Joseph and Roger had an agenda to which the Jedburghs were not privy: to turn the Vercors Plateau, where the *maquisards* had risen in open revolt as soon as news of the Normandy landings reached them, into an impregnable redoubt. From here forces could sortie to support the Allied advance up the Rhône Valley and – crucially – up the *Route Napoléon* to the east of the Massif, an alternative way north from the Côte-d'Azur, through Gap, to Grenoble, which the Emperor himself had followed in his northward passage to reclaim his throne after his escape from Elba in 1815. To assure the invulnerability of the Vercors, Roger avowed, it would be necessary to bring in all the partisan units from the surrounding area, which, of course, immediately rendered the Jedburgh team redundant. Nor was that the only surprise in store for Vuchot:

> Our interviewers were firm; Roger was persuasive. I noticed that Marten was silent; it seemed as if he were assisting [this in the French sense, of being a spectator at an event] at a discussion that did not concern him. As he was the team leader I hesitated at times, to say something. It was only after the conference that I found out he had other functions; Marten thought I knew what it was all about; he had evidently sent me a letter informing me about it; that letter had never reached me unfortunately.

One of the 'other functions' was apparently to act as a courier/emissary; Marten boarded a Westland Lysander aircraft at an LZ known as Spitfire, south of Sault in the Vaucluse, on the night of 10 July and returned to Algiers via Corsica; according to some reports the purpose of his return was to press Joseph's plan to utilise the *Route Napoléon*, though this may have been justification for withdrawing him. (In fact, Joseph himself was brought out of France, also by Lysander from Spitfire, on the night of 2 August, and it was he who, during a lengthy meeting at his headquarters in Naples, persuaded Lt-Gen Alexander Patch, the Supreme Commander of Operation Anvil/Dragoon, to make use of the *Route Napoléon*; as a result of adopting Zeller's suggestion, the Allies were in Grenoble on D+6, instead of D+90, as the original plan had predicted. If one relatively low-ranking officer personally shortened World War Two in Europe, it was probably Henri Zeller.)

Perhaps Vuchot was an able negotiator, or perhaps Roger (and/or his colleagues; Hervieux, for one, was no friend of the Communists) had foreseen problems integrating the FTP into the overall structure of resistance on the Vercors Plateau. In any event, a compromise was finally struck on the matter of the disposition of forces: Vuchot and Manierre would be allowed to remain in the valley and operate there in the conventional Jedburgh role, and would keep the 'troublesome' FTP, along with two AS companies of their choosing. They opted for the *maquisards* from St-Uze, under 'Malaboux', and another group which had taken the *nom de guerre* of its rather idiosyncratic leader 'Bozambo' (Lt Marcellin) as its own. Roger, however, insisted on retaining the radio operator, Sgt Durocher, arguing that Manierre and Vuchot would have little need of a direct conduit to Algiers, and that any messages they did need to send could be transmitted, with the highest priority, by Roger's headquarters. Vuchot gave in, but 'with rage in my heart I descended to the valley. It seemed to me essential to organise something in the northern sector of the Drôme. If not, who would utilise this region, useful as it was for work on the lines of communication running along the Rhône valley?

It is clear from Vuchot's account that he had an uphill struggle to turn the *maquisards* at his disposal, barely 200 men in all, into anything like an effective fighting force, and he had to resort to most extreme measures to get his message across:

The maquis chiefs ... each wanted to raise, organise and dispose his little band at his own will and pleasure. The principal interest was feeding. Good fare being the condition of recruitment, it was the maquis where one ate the best that was the most prosperous and the chief the most famous. Malboux ... did not hesitate at forgery, and used my name to make more or less unreasonable requisitions. He took arms destined for others at parachutages, to equip his men better. His maquis he felt should be the only one in the region; he attempted to organise his own personal police etc.

One might ask why with so many drawbacks I kept people like Bozambo and Malboux. Malboux was remarkably brave and audacious, with no military experience, he had a genius for coups de main and ambushes. If he was without scruple, he was on the other hand, almost the only chief of a Corps Franc on whom I could depend at all. He died heroically at the very moment when I was planning to have him arrested.

Bozambo was unbalanced, versatile, susceptible, always listening to the last who spoke, getting enthusiastic, and loosing [sic] enthusiasm with equal rapidity. He seemed to me to be the perfect example of the maquis leader to get rid of. But he had a very real popularity in the region ...

This search for independence, this desire to play the Big Chief, was to be found at all levels. The section which organised the supply of food for the Bozambo maquis, called the Special Section, tried to free itself from the yoke of the chief. The four principals of this section began a systematic pillage of the southern section of the department of the Isère, where for a time they had a very bad reputation with the FFI chiefs. An attempt was made to organise for them a proper maquis. Neither advice nor observations had any effect on them. I handed them over to the Gendarmes of the Vercors, who allowed them to escape when La Chapelle was bombed for the first time.

I then gave the order for their arrest. A detachment awaited them at their home one night. They defended themselves with pistols. Two of the four were killed, the others taken as prisoners. After a short meeting between myself, my adjutant, the intelligence officer and Bozambo, the prisoners were shot. This example had a most salutary effect on the maquis.

Manierre gave a more spirited account of the incident:

The 'équipe spéciale' [which numbered six, he said] had set themselves up in a deserted château where they were living with their women and from which they would make wild excursions in automobiles decorated with tricolors and the Cross of Lorraine, the object of these trips being robbery and banditry. They were known to have entered houses, taken everything out from money and silverware to bed linen and household effects and they were keeping all this property in the stables and the barn of the château where they were living. Naturally their activities were creating a terrible impression throughout the region and causing ill feeling towards the French resistance. The 'équipe spéciale' had not turned over the money or supplies they had got but kept them for themselves. Therefore it was determined that we would arrest them, try them by court martial, and either execute them or put them in jail.

We surrounded their château early one morning and called on them to give themselves up. This they refused to do. A brisk fire fight ensued, reminiscent of prohibition days in Chicago, the result was that two of the six were killed and two of the women were killed, the others wounded. Then we threw four hand grenades in through a window and fired rockets into the house. The 'équipe spéciale' was very effectively liquidated …

Apparently, the days of Jedburgh justice were not past …

*

The most frustrating effect of the indiscipline of the partisans was that which it had on *sédentaires* who had yet to 'come out'; among them were many men with military experience, the very people Vuchot needed as leaders and instructors if he was to increase the effectiveness of the bands, but almost to a man they refused to join him, claiming that those bands were no better than terrorists intent on pillage, and Vuchot found no way to break this vicious circle. Other men who declined to join the struggle argued that the time (it was by now the beginning of July, and the Allies had been in France for almost a month) was not yet ripe, and once again, Vuchot was unable to change their minds. Not surprisingly perhaps, many of those who *did* join the partisans were attracted to them for the very worst of reasons, and thus the situation was exacerbated still further.

Eventually, some of the partisans, chiefly from the FTP, gave up any pretence of making war on the forces of occupation, and set about pillaging in earnest, taking money and valuables to a plan hatched by 'a Lyonnais committee' which was aimed at building up a war chest for the power struggle which would follow the liberation. Vuchot admitted: 'There was no possible means of restraining them except by the firing squad. I sent people at first to execute them, later however, I gave up. The groups defended themselves and their comrades came to avenge them. It was like a small civil war.'

By this time – mid-July – events were starting to come to a head up on the Vercors Plateau. The Vercors *maquisards* had received their first big *parachutage* of weapons and equipment as part of Operation Zebra on 25 June, when thirty-five aircraft dropped a total of 420 containers; and the arrival of the advanced elements of an Inter-Allied Mission, Eucalyptus, and a fifteen-strong Operational Group, Justine, on the night of 29 June, seemed to indicate that SHAEF was, at least belatedly, taking the rising seriously. The partisans, however, mistakenly assumed the parachutists to be the advance party for a much larger airborne force, and that impression was reinforced when a French military engineering team, Mission Paquebot, was parachuted in on 6 July to begin work on fashioning a landing strip big enough to take a twin-engined aircraft at Vassieux, in a large, shallow bowl near the geographical centre of the plateau. By 14 July, Hervieux having issued a proclamation calling for every able-bodied man in the region around the plateau to join the rising, there were around 4,000 partisans assembled at Vassieux, many of them already armed. That morning, even as they began to assemble for a Bastille Day parade, seventy-two B-17 Flying Fortresses dropped

862 canisters of arms, suspended beneath red, white and blue parachutes, as part of Operation Cadillac, whereupon the *Luftwaffe* promptly reacted, dropping incendiary bombs and strafing the DZ with machine-gun fire. The pick-up operation had to wait until nightfall, but by the end of the next day there were weapons – though only, and this was to be crucial, *light* weapons – for all.

Over the course of the next week, Major Desmond Longe, the leader of Eucalyptus, sent urgent radio messages to London and Algiers, asking for reinforcements, heavier weapons and air support, while Roger attempted to persuade London to launch air raids on local airfields, where he had seen troop-carrying gliders being readied for action. The pleas fell on deaf ears, but it was probably too late anyway.

When the German assault came, on 18 July, it was rebuffed initially by defenders on the heights who were able to control the roads up on to the plateau, but on 21 July troop-carrying gliders landed in the zone at Vassieux which the partisans had just finished clearing for Allied airborne operations. The German airborne forces were soon reinforced, and the perimeter they established and held was never in serious danger. Assaults from St-Nizier-du-Moucherotte, as well as from the south and east, followed and proved to be overwhelming. On 23 July, Hervieux gave the order for the *maquisards* to disperse, but by that time a reinforced division of German mountain troops, with artillery and heavy armour, had spread out over the plateau and were blocking every road that led down from it. Those who escaped did so chiefly in ones and twos, and even the men of the Operational Group were sorely tested.

Hervieux's decision to delay the order to disperse until long after it had become the only obvious course of action has been criticised widely ever since. The death toll was high: at least 630 men died in the fighting on the plateau, and more were taken, the majority of them killed out of hand while trying to get away; some 200 non-*résistants* were killed in reprisals, which saw whole villages levelled and many hundreds of houses burned.

The arrival of the rest of Mission Eucalyptus, which had no less than three radio operators, freed Sgt Durocher, and he returned to the Jedburgh team about 10 July, by which time Veganin/Dodge was starting to get its activities on a more level footing. While Vuchot was trying to increase the numbers of men at his disposal, to introduce a more stable element and instill some discipline into them, Manierre – a career soldier who had graduated from West Point in 1942 – was trying to improve their military effectiveness, instructing the more reliable elements in the handling of weapons and explosives and leading them on raids. He achieved little at first, but as July wore on, the men's confidence began to grow, and he was able to turn his attention to more important targets, among them the power station at Beaumont-Monteux.

Manierre had to work harder, and take greater risks, to cut the railway lines in the Rhône and Isère Valleys, as the Germans improved protective measures along them – reducing the distance between sentry posts from 500 to 200 metres; increasing patrols; installing lighting at key points and cutting down undergrowth near the permanent way. Some opportunities, however, were simply too good to ignore. When he received intelligence that a train carrying German troops was to move north up the Rhône Valley, Manierre resolved to ambush it at St-Vallier, where the valley narrows almost into a low gorge, with roads and railway lines on both banks. He chose a spot where the line crossed a culvert beneath a bluff; when the line was blown and the train derailed, his ambush party on the crest created carnage among the Germans at no cost to itself.

By the end of July Manierre was no longer participating personally in operations, but was persuaded, over Vuchot's objections, to work for a time with a group based near Chantmerle-les-Blés, a little way northeast of Tain, in an attempt to cut definitively the railway on the left bank of the Rhône. The group in question 'composed of young men of an exceptionally superior quality', many of whom had been cadets at the St-Cyr military academy, was under the leadership of 'Capt Martin', a man in his fifties, for whom Manierre clearly had the highest respect. Manierre decided that the best way to take the line out of commission was to demolish a bridge at Serves-sur-Rhône, and planned the operation to coincide with the passage of a train carrying elements of a Panzer Division (and its vehicles), which intelligence said was due on the night of 5 August. Reconnoitring the bridge on 4 August, he elected to place a total of seventy kilograms of plastic explosive in peach baskets (an important local crop, the peaches were just then being picked), and wire them to the rails from beneath, the charges to be fired both by pull switches and fog signals placed on the tracks.

The next day he set off in a borrowed truck to collect the explosives, which were cached near Beaurepaire, and met up with Vuchot, who tried to dissuade him from blowing the bridge. On his way back to Chantmerles the truck overheated, and while the driver was looking for water to replenish the radiator, two men wearing tricolor armbands embroidered with the Cross of Lorraine, and carrying submachine-guns, approached them. They claimed to be from a local *maquis* which had set up a road-block a little way down the road; hearing the truck, they had come to investigate. The men climbed into the back and the truck set off, down a hill and around a bend, where it was confronted by two trees felled across the road, manned by a group of about thirty partisans armed with Brens, rifles and SMGs. 'The atmosphere was that of any Maquis', said Manierre, 'and I felt no suspicion or misgivings.' The driver got down, and was soon involved in a loud argument. Manierre gathered that the truck was going to be 'confiscated', so, to prevent that, he got down too, and went around to the back:

> I began to protest, when the man in charge pushed his Sten gun into my stomach and told me to hold out my hands. I did so. Somebody handcuffed them, and I was ordered to sit in a deep hole by the side of the road. Still believing there had been a mistake, I sat in the hole and decided to keep quiet until some responsible person appeared to whom I could explain my identity, and who I expected would give me back my truck and send me on my way.
>
> Shortly afterwards I was searched and my American Army dog-tags were found in my pocket. The man in charge, on seeing them, said in French: 'You Yankees must understand that there is only one chief in France, and he is Marshal Pétain.' Then I realised I was in the hands of the Milice.

Manierre was taken first to Valence, and interrogated with what he described as 'mild third-degree treatment', before being transferred to Lyon, ostensibly to the regional *Milice* headquarters. On the way he tried to persuade his escort to release him; he failed, but managed to talk them into allowing him to change his clothes for those in his knapsack, which he had been permitted to retain. Thus, when he arrived at Lyon he was wearing military clothing and a green 'commando' beret, albeit without any insignia or badges. When he reached Lyon he was given over to the *Sipo-SD*, who beat him up in a desultory fashion, 'which consisted of three Gestapo agents punching me, pulling my hair, and knocking me down and kicking me until I got up off the floor. These blows did not seem particularly hard to me, and I daresay that no effort was made to seriously hurt or punish me, nevertheless it was most unpleasant'. This, by his own account, was the only ill-treatment that Manierre received, although the version of his experiences in German hands which passed into the Jedburgh canon has him savagely tortured.

It is hard to understand why Manierre got off lightly, for *Sipo-SD* knew perfectly well that he was an American 'terrorist', and he was informed that he was to be tried by a (German) civilian tribunal and would inevitably be found guilty and sentenced to death. Then fate intervened again; on the night of 15 August the FFI attacked *Gestapo* headquarters, destroying much of it and killing and capturing many of the personnel, the rest of whom fled, leaving no instructions as to what should become of their prisoners. The following day a *Wehrmacht* officer interviewed Manierre, who told him that he was a flyer shot down near Valence, and had been arrested while the *Maquis* was trying to smuggle him to Spain. The German officer 'appeared to swallow my story hook, line and sinker. He said that he would send me to a prisoner of war camp right away.' In fact, it was eighteen days before he was put on a train east, in company with Lt Chester Myers of OG Justine, who had been captured in a *maquisard* hospital bed, recovering from an appendectomy. He was questioned again, at the *Luftwaffe* interrogation centre at Oberürsel, near Frankfurt, where by the purest chance he met his brother. The two were sent to Stalag Luft 1 at Barth, on the Baltic, and were liberated by Russian forces on 2 May 1945. The American officer who deployed with team Monocle, Lt Ray Foster, goes into some detail in his appendix to that team's report regarding an abortive mission he mounted to rescue Manierre; this is described below.

For no clear reason, Vuchot's report ends with his account of other events of 5 August – he relates how there were German convoys on most roads, and that *maquisards* led by Marboux and Bozambo had attacked two of them, causing little damage but losing some of their own men. Of later events, he simply says that after 15 August (the date of the Anvil/Dragoon landings on the south coast) 'part of the maquis stayed in the interior [presumably the area between the Rhône Valley and the Vercors] to serve as a reserve and to blow bridges if the Germans attempted to enter and use them. The larger part of the maquis was stationed in the immediate proximity of the RN7 [the main road down the valley] and the Lyon–Marseilles railway and carried out practically non-stop raids on these with groups up to a company strong.'

Claude Vuchot later rejoined his regiment and fought through to the Vosges, where he was killed in action. Sgt Durocher returned to the United Kingdom on 14 October. After arriving back in Algiers on 25 July, Neil Marten served at SPOC, and later at 4 Special Forces Unit HQ in France, in a staff capacity, and was responsible for debriefing many of the Massingham teams.

Willys

Willys left Blida on the night of 28 June, to be inserted into the eastern Ardèche some thirty kilometres west of the Rhône, roughly equidistant from Valence to the north and Montélimar. They were to operate initially north-west of Privas and north of the adjacent towns of Aubenas and Vals-les-Bains, all of which had German garrisons, across the river from the area where Veganin/Dodge was located. The team was led by Capt Georges Marchal, who called himself Granier ('Simon'), together with Capt John Montague ('Honan') and Sgt Ted Cornick ('Chansi'), both of the Royal Armoured Corps, and was to work to the direction of an Allied Military Mission, Pectoral, which was composed of two French and one French-Canadian officers. It is clear from the team's report that their relationship with Pectoral was poor right from the start. They were misemployed and never permitted to operate in the role envisaged for them, and were considerably less effective than they might have been as a result. To quote Neil Marten, who debriefed Montague and Cornick at 4 SFU HQ:

> The reason for the Allied Mission trying to make the Jeds work on intelligence only, which was strictly not their role, appeared to be a deliberate desire not to make any use of them as they did not want any glory taken away from their work. No advice given by the Jeds on military matters was accepted and the Allied Mission appeared to be concerned only with arming the greatest number of people regardless of their fighting capabilities, and they failed to co-ordinate the resistance movements in this area.

As well as the direct effect of Pectoral's shortcomings on the team, the mission's failure to impose anything like a unified command structure on the partisan groups, and to contain their politically-motivated activities, meant that the resistance effort was much diluted. The Jedburgh team's effectiveness was further reduced by SPOC's failure to respond to many of its requests.

Pectoral had been inserted just a fortnight before Willys arrived on the scene. Its leader, 'Vanel' (Cmdt Paul Vaucheret), was a career army officer who was fervently anti-Communist, which was unfortunate, to say the least, since the strongest and best-led partisan groups in the region were FTP. Since he was EMFFI's choice as DMD, Vaucheret had considerable authority, but seems to have made a string of poor decisions; eventually his influence was to be limited by the DMR, Col Henri Provisor, who appointed the local *Armée Secrète* chief, Cmdt René Calloud, in his place; after that matters began to improve, but only very slowly.

There is no report of any mishap during the team's insertion, to a ground known as Tandem in the hills near Devesset, fifteen kilometres north of Le Cheylard, where the FFI command post was located, and all equipment seems to have been recovered intact. (This was in contrast to Pectoral's insertion at the same site; Vaucheret got hung up in a tall poplar tree, and his French assistant, Capt Williams, landed in a midden. Only the Canadian, Maj Chassée, was unscathed.) From the outset, Marchal and Montague were instructed to restrict their activities to gathering intelligence, and were somewhat mystified by this, since an SOE F Section agent, a French naval officer, had been in place in the region for three years, and had established an excellent network of agents. After two weeks Montague rebelled, and asked Vaucheret for 'military work'; he was told he could seek out the men responsible for training individual partisan groups, to assess their equipment needs, but was provided with no transport and no assistance. Some days later Calloud replaced Vaucheret as DMD, and he put a stop to Montague's efforts in that direction, claiming to have the matter in hand himself. Montague continued to visit partisan bands, however, and tells us that he made several suggestions as to how their disposition and tactics could be improved, but his advice was pointedly ignored. Marchal continued to work at gathering intelligence, a role he played throughout Willys' time in France. In a brief supplement to Montague's report he described this work as 'quite unsuited to the dynamism of Capt Montague', but was no happier in the role than the Englishman, and no less critical of Vaucheret and the other members of Pectoral, and of the *maquisard* leaders, than was his colleague, saying:

> To sum up, I carried out to the best of my ability the task which I was given, seeing that the Maquis of Ardèche and the groups francs were too jealous of their rights and too obstinate in their desire to do everything themselves, to allow me to exercise an effective command. Moreover, either through ignorance of our formation [he perhaps meant 'training'], or by some other deep rooted idea, Comdt Vanel did not wish us to undertake demolitions ourselves, or take over any command.

In the fortnight before Willys' deployment, German forces based in Privas had made two sorties against the Ardèchois FFI; the first was blocked at Le Pont de Boyon, but the second, in considerably greater strength and supported by the *Luftwaffe* and light armour, managed to penetrate as far as Le Cheylard and caused considerable damage before the partisans were able to escape. On 5 July, the Germans came back in brigade strength, and fought engagements on the Col de la Faye and at Le Cheylard itself, bombing the town and surrounding villages. The casualty figures from different sources are somewhat contradictory, but make it clear that this was a major action; Montague says the Germans suffered around eighty killed or wounded in the first engagement and more than twice that in the second, with Resistance losses put at around fifty killed and the same number wounded. German sources state that in the course of the two actions around 200 maquisards were killed in the fighting, and that 135 men were shot in reprisals (Montague says the Germans shot all the French wounded they found; from that time on, at least until late August, the *résistants* took no prisoners). It was as a direct consequence of these raids that Vaucheret was replaced as DMD, and after that he faded into relative obscurity, the Canadian Chassée having taken over leadership of Pectoral. The changes at the top did not profit Montague, however, and he decided to take matters into his own hands, and cut himself off entirely from the mission. He moved down into the valley, made contact with partisans based there, and began a campaign of sabotaging the railway lines and laying ambushes on the N86, the main road on the right bank of the Rhône. Almost at once he ran into supply problems; requests to Algiers passed to Ted Cornick for onward transmission went unheeded, and pleas to Vaucheret and Calloud to allocate resources to disrupting traffic along the river were ignored.

By now the Allied landings on the Mediterranean coast of France, Operation Anvil/Dragoon, were only a month away, and SHAEF decided to augment the Special Forces assets in the Rhône Valley by the addition of two Operational Groups: Louise, which arrived at the Tandem DZ in the early hours of 18 July, and Betsy, two nights later. Betsy was to operate further north, near Annonay, and was co-located with a partisan group based at Vanosc. It had some success against bridges in the Rhône valley, but lost two men killed, one as a result of wounds he sustained in an air raid on the Vanosc campsite on 10 August, another in a strafing attack on 29 August. One of the officers was seriously wounded in that latter incident. Louise began well, demolishing a suspension bridge and blocking the Rhône to barge traffic on 22 July, but soon began to experience the same obstructive attitude that Vaucheret and Calloud displayed to Montague. It was involved in a major ambush near Les Vans, some way south-west of Aubenas, on 29

July, in which perhaps a hundred German troops were killed and a tank and a number of lorries were destroyed, but was otherwise under-employed during the period leading up to the Anvil/Dragoon landings.

The fact that the Americans seemed to receive everything they requested from Algiers almost as soon as the ink was dry on the signals pad, while Willys and Pectoral had to wait, sometimes for weeks, for scraps, was clearly a source of some resentment. Neil Marten, in his report on the team's debriefing, says: 'Too much was sent to the OGs in the way of resupply considering the small amount of work they were given to do. The food and comforts sent to them were too lavish and gave cause to some irritation to the French.' And not only to the French; reading between the lines of Montague's report it is clear that the Jed-burghs compared their own situation very unfavourably with that of Louise and Betsy.

The high point of the OG's resupply came on 15 August, when – fol-lowing a request by Vaucheret, and against the better judgement of Lt Mackenzie (Louise's leader) – four 37mm anti-tank guns were dropped, one of which killed a *maquisard* when its parachute failed to deploy properly. These were American M3A1s, a substantially lighter piece than the British 6pdr, two of which were dropped to SAS troops carry-ing out Operation Houndsworth in the Morvan. Whether the considerable effort required to send the guns was worthwhile is debat-able – they were an obsolete type, too small to be really effective – and only one was ever employed with any substantial result, served by a crew composed of three downed RAF flyers, who used it to bombard a strong German column moving northward from Vallon-Pont-d'Arc in the direction of Aubenas and Privas.

Montague divided the liberation of the Ardèche into two quite con-ventional phases: the ambush and sabotage phase which preceded the Allied landings on the Côte-d'Azur in mid-August, and the all-out guer-rilla offensive which followed it, but it is clear from Willys' report that from the team's standpoint the second was scarcely any more satisfac-tory than the first, and that opportunities to kill or capture Axis forces moving up the Rhône Valley and on routes parallel to it were lost because of the *maquisard* leaders' mishandling of the situation and their continued unwillingness to accept advice. This was clearly the sort of situation in which a Jedburgh team had been expected to take control, but the presence of the Pectoral mission rendered that impossible. The situation improved eventually, however, and by the end of August the Ardèchois *maquisards* had succeeded in paralysing road and rail traffic on the west bank of the Rhône, and had taken 7,000 Axis troops prisoner and killed many more. The vanguard of the French *Armée B* arrived in the area on 1 September, and without further delay, and clearly glad of the opportunity, Montague and Sgt Cornick left to travel to Brignoles, in the Var, where 4 SFU's field headquarters had been established. Montague moved to Grenoble along with the HQ staff, and returned to London on 26 September, but Ted Cornick returned to the Ardèche, to continue as Pectoral's link with Algiers. He was later withdrawn to Avignon, where – in company with two other radio operators – he volunteered for a mission in northern Italy. It was cancelled before he was deployed, and he returned to the United Kingdom.

Packard

It was more than a month after Willys' insertion before the next Massingham-based team, Packard, was dropped into France. It has been suggested that this delay was due to confusion within the command structure – we may recall that EMFFI officially took over control of SFHQ's activities in France from 1 July – but internal politics within the French High Command may also be blamed. In any event, while SFHQ, with SHAEF's backing, could still exert a degree of pressure in London (and was able to get ten more teams inserted from the United Kingdom during the month of July), that was certainly not the case in Algiers, where it had very little influence. We have already found evidence of friction between some Inter-Allied Missions and Jedburgh teams, and the mission handed to team Packard – 'To work with the Allied Mission [Isotrope] in a strictly military capacity and to carry on guerrilla activity *whether the Mission was in accord or not* [italics added]' – seems to reflect a certain dissatisfaction with the degree of co-operation and understanding that the Jedburghs (and perhaps their controllers) were receiving from the Missions.

Packard was led by Capt Aaron Bank ('Chechwan'), with Lt Henri Denis, who called himself Boineau ('Fukien') as his deputy; the radio operator originally assigned to the team, T/Sgt Howard V Palmer ('Formosa'), was replaced by 'F Montfort', who is stated by most sources (including the team's report header sheet) to have been a French subaltern. A note on the sheet states that Monfort was 'not a Jed', and he was presumably recruited in Algiers. Sgt Palmer later joined team Sceptre, as a replacement for the invalided Sgt Thomas Tracy.

Packard left Blida aboard an RAF Halifax a few minutes before midnight on 31 July, and was dropped on to a ground known as Quincaille, near Barre-des-Cevénnes, some eight kilometres south-east of Florac in the Lozère *département*. The three men landed safely, although Bank was temporarily stunned, and were met by a reception committee. Bank, in his official report, states that it included 'Cmdt Jean' ('Isotrope'; Cmdt Jean Baldensperger) and 'Maj Hampson' ('Étoile'; Maj Denys Hampson) of the Inter-Allied Mission 'Isotrope', who had arrived in the area on 9 June.

There was antagonism between Packard and Isotrope right from the start. The Jedburgh team set up its command post near Le Collet-de-Dèze, near the border with the Gard, in the northern margin of the sparsely inhabited Cévennes mountains but only about fifteen kilometres from Alès, the *département*'s second city, and soon began a close collaboration with 'Cmdt Audibert' (Michel Brugier), the FFI chief in the Gard, and 'Cmdt Bonbix', who was his military commander. Bank clearly held these men, both of whom were career soldiers, in high regard, but this was at odds with Isotrope's judgement, for he favoured the FTP leader 'M. Barry', whom Bank described as 'a rabid communist'. Matters soon came to a head. Isotrope ordered that the standard load of containers dropped with the team – five Brens and forty rifles, plus ammunition – should be handed over to the FTP. Bank, who had intended to distribute these weapons to the FFI and thus cement his relationship with them, demurred, but was overruled, with the promise that the team would receive a consignment of arms from a future *parachutage* (it did, but lost out on the deal in terms of both quantity and quality).

It may have been the ideological difference which caused the rift between Jedburghs and Missionaries, but the situation was certainly not improved by Isotrope believing the Jeds to be under his command and Bank believing them to be independent. In fact, there was little Bank could do but follow Isotrope's lead, since the Resistance in the area was dominated by the FTP, who outnumbered the others by three to one; any attempt to usurp control would have been both futile and foolish. As it was, relations between the two factions were already strained – the FTP had hijacked a train-load of food the FFI had captured and distributed it themselves, gaining much kudos in the process – and were to deteriorate still further thanks to incidents such as FTP elements surrounding DZs and taking over at gun-point *parachutages* of arms and ammunition intended for other groups.

The night prior to the Côte-d'Azur invasion, Packard manned the DZ near Barre and received the two-man team Minaret, which was to operate immediately to the east; Minaret left the following day (says Bank; its own report tells a somewhat different story), and with it went Mission Isotrope, to establish a new base near Valleraugue, twenty-five kilometres south-west of Le Collet.

The period immediately after the Anvil/Dragoon landings on 15 August seems to have been one of enforced idleness for Bank and Denis. Preparations for harassing Axis columns moving along the roads had been made, but for almost a week, nothing happened. Then, on 22 August, the sizeable German garrison at Alès moved out, some in the direction of Nîmes, others towards Uzès, and the *maquisards*, both the FTP under Barry and the FFI under Bonbix, moved into the town. To begin with the two factions seem to have been under something like unified command – at least, they operated from the same headquarters in the town hall – and the demanding work began of rooting out small pockets of Axis troops who had gone to ground in the surrounding villages. Two days later, however, when news came that the German garrison at Nîmes was withdrawing, the FTP contingent, which numbered about 600 men, left Alès without warning, and moved south to take control of the city, substantially weakening the Resistance forces in the northern part of the *département*. A decision by Cmdt Audibert also to take some of his contingent to Nîmes, in the hope of gaining at least a foothold there, and not allowing it to fall entirely into Communist hands, further depleted the fighting forces. It proved to be precisely the worst time for such a dilution, for that same day Axis troops from as far away as Toulouse and Perpignan, anxious to quit the south before they were cut off, began to pour eastward through the region, heading for the Rhône Valley. With the FTP intent on strengthening their hold on the *département*'s capital, and much of the FFI contingent deploying to prevent that, neither faction showed much interest in harassing the retreating forces of occupation other than in executing captured *miliciens* and collaborators. Frustrated, Bank went to Avignon, to the Advance HQ of the French *Armée B*, on 28 August, to plead for support, but received none, and returned to Alès to continue trying to make the best of a poor situation. In fact, the exodus was almost over. By 30 August the flood had slowed to a trickle, and the following day, when the advance elements of *Armée B* finally arrived, there was little left for them to do.

Its task in the Gard finished, Packard paused only for a night of debauchery in a Nîmes bordello (the proprietor of which, like many of his kind, had proved to be an excellent source of intelligence throughout the German occupation) before moving eastward to Brignoles, to the 4

SFU base there, arriving on 3 September, and from there to Grenoble, where Bank was debriefed before returning to London.

Aaron Bank later conceived Operation Iron Cross, which had the assassination of Adolf Hitler as one of its objectives, but the mission was aborted before the team Bank trained and led, which included Sgt Ted Baumgold, team Collodion's W/T operator, could be inserted into the area around the *Führer*'s mountain retreat at Berchtesgaden. He remained in the United States Army, retiring with the rank of colonel after having been instrumental in creating the 10th Special Forces Group – the Green Berets – raised at Fort Bragg in 1952 and the US Army's prototype special forces unit. Bank drew heavily on his experience with the Jedburghs in developing this concept, though in truth, the Green Berets' real antecedents were probably the Operational Groups.

Minaret

Team Minaret consisted of Maj Lancelot Hartley-Sharpe ('Edmond') and Sgt John Ellis ('Arsène'); the third member, Capt Cros of the French Army, who called himself Mutin, did not go into the field due to illness. The team of Sharpe, Cros and Ellis had earlier been briefed as Jock, 'To assist in organising resistance in Lackey circuit', which is confusing, for the SOE F Section circuit of that name, an adjunct to 'Ditcher' was based in Burgundy, well outside Massingham's area of responsibility, and had never been active. There is no record of when the team was briefed for the mission, but the file header sheet is marked 'Operation cancelled, see telegram to SPOC of 2.8.44'.

Minaret was inserted into the Quincaille DZ near Barre-des-Cevénnes on the night of 13 August; the two men landed safely (though the RAF Halifax which brought them was shot down by an anti-aircraft battery over the Spanish frontier on its way back to Blida, with the loss of the entire crew), and were met by Aaron Bank of team Packard and members of Mission Isotrope. Cmdt Baldensperger suggested the team would be best served by associating itself with the Aigoual *maquis*, which took its name from a prominent peak about fifty kilometres due west of Alès; this was to prove an inspired choice.

The Aigoual group numbered between five and six hundred men under the command of an Air Force officer, 'Cmdt Colas' (Lt-Col Matignon). Its headquarters were situated initially at L'Espérou and later at Valleraugue. It was well armed and had a truly enormous reserve of explosives – some two tonnes of plastic – but had not fired a shot in anger for months, since a desultory action in which the previous military commander had been killed. Sharpe immediately began making plans to employ the men and their stock of *matériel*. The main route through the area was the N99, which left the north–south N9 at La Cavalerie to wind eastward through Nant and Le Vigan to Ganges, where it split to continue to Montpellier and Nîmes; it was decided to cut this road in two places, by blowing a tunnel at Alzon and the bridge at Pont de l'Herault, north of Ganges. Both demolitions were achieved, but only after some delay when the group's 'demolitions experts' proved to be anything but, and Sharpe had to set up a short course to teach them the necessary techniques.

'There followed a period of three weeks during which the Maquis de l'Aigoual was continuously in action', Sharpe tells us. Ambushes were mounted on the main road and those secondary routes the Axis troops were forced to take to circumvent the two cuts, and further demolitions destroyed four more bridges; the most effective ambush took place at Ganges, where a sizeable German column was held up for four hours and eventually forced to retreat southward, with forty to fifty dead at the cost of three *maquisards*' lives. Sharpe estimated, in this three-week period, that Axis losses amounted to about 300 dead and 2,000 prisoners, about 200 of them Armenians who were 'seduced from their HQ at Le Vigan, collected at dead of night by trucks and transported to their new abode in the form of a prison camp fifteen miles away – all this without the knowledge of their 45 German officers and NCOs left behind to the subsequent mercy of a later mopping-up operation', thanks largely to the actions of a Russian girl among the *maquisards*.

By the first week of September, with most of the German forces in the area either driven out or in captivity, the *maquisards* began to turn their attention to other matters, and descended on Nîmes and Montpellier, where 'our activities ... were mostly of a social nature', but included a parade at which Gen de Lattre de Tassigny took the salute. They met up with other Jedburghs too, and on 6 September Minaret 'took a tearful farewell of the maquis' and travelled northward, first to Vals-les-Bains and then to Lyon, where the pair parted company, Sharpe to travel to Italy by way of Marseilles and Sgt Ellis to return, by a somewhat circuitous route, to London.

Citroën

In all, ten Jedburgh teams were deployed to France during the twenty-four hours immediately before the Allied landings on the Côte d'Azur on 15 August, two of which were to operate in the area immediately to the east of the Rhône Valley. Both were dropped on the night of 13 August to a reception committee led by 'Archiduc' (Camille Rayon) at a ground known as Armature, near St-Christol, twenty-five kilometres north-east of Apt, in the Vaucluse. The DZ, which was very rocky, had actually been approved for *matériel* only, and the reception committee was surprised to receive bodies (and many bodies, at that – as well as Citroën and the other Jedburgh team, Monocle, a fifteen-strong Operational Group, Nancy, was also inserted there that night). The despatching of the Jedburghs, in particular, was handled badly, the American pilot of the B-24 Liberator dropping Citroën at a height of 600m and the despatcher quite unnecessarily pushing all three members out of the hatch, which was most unsettling. Despite that the team landed safely, although one of its panniers (containing the B2 radio set and the W/T operator's personal kit) was smashed.

That night the team – Cmdt René-Clément Bloch, who called himself Alcée ('Laurent'); Capt John Smallwood of the 24th Lancers ('Anne') and Sgt Fred Bailey ('Rétif') – met 'Cmdt Beyne', the leader of the Mont Ventoux *maquis*. On 16 August they travelled to his HQ at Sault, and met a Canadian major, Labelle ('Paul'), who had been parachuted in a month earlier as part of a Mission known as Nartex. Paul, said Bloch, 'had never heard of a Jed and was not very interested in us anyway, and not helpful'. Beyne gave the Jedburghs two companies of *Corps Francs* and sent them off to the Luberon, south of Apt, to make nuisances of themselves. It was 19 August by now, however, and their capacity for mischief was severely constrained by a distinct absence of German troops in the area; they did become involved in a small and seemingly rather desultory engagement south of Pertuis on the following day. On 22 August – by which time the team was in contact with American spearhead elements advancing from the east – Citroën took command of a mixed bag of partisans (including a group from the *Gendarmerie Maritime* and one of Indo-Chinese, as well as the group from Pertuis), and organised the blockade of the road out of Apt towards Avignon.

Another Jedburgh team, Graham, was also present at this incident, and its leader was to be highly critical of the blocking party, but perhaps not surprisingly, Citroën's account is rather different, saying only that 'the results were almost nil as the Germans had practically all withdrawn, owing to the delay in the attack'.

Smallwood, with a company of *maquisards*, followed on behind the retreating Germans, reaching Cavaillon on the evening of 24 August and spending the night there, before entering now-abandoned Avignon the following day and then pushing on up the Rhône towards Orange. At Courthézon, some five kilometres short of the town, the group got rather ahead of itself, and found itself surrounded by Axis troops; a sharp fire-fight ensued, during which the partisans had six men wounded, but managed to break off and retire taking with them four prisoners; the bus in which they were travelling was hit repeatedly, and they were lucky to escape before the 300kg of plastic explosive aboard was detonated. Meanwhile, Bloch was engaged in securing the area south and west of Apt and trying to smooth over the obvious (and growing) differences between the FFI and the FTP. Smallwood arrived back from his excursion up the lower Rhône on 26 August, and five days later the team reported to 4 SFU at Brignolles.

Monocle

Monocle dropped on to the Armature DZ while the members of Team Citroën were still collecting themselves. It was led by Capt Jacques Fiardo, who took the name Tosel ('Immense'), with two Americans, Lt Ray H Foster ('Solide') and T/Sgt Robert J Anderson ('Raieux'), who were to work in the Drôme, under the control of the FFI chief, 'Maj Legrande' (Cmdt de Lassus de St-Geniez). Like Citroën, Monocle's insertion was poorly handled, largely because the B-24 Liberator pilot insisted on flying across the lights, not down them, and dropping his charges at undiminished speed from a height of 600m. Fiardo and Anderson landed on opposite sides of the small, rocky ground and were unscathed, but Foster came down some distance away, on a steep slope, and badly sprained an ankle and a knee. Despite the reception party, led by 'Archiduc' (Camille Rayon) not expecting bodies, Fiardo records that 'his work that night was perfectly executed.'

It was two days before transport could be organised to take Monocle north into the Drôme, but eventually it travelled to Buis-les-Baronnies, just across the departmental boundary, where it distributed weapons given to it by OG Nancy, and gave some instruction in demolition techniques to an FTP group. Fiardo and Foster made contact with Legrande on 16 August, and the following day set up their command post some ten kilometres south of Dieulefit, though Fiardo was to remain at the FFI HQ with Legrande 'who was at times rather difficult to get on with' while Foster protected Anderson in the 'classic' arrangement which had been devised when the original Jedburgh concept was being refined, back in 1942. One or other of the officers went out with a Resistance *coup-de-main* party most nights, and Foster led a group which blew up the fuel dump at Valence-Chabieul airfield, which was still in use by the *Luftwaffe*. Most operations, however, were concentrated on cutting the N7 and the railway lines which parallel and cross it.

On 22 August, the Jedburghs made their first contact with the American forces arriving from the south, and from that time on their mission changed to one of liaison and intelligence-gathering. But they did take part in the liberation of Valence, which was carried out by the FFI, the American commander, Gen Butler, having elected to bypass the city. The team's report – which is very brief – does not tell us when it stood down, though Foster and Sgt Anderson are reported as being back in the United Kingdom by 1 October. Before that, however, Ray Foster had set off on a one-man rescue mission, to try to effect the release of Cy Manierre. In his report he says:

It seems ... that Cy had a habit of meeting with his agents and then when the police came, he would jump out of the window and beat it. I say this as it comes in later on [it never does]. He was taken by the Milice and taken to Valence. At the time he was in civilian clothes. I questioned a man who later worked for me, by the name of Esve. He said, and it is true, that Manniere [sic] was taken on a Friday or a Saturday night [it was Saturday, 5 August], taken to Valence and held there by the Milice until Tuesday night. Le Grance [sic; actually, Legrande] was asked to help on this case but refused. Legrande said his agents said Manniere left on Monday night but later found he was wrong. Capt John [one of Legrande's lieutenants] had a relation who worked for the police in Valence. Manniere could have been sprung at this point. He left Valence under Gestapo orders for Lyon. In Valence the Milice turned him over to the Gestapo. He was in Montluc Prison until August 26th when he left for Belfort with four other Americans including Lt Meyer [sic; actually, Myers] of O.G.'s, who was captured in the Vercors. I contacted the chief of the Resistance in Lyon and he said he had connections in Belfort. My plan was to take three women along in a civilian car. First after Drome was liberated I returned to

4,S.F.U., headquarters and got 300,000,000 Francs from Col. Bartlet, to buy out Manniere. I was too late. Continuing my plan I was to follow the civilian car in a jeep. In Bourg [which 'Bourg' he means is unclear; Bourg-en-Bresse seems the obvious candidate] the Resistance there was to furnish a guide and take us up into the mountains and we would use only the small mountain roads and trails getting to Belfort. Alongside of Belfort I was to make my headquarters and the women were to go to Belfort and establish contacts. The woman who used to buy vegetables and rations for the prison in Lyon was one of the women with me. She knew that it was possible to get Manniere out with money. The reason I knew Manniere was there was that she got a note from a girl friend who left in the same truck as Manniere [presumably only as far as the nearest railway station, for Manierre and Myers travelled to Germany by train, by Manierre's own account]. This girl was held because of some difficulty in obtaining help along the way. She also worked for the Resistance. I firmly believe this mission could have been successful, had it been carried out, but I was ordered back to Grenoble by Major Bonner of O.S.S.

It is unclear which point in his plan Foster had reached – or indeed, if he had actually begun to put it into effect – when he was ordered back to Grenoble. In his report on the team's de-briefing, Neil Marten said:

The reason why Lt Foster was not allowed to follow up the plan for effecting the release of Major [sic] Manniere is NOT understood [emphasis in the original]. From conversation it would appear that he had a very good chance of success, and it is the greatest pity that he was stopped

which assertion seems as fanciful as the plan itself.

Jude

The day following the Anvil/Dragoon landings, team Jude was despatched from the United Kingdom to operate further north, in the area immediately to the south of Lyon. Like team Alan, inserted just a few days earlier, Jude was to accompany a party from 3 SAS, this time the group which was to mount Operation Jockworth. It, too, was to contact an FFI Mission – Gingembre – and provide communications between the SAS party and its Brigade Headquarters in the United Kingdom. It would also harrass enemy lines of communication, particularly those in the Giers Valley, between Lyon and St-Étienne, as a secondary objective. Team Jude had Capt William Evans of the King's Liverpool Regiment ('Glamorgan') as its leader, together with Capt Jean Larrieu, who called himself Lavisme ('Rence') and Sgt Alfred Holdham ('Guinea'). Evans and Larrieu were to work very closely with elements of the SAS party since it was split into small operational groups, some of which lacked experienced leaders; in particular, they directed reconnaissance patrols and ordered, planned and led ambushes.

The four Stirlings carrying the party had no trouble locating the DZ, north-east of St-Étienne but there was considerable confusion on the ground due to the organiser of the reception committee having misinterpreted the warning message transmitted by the BBC, which told him to expect 'forty friends'; he took this to mean forty aircraft, rather than forty men, and had assembled some 2,000 *maquisards* from all over the region, together with a hundred assorted vehicles, to clear the mass of containers he envisaged being dropped. The general state of chaos was enhanced when many of the containers of demolition stores for the SAS party exploded on impact – a common occurrence, due to detonators and plastic explosive being packed together.

The partisan groups in the area were, according to William Evans, willing but poorly armed, and their training was negligible, but within days of his arrival he and 'Mary' (Raymond Basset), the leader of Gingembre, had begun to define a unified command structure; identified suitable DZs for *parachutages* and assembled reception committees for them; set up a network of young people to act as couriers and messengers between the command post and the individual partisan groups, and even established a rudimentary medical service, with a field hospital staffed by qualified volunteers.

Within two weeks of Jude's arriving in the field, those elements of the US 7th Army which were proceeding directly up the Rhône Valley had finally succeeded in breaking through the block created by the German 11. Panzer Division at Montélimar, and were advancing rapidly on Lyon. With the battle for control of the city imminent, Jude's role changed to one of co-ordination, Evans mentions (though once more, one is struck by the absence of any reference in his report to the activities of other Jedburgh teams in the area), in particular the briefing of 'anti-scorch' teams whose tasks were to prevent the destruction of essential public services. In this they were only marginally successful –

just one of the many bridges across the Rhône and Saône, which converge in the city, was saved from destruction, largely because the teams protecting them failed to follow instructions.

Following the liberation of Lyon, Jude turned its attention to setting up an officers' and junior leaders' school at St-Genis-Laval in the city's southern suburbs, running a course which lasted for four weeks. This was a marked success, and when Jude was stood down and returned to London, on 22 October, urgent representations were made to SFHQ to allow the team to return to France and run further courses; they returned to Lyon on 7 November for what was officially known as Operation Jude II, and returned just before the end of the year.

Jeremy

The header sheet to the report of team Jeremy indicates that it was despatched from Algiers on the night of 16 August, but the report itself makes it clear that that is an error, and it was a further eight days before it actually went into the field. The team comprised Capt George Hallowes of the Gordon Highlanders ('Aimable'), Lt Henri-Charles Giese, who took the name Fontcroise ('Dur') and Sgt Roger Leney ('Ferme'), and was deployed to the Haute-Loire, to operate under the control of 'Diane', the redoubtable Virgina Hall, one of the most celebrated of SOE/OSS's female operatives.

Hall – known in the Haute-Loire as 'La dame qui boite' (the limping lady) – was an American citizen, born in Maryland in 1906. She lost her lower left leg after she accidentally shot herself in the foot while hunting, in the mid-1930s. The outbreak of World War Two found her living in France, and in May 1940 she joined the ambulance service. After the fall of France she made her way to London, and was an early recruit to SOE's F Section. Sent back into France (by felucca from Gibraltar) in 1941, she operated in the Unoccupied Zone until the Germans arrived in November 1942, escaping to Spain by walking across the Pyrénées. Having transferred to OSS's Special Operations Branch, she was reinserted, this time by a motor torpedo boat on the Brittany coast (her disability made parachuting an unacceptable risk) in March, 1944, and established the Hector network in the Haute-Loire.

Jeremy's first attempt at insertion, on the night of 22 August, failed, but two nights later it succeeded, and was met by Diane on a ground near her base at Le Chambon-sur-Lignon, some thirty kilometres east of Le Puy-en-Velay. The next day Sgt Leney remained with her, to establish contact with Algiers, while Hallowes and Giese moved to Le Puy, the departmental HQ of the FFI. By that time the Haute-Loire had been largely cleared of its German garrisons, but there was still a perceived danger from Axis troops arriving from further south, and Hallowes decided to try to arm those *résistants* – about 800 of the total of 1,500 available – who as yet had no weapons. (It was to be 2 September before the first consignment of arms, which amounted to thirty containers, enough to arm perhaps a hundred, arrived, and by then, of course, events had moved on.) His biggest headache was created by *résistants du vingt-cinquième heure* – men who, as Hallowes said,

> had just recently put on uniform, stuck on Major's badges of rank and were out only for themselves, and the profit they could make from it. Many times I heard them state how they had done this and that, when it was the Maquis men who were the true basis of Resistance. Many of these 'Majors' had only been in the Resistance for about a week since the Germans left. Feeling ran high in one or two quarters because of this, and some were reluctant to obey the orders of these 'officers' who were all more or less installed at the Headquarters in Le Puy.

He encountered further problems when he visited St-Étienne, the nearest large city, to which all the left-leaning *résistants* armed by the Hector network had gravitated. In consequence, FTP members remaining in the Haute-Loire were told that they would be armed only if they took orders from Jeremy. 'They decided they did not want to obey any orders other than FTP, so they remain unarmed.'

Hallowes met the first representatives of the French *Armée B*, advancing up the right bank of the Rhône, on 1 September, and with the danger of a flood of escaping Germans over, began to formulate a plan for the continuing employment of its three 'battalions' of *maquisards*, each of them composed of two 150-man companies. By 3 September, the day the FFI liberated Lyon, see below, he had hit upon the notion of moving them to the area around Vichy, around 100 kilometres away to the north-west, and put the plan to 'Gaspard', the Departmental FFI chief, who approved it. This move took place, largely by rail, on 12 September, by which time all the partisans were armed, but it soon became apparent that there was no more need for the Haute-Loire *bataillons* here than there was in their own territory, and on 17 September they moved again, this time to Pontailler-sur-Saône, twenty-five kilometres east of Dijon, where they would be incorporated into the French Army.

Hallowes' report ends abruptly at this point – he had been ordered to compile it while still in the field, on 16 September – and it is impossible to trace Jeremy's subsequent movements. It is safe to say that the team did not accompany the Haute-Loire *bataillons*, though Henri Giese, who disappears from the narrative at this point, may well have done so. As for Hallowes and Leney, rather than returning to London to be stood down, they travelled via 4 SFU's base at Avignon, where they were debriefed, and Marseilles to Bari, where they were put on stand-by for a mission in northern Italy. That came to nothing, and they returned to the United Kingdom on 24 October.

Masque and Scion

The last two Massingham-based teams to be deployed were both instructed to contact Claude Vuchot of Veganin/Dodge, who had been alone in the field with his radio operator, the Canadian, Sgt Durocher, since Cy Manierre's capture. Team Masque, composed of Capt Nelson E Guillot ('Harmonieux'), Lt Jacques Bouvery, alias Gramont ('Succulent') and 1/Sgt Francis M Poche of the USAAF ('Idéal') was the first to be inserted, on the night of 27 August, and Scion – Maj Osborne Grenfell of the Royal Armoured Corps ('Scintillating'), Lt Roger Gruppo, who used the name Revard ('Vif') and Sgt Thomas 'Cobber' Cain, of the Fife and Forfar Yeomanry ('Vibrant') – followed two nights later. Both were to be dropped to Tandem, the ground where team Willys had dropped, two months earlier, and very close to the area where team Jeremy was now operating, near St-Agrève, in the Ardèche, just forty kilometres east of Le Puy-en-Velay and at least 100 kilometres from the western extremity of the Isère, where Vuchot was by then located; Scion's report tells us that its pilot failed to find the first-choice ground, 'Lee', which was close to Vuchot's base, and dropped to the alternate, and Masque's pilot may have encountered the same difficulty. As well as the two Jedburgh teams, two more Operational Groups were also dropped to Tandem during the last days of August (Guillot's report says that both Jedburghs and both OGs were inserted the same night, 27 August – his team-mate Bouvery says that seven aircraft dropped loads onto the ground that night – but other reports tell contradictory stories) and all were assembled at the local *maquis* command post at Devesset, where they were accommodated at a hotel; all concerned commented on the high quality of the food.

Masque's and Scion's reports tell us they met with the DMD for the Ardèche, 'Cmdt Vanel' (Cmdt Paul Vaucheret), the leader of Mission Pectoral (see above), who gave them the option of either trying to cross the Rhône Valley and attempting to join Vuchot, or of remaining in the Ardèche and putting themselves at his disposal. (Guillot's report seems to indicate that this latter may have been suggested at the teams' briefings as an alternative to seeking out Vuchot. He says 'As per briefing, upon not being able to contact Commandant Noir [i.e. Vuchot], we reported to Commandant Vanel'.) The first option involved a potentially hazardous journey, and it would be four or five days before they could expect to be in position, and Grenfell says they 'insisted on the second course, as we wanted to get in combat as quickly as possible'. (There is an anomaly here. Willys' report tells us that Vaucheret had been removed as DMD some time in July by the DMR, Col Henri Provisor, and the local *Armée Secrète* chief, Cmdt René Calloud, put in his place; in any event, it was with Calloud that the teams were to be most closely associated, and following the initial references to him, Vaucheret is barely mentioned thereafter in either report.)

Both teams proceeded to St-Étienne on 30 or 31 August, and became involved in the preparations for the liberation of Lyon. This operation was to involve most of the *maquisards* from the surrounding district – a total of 5,000 or more men – in addition to elements of the Allied army advancing northward from Provence. The advance towards the jumping-off points began on 1 September, and the following day partisan units began linking up with regular units arriving from the south. H-Hour for the assault was 0600 on 3 September, and despite the bulk of the French forces being only lightly armed, by 1000 the city was largely in their hands. There were the inevitable pockets of resistance to be mopped up, a task to which the FFI were not well suited –the guerrilla troops having little or no experience of fighting in built-up areas – and many 'friendly fire' casualties resulted. During this period, according to Grenfell, all the Jedburghs (save for Sgt Cain, who had been seconded to Pectoral) fought as simple infantrymen.

Both teams were withdrawn to 4 SFU at Avignon soon after Lyon was secured. They were very critical of the delay in inserting them, stressing that many of the *maquisards* viewed them as *arrivistes*, 'men of the eleventh hour'. Hence their resolve to fight as 'simple infantrymen', hints Grenfell; the decision paid off, and the Jeds' stock rose considerably in consequence, especially when it became clear that they knew a thing or two about house-to-house fighting. None the less, their objections to being held back until such a late date have perfect validity, and the decision to send them into action at a time when the battle in the area was clearly won, and there were no 'Jedburgh tasks' to be undertaken, appears to have been made more as a way of getting them off SPOC's hands than as a real contribution to the war effort. Frustration shines through the conclusion to Grenfell's report, especially its final paragraph: 'Team Scion had only one regret: that it was not parachuted earlier. It had only one desire: to be used as quickly as possible. It remains volunteer [sic] for any mission in any theatre of operations.'

Part Six

THE SOUTH EAST

Chloroform

Team Chloroform, which was led by Capt Jacques Martin, who called himself Martino ('Joshua'), assisted by Lt Henry D McIntosh ('Lionel') and with S/Lt Jean Sassi, who used the name Nicole ('Latimer') as its W/T operator, had originally been briefed as early as 8 June for a mission to the region south of the Vercors Plateau, where it would operate as a mirror of Veganin/Dodge, but was unable to depart until the very end of the month due to bad weather. By that time its aims had been changed, and it was 'to regulate some political misunderstandings which existed in the Drôme region, particularly in the groups of Alain; second, to strengthen and further organise the groups; third, to cut the railroad line Valence, Crest, Die, Gap'. In fact, when Chloroform arrived it became clear that the political dispute – between 'Alain' (Pierre Raynaud, one of 'Roger''s assistants) and 'Hermine' (Cmdt Druout) – had been resolved; that the railway line in question had been out of commission since 6 June, and would be kept that way, and that the partisans in the area were already organised and partially trained and armed.

Chloroform's insertion, in the early hours of 30 June at a ground near Dieulefit, some thirty-five kilometres east of Montélimar and the same distance south of Crest, was successful, despite the team having been dropped from a height of 800m, and being widely dispersed on landing. They were met by a reception party, and taken north to Léoncel, on the edge of the Vercors, where 'Richard' (Capt René, commander of the Northern Battalion of the *Régiment du Drôme*) was then based, and through him, by 2 July they had made contact with all the appropriate Resistance leaders – Alain, Roger (Lt-Col Francis Cammaerts) and 'Col Joseph' (Henri Zeller, who had overall command of the FFI in south-eastern France), together with Neil Marten of team Veganin, and Hermine. By this time, the tensions between the right-leaning Hermine and Alain, who had allied himself with the FTP, had come to a head, and

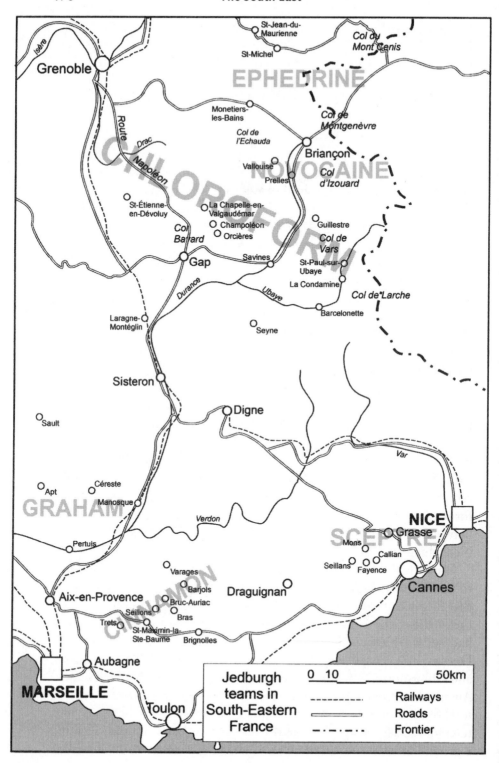

Jedburgh teams in South-Eastern France

0 10 50km

Railways
Roads
Frontier

Col Joseph had reassigned the former to the Hautes-Alpes, to the east. Jacques Martin reviewed the situation, and since there was little work for the team in the Drôme, decided that Chloroform – whose operational area covered both *départements* – would be best employed accompanying him; with Joseph's and SPOC's agreement, they set out eastward, in a car and a truck.

At St-Étienne-en-Dévoluy Chloroform split away from Hermine, and contacted the local Resistance chief, 'Cmdt Terrasson'; from his evaluation of the situation – less than fifty would-be *résistants*, with no arms to speak of and very little training – Martin decided to remain there, and operate from a base in the Vallée du Drac de Champoléon, to the east of the *Route Napoléon* but adjacent both to it and the main east–west route in the region, which intersect it at Gap. They began their journey up the valley on 8 July, and everywhere were taken for Germans; pausing to eat lunch in a restaurant at Pont du Fosse, they were surprised by partisans ('a kid with a Sten' according to McIntosh, but four *maquisards* by Martin's account) who came close to shooting them out of hand.

As word of the Jedburghs' presence spread, more and more volunteers came forward, and an eight-day basic training course, covering weapons handling and fieldcraft, was set up at a base near Les Baumes. Men who had completed their military service were soon able to act as instructors, and the shortfall in weaponry was initially made up from a stock of World War One-vintage *Modèle* '07 Lebel rifles, which the priest at Champoléon had hidden in his church. Later other weapons, cached the previous year when a number of *parachutages* had been received, were also unearthed. The first partisans trained by Chloroform were in action by the second week of July, cutting the railway between Gap and Briançon and ambushing German vehicles on the N94 which links the two towns.

On 17 July, Martin received a message from Roger, instructing him to return to the Drôme, and chose to disregard it, apparently unaware that Roger had authority over all the Jedburgh teams in the area. Then, the next day, the German assault on the Vercors began. Hermine, who had set up his headquarters near Gap, returned to St-Étienne-en-Dévoluy to organise and help regroup any escapees from the plateau, and Chloroform joined him there, and remained until the beginning of August. During that period the first resupply missions were flown and a total of nine aircraft dropped containers of arms and ammunition, plus ten radio sets for distribution to the partisan leaders in the region, on to a ground known as Weasel, on the Plateau d'Auronze; thanks to poor packing, more than a quarter of all the supplies dropped were destroyed. On 2 August the team moved east, and set up a base at La Chapelle-en-Valgaudémar, where Martin and McIntosh ran a course for *maquisard* officers and NCOs before returning on 10 August to the Champoléon valley, to Orcières, where a camp was established which was to serve the team as a base until the end of its operations.

One day prior to the Anvil/Dragoon landings, Choloroform set off with around sixty partisans to cross the mountains which separate Orcières from the valley of the Durance, to the south, where the routes between Gap and Briançon run; by 1600 the following afternoon they had blown the railway bridge across the river at Savines, and established ambush parties on the N94, making contact in the process with team Novocaine, which had been inserted a week earlier and was now operating around Briançon.

The master plan for the region entailed supporting Col Joseph's scheme to use the *Route Napoléon* to supplement the main roads up the Rhône Valley, and called for the partisans to take control of Gap and the Col Bayard, to the north, which had the secondary effect of denying the route to German forces retreating in the face of the invading Allies. On 19 August Hermine gave the executive orders, and his forces were in place by that night. On hearing that American units had been seen as close as Laragne-Montéglin, north of Sisteron, Martin sought them out, and obtained the assistance of an armoured detachment. At 1700 the partisans began the assault of Gap, a request to the German garrison to surrender having been turned down; within two hours the town was liberated, and over 1,200 Axis troops, including forty officers, were made prisoner (the ORs were held in the cinema, and it was judged safe to leave just two partisans to guard them, so low was their morale). The following morning, about 1,500 Axis troops arrived from further north, but were stopped and driven back long before they reached the pass; by the evening of 21 August, virtually the whole of the Hautes-Alpes had been liberated.

The situation to the east, in the Basses-Alpes (now known as the Alpes de Haute-Provence), was less clear, and in response to German activity at Col de Larche on the old Franco-Italian frontier, Chloroform and a small American unit comprising two armoured cars and four jeeps accompanied two platoons of partisans to La Condamine, at the foot of the pass. For seven days they managed to convince the enemy that they were present in sufficient strength to deny them the route down towards Barcelonette; they were relieved by an American airborne battalion, and the Jedburghs then returned to Gap. The area being completely free of

Axis troops by 15 September, McIntosh travelled to 4 SFU HQ at Grenoble for orders, and then returned to meet up with the rest of the team at Avignon where, says Martin, 'we celebrated'.

Novocaine

Team Novocaine was somewhat unusual – though by no means unique – in that it had no officer of a rank higher than lieutenant, and thus, at least by its own account, it struggled to make an impact on the *maquisards* it encountered. It was led, at least nominally, by Lt Charles J Gennerich ('Mathieu'), assisted by Lt Jean-Yves Pronost, calling himself Le Lann ('Herve') and Sgt William T Thompson ('Gilles'), and was deployed, like all the other teams sent into the region east of the Rhône, to operate at Roger's orders. Novocaine left Blida in the late evening of 6 August, and landed at 0130 on 7 August on a DZ near Roger's long-time headquarters at Seyne in the Basses-Alpes. Despite the ground being unsuitable, all members of the team landed safely, and just one container was lost when its parachute failed to open.

It was some days before Gennerich could report to Roger, and in the meantime the team busied itself teaching partisans how to handle some of the weaponry at their disposal. On 10 August they received orders to move to the upper Durance Valley, to Vallouise, just south-west of Briançon, and cut the route into Italy across the Col de Montgenèvre. A truck was provided to carry them, but they were forced to leave behind the containers of weapons they had brought, taking only two Brens and quantities of explosives and grenades. The team paused for a day and a night near Guillestre in the company of a partisan group commanded by 'Gilbert' (Garletti), an AS group composed largely of men who had served with the *Chasseurs Alpins*, the French Army's élite mountain troops; there they recruited two South Africans who had been taken prisoner in the Western Desert, had escaped from Italian custody and fought with Italian partisans before crossing into France. They also cut the water supply to nearby Fort Mont Dauphin, one of the many fortifications in the area, which was home to a small Axis garrison. On 14 August they moved to Vallouise, and that night demolished a stone bridge carrying the main road into Briançon, and blocked a tunnel carrying a parallel secondary road, near the village of Prelles; this effectively cut communications between Briançon and points south, the only alternative road, which crossed the Col d'Izouard at a height of

2360m, being very susceptible to ambuscade. It also isolated Guillestre, the road west between there and Gap having been cut at Savines by team Chloroform, and two days later the eighty-strong garrison in the fort surrendered, yielding up considerable quantities of arms and ammunition as well as valuable motor vehicles.

By 22 August, the spearhead units of the American forces in the area had reached Guillestre, and rumours of the imminent evacuation of Briançon were spreading. The following day Gennerich and Pronost led a strong force of partisans against the town, only to discover that the Germans had already left, and that American troops, albeit only a motorised reconnaissance patrol, had actually beaten them to it. With the German garrison dispersed, the partisans began setting up defensive positions, and were later reinforced by elements of an American armoured unit, but they soon found themselves coming under sustained artillery fire, for rather than trying to fight their way through to the north, Axis forces effectively trapped in that section of southern Savoie had again turned their attention on the town. Although the *maquisards* were driven out on 29 August, it was only a matter of time before reinforcements arrived, and on 6 September, supported by partisans, regular French forces finally liberated the town. With that Novocaine retired to Grenoble, to be debriefed and returned to the United Kingdom.

Graham

Team Graham was finally deployed, after an unnecessary series of delays, on the night of 10 August. It was one of the more unusual Jedburgh teams in that its two members – its W/T operator Sgt William H Adams ('Desire') was supposed to follow them, but did not – were semi-invalids. In his book *Irregular Soldier*, 'Bing' Crosby, the team's leader, tells how he was born with deformed feet; that he was only able to walk at all after extensive surgery and that thereafter it was necessary for him to 'talk very firmly with 'official' doctors in order to persuade them that I was capable of doing whatever I wanted to do at the time'. He tells us, too, that during Jedburgh training at Milton Hall, he teamed up with one of the more senior French officers, Pierre Gavet, who changed his name to Gouvet, 'as an old crocks team' (Crosby was then thirty-three; Gavet, of similar age and known as 'Papa' among the volunteers, had suffered a back injury during a training jump). Crosby relates how they had problems keeping up with their younger colleagues in some areas during training, though not on the long endurance marches in the coastal mountains of Algeria, and that it was decided that the pair should be given an extra chance of arriving in one piece by the rather unlikely stratagem of parachuting them into a lake.

In the event, that mission – to the Ariège or perhaps the Hautes-Pyrénées – was aborted, and they were rebriefed for another in the Basses-Alpes, where they were to be inserted in (rather cramped) luxury by Lysander aircraft from Corsica. Maj Crosby ('Huge') and Cmdt Gavet ('Crispin') left Algiers on 29 July, and were scheduled to be inserted at the Spitfire LZ midway between Apt and Sault in the Vaucluse, on the night of 31 July. Confusion reigned in Corsica, and it was the night of 10 August before they finally landed in France, aboard an RAF Dakota operating out of Cecina in Italy.

Crosby – who, although not a Scot, like Tommy Macpherson, was a member of a Highland regiment, the Gordons, and also operated in France in his kilt – describes events after arriving at the *Maquis*:

> Four days were wasted while the new 'chefs' held discussions with all and sundry, and appointed new departmental chiefs, etc. During this time, despite repreated requests, it was impossible to make any movement to a more active area. Finally, Col St Sauveur appointed us as mission to Noel – chef FFI Basses Alpes, and on the night of 14th we moved to a maquis ... north of Cereste. Noel was too elusive to be found, so having sent various couriers to tell him where we were, we decided to work with this maquis until such time as he appeared.
>
> On the morning of August 15, we carried out some instruction in explosives and arms – the men being well organised but badly in need of training. When the news of the [Anvil/Dragoon] landing came through we helped 'mobilise' the maquis and on the evening of the 15th placed men in ambush positions on all roads in the sector, to prevent enemy movement.

Crosby and Gavet spent the following days touring the region, never catching sight of a German uniform, offering advice on choosing key features for mining, and helping to organise the partisan group, which grew from sixty to 250 almost overnight. On 19 August they made contact with American forces moving up the valley of the Durance, and Crosby agreed that they would move north, to the area west of Sisteron, and help to organise a force to protect the left flank of their lines of communication. Save for a brief excursion to Apt to check on a (false) rumour that the Germans had retaken the town, they worked at this task for three days. On 22 August a better-founded rumour of the reoccupation of Apt started circulating, with a rider that Cereste would be next; Crosby set out and 'took the law into [his] own hands, and mobilised a large force of FFI from the surrounding area, and thus by evening had gathered an army of some 600/700 armed and lorried FFI at Cereste'. These men he placed in positions to cover all the exits from Apt save for the road west, to Avignon, which was covered by a group from Pertuis, and settled down to wait for reinforcements in the shape of four American tanks and a company of infantry. What followed was something of a fiasco:

> Unfortunately, the American forces who started to arrive at 0700 required six hours personal recce before attacking – not believing, as usual, that there were really any FFI to do the job, and not believing our reports on the terrains, etc. Naturally, the Boche saw their activity – which was far from hidden – and just before we attacked, all withdrew from the town towards Avignon. The force from Pertuis ... had decided it was 'too dangerous' to approach nearer than some four kilometres from [the road], and therefore let pass the entire column ...

The following morning, Crosby received a message from Noel reporting that a large German force had crossed the Col de Larche (from Italy) and were advancing on Barcelonette, and asking him to obtain regular troops to deal with the matter. He and Gavet went first to 'Army HQ' (presumably the Divisional HQ at Sisteron), and from there to Barcelonette, where they met Captain Halsey, a member of yet another Allied Mission inserted into the area; they then headed on up the Ubaye valley to Condamine, where they came under sustained German fire. Cut off from the car in which they had been travelling, they set out to hike the fifteen kilometres back to Barcelonette, but came under fire again at Jausiers, and were forced to take to the hills. Crosby's chronology rather breaks down at this point, and the next we know, he is taking a party of ten men 'by a roundabout route into Italy, over the mountains to attempt to bring back a prisoner for identification'. In the event, the effort proved futile, and Crosby had to content himself with fooling the locals into believing that he had a large force at his disposal.

Returning to Barcelonette, it became obvious that Graham's task was over, and Crosby and Gavet made their way to Grenoble to be debriefed and stood down. Pierre Gavet remained in France, and rejoined his unit – a colonial artillery regiment – while Bing Crosby returned to the United Kingdom, arriving in London on 25 September.

Ephedrine

Six days after Novocaine was dropped to operate in the mountainous region which borders Italy, on the night of 12 August, another team, Ephedrine, was despatched to the same area. Made up of Lt Louis Donnard, who used the name Rabeau ('Julien'), Lt Lawrence E Swank ('Gantor') and S/Lt Robert Desplechin, who took the name Bourgoin ('Léon'), the team was dropped on the ground near Seyne together with a three-man Allied Mission known as Progression and four French officers, a total of ten men, with around fifty containers and many packages. Despite the pilot of the Liberator in which Ephedrine was flying dropping them from a height of 800m, all landed safely within the confines of the rather small DZ, though perhaps a dozen containers were destroyed when their parachutes failed to open. As the reception committee had been briefed to expect only the Jedburghs and their standard load of containers, there was a certain amount of confusion on the ground, and it was some hours before the DZ was cleared.

Ephedrine had been given only an outline briefing of its own, and was to have received detailed instructions from Roger, but unfortunately he had been arrested by *Sipo*-SD two days earlier, near Digne, together with the recently arrived Xan Fielding. (They were to be freed in a most audacious manner by Roger's assistant, 'Pauline', known as Christine Granville, but actually Krystyna Giżycka, who, in the words of MRD Foot, one of SOE's official historians, 'by a combination of steady nerve, feminine cunning and sheer brass persuaded his captors that the Americans' arrival was imminent, and secured the party's release three hours before they were to have been shot'. The sum of two million francs in cash changed hands, too.) The team remained on the DZ until the evening of 13 August, waiting for Roger, and eventually was put into contact with Pauline, who provided a small truck to take them, and the party to their operational areas in Savoie and Haute-Savoie. They set out on the following afternoon, intending to travel by way of Barcelonette and the Col De Vars to Guillestre, where they would be received by Gilbert's group. They reached Barcelonette at about 1900, and two hours later were just short of the village of St-Paul, at the foot of the climb up to the Col, when a loaded rifle, issued to one of the French officers but left loose on the floor of the truck with the party's luggage, discharged when someone leaned or fell on it while the vehicle was negotiating a bend. The round hit Lawrence Swank in the right armpit, touched a bone and fragmented before exiting under the right shoulder blade. The American lieutenant died from loss of blood at about 0200 the next morning, a local doctor who attended having been unable to do anything for him save administer morphine; he was buried incognito at St-Paul on 15 August.

The party continued, and reached Vallouise, where Novocaine was then located, on 17 August; the following morning Donnard and Desplechin set out, together with the Mission members and the four French officers, for Le Monêtiers-les-Bains – some fifteen kilometres due north on the N91 which links Briançon with Grenoble – by way of the Col de l'Eychauda, their baggage carried on mules. In the course of the journey, which Donnard was to describe as 'particularly tiresome', the harness of one mule parted, and the muleteer abandoned the team's personal kit, which was pillaged, and their operational funds, totalling 250,000 francs, stolen. On their arrival at Le Monêtiers, the team passed over 200kg of explosives to the leader of the local *maquisards*, who put some of it to good use immediately, blocking the N91 for twenty-four hours. Continuing their journey northward, the party arrived in the Maurienne, the valley along which runs the N6 which links France and Italy by way of the Col du Mont-Cenis. This was to be the Jedburgh team's base for the remainder of its time in France, and Donnard and Desplanchin set up a command post adjacent to that of 'Capt Villon' (Gerlotto), a regular soldier who was the *de facto* leader of all the *maquis-ards*, both AS and FTP, in the valley; the Progression Mission based itself close by, but the four French officers continued on their way, to help with the training and organisation of groups further north.

The situation Ephedrine found in the Maurienne was not entirely encouraging. Since this was a main supply route for the German forces fighting in Italy, the road was heavily patrolled; garrisons in the valley totalled perhaps 600 men and key positions were fortified. The partisan forces were weak and poorly armed; well over half were *sédentaires* who had not yet left their homes to join a fighting unit, and whereas their morale was relatively good, they had little *esprit de corps*. Villon was competent and a good organiser, in Donnard's judgement, but the task of turning all the would-be partisans in the valley into an effective fighting force was more than he could be expected to carry out. The area had received one supply drop amounting to perhaps thirty containers in April, but most of them had been taken by the Germans; in addition the team's report tells us: 'There were also some arms (10 MGs and about 50 rifles) which had been dropped to the Col des Saisies at the beginning of August'.

Donnard turned over to Villon all the arms the party had brought on

22 August, and straight away decided to open a campaign against the traffic using the N6. Over the following two days, four major ambushes were mounted, a total of thirteen vehicles destroyed and well over a hundred German troops, including at least three officers, killed or captured. The occupying forces reacted swiftly, burning eight villages and shooting thirty men and women, as well as combing the valley for guerrilla bases, and Villon hastily called off his campaign. From then until the end of the month there was an uneasy truce, although throughout the week German combat engineers prepared bridges and factories for demolition. On 1 September *maquisard* reinforcements started arriving from the Tarentaise to the north, and the following day an assault was mounted on the garrison at St-Jean-de-Maurienne, the main town in the valley. Fighting was heavy, but the attack could not be pushed home due to very heavy rain, under cover of which the German forces withdrew up the valley, south to St-Michel, followed by partisans who harried them all the way. Sporadic fighting continued over the next three days, and on 5 September Donnard was able to contact a regular unit, the 5th *Tirailleurs Marocains*, who took charge of the situation. On 8 September Ephedrine left to travel to Grenoble, to report to 4 SFU, and were stood down.

Cinnamon

The night after Ephedrine arrived in France it was the turn of team Cinnamon, comprising Capt Henri Lespinasse-Fonsegrieve, who called himself François Ferandon ('Orthon'), Capt Robert Harcourt of the Royal Armoured Corps ('Louis') and S/Lt Jacques Marineau, who took Maurin as his *nom de guerre* ('Luc'). The team was inserted by a USAAF B-17 Flying Fortress operating out of Blida, the pilot of which was either incompetent or ill trained (the latter is perhaps more likely; B-17s were seldom used to insert men). He arrived over the DZ fifteen minutes ahead of schedule and then circled for half an hour; in all, he made four passes over the ground, and on the last of them – well to the right of the line of the lights and flying at an altitude of around 600m – he gave the Jedburghs the green light prematurely, and without slowing the aircraft. Harcourt, the first to jump and disoriented after having somersaulted in the course of his fall, landed 900m away from the lights, in an oak wood, and broke both his lower legs; Marineau and Lespinasse also landed in the wood, but were unhurt. The team's containers, though dispersed over a very wide area, were eventually recovered intact, but they soon discovered that due to a mix-up at Blida, some of the containers meant for them had been loaded aboard the aircraft which inserted team Citroën, one of the other four teams dropped that same night, and they had some of Citroën's, and there were deficiencies and equipment mismatches as a result. The last straw, perhaps, was the realisation that the meagre briefing they had received at SPOC was hopelessly out of date, and that following the directions given to the safe house would have landed them directly in German hands.

The ground – Fantôme – was three kilometres south-west of Brue-Auriac, between St-Maximin-la-Ste-Baume and Barjols, in the western Var (although the team's orders said they were to work with the Perpendiculaire circuit, which was located in the Vaucluse, to the north and west). They were met by the organiser of F Section's Carpenter circuit, 'Maj Firmin' (Robert Boiteaux), who was based closer to hand in Marseilles but had to return there urgently. (Boiteaux had been given the mission since he had to receive two sabotage instructors to work with his own circuit on the same ground that night.) After a hurried consultation with Lespinasse, during the course of which he tried to persuade him to accompany him back to Marseilles and work from there – a wholly unrealistic suggestion – he left, taking half the reception party with him; it was well after dawn before the team – which was probably more concerned, in any event, with Harcourt's plight than in recovering containers, some of which would be useless to them – was able to clear the DZ.

French sources say that Cinnamon's instructions were to contact 'Vernie' (or Vernis; Col Joseph Lelaquet, the chief of the ORA in the Var), but the team's report makes only a dismissive passing mention of him, saying he had 'no influence'. Their contact, it says, was Col Joseph Gouzy, and they had been given directions to his safe house in St-Maximin; as luck would have it, one of Gouzy's liaison agents was present at the DZ that night, and told them that the house in question had long been requisitioned by the Germans – St-Maximin was the only town they occupied in that part of the Var – and that the colonel had shifted his base to Varages, north of Barjols. The agent was sent off to fetch the colonel, who arrived the next morning at the small base Cinnamon had made for themselves in the wood.

Harcourt's brief report tells us that Gouzy had a *maquis* divided into twelve small groups, each under the command of a regular officer, and that he advocated their working with him; Lespinasse, however, was seduced by the offer made by a young officer from the French *Service de*

Renseignements, Lt Pavlovitch or Pawilovitch, that the team should set up its command post at his safe house in Seillons-Source-d'Argens, seven kilometres away from the DZ in the direction of St-Maximin, and operate alongside a partisan band from nearby Trets. With that, Lespinasse and Marineau set off for Seillons, and Harcourt was taken off, under the care of Mme Gouzy, to a safe house he calls 'La Ferme Americaine' near Varages; he had no further contact with Lespinasse until after the *département* had been liberated, by which time he had been taken to an American field hospital. He later worked alongside Neil Marten at 4 SFU's interim HQ at Brignoles until returning to the United Kingdom on 24 October.

Lespinasse decided that his first act would be to demolish a bridge which carried the N7 road over the main railway through the area, thus putting both out of action at a stroke. Unfortunately, the Trets partisans, who had already placed demolition charges on the bridge, proved to be less reliable than he had hoped. He and Pavlovitch, together with a boy scout of indeterminate age named Capst, who was to be invaluable as a messenger, arrived at the RV at the appointed time in the very early hours of 16 August, but the *maquisards* did not; he waited until dawn and then cleared the area, having to content himself with firing a few unaimed bursts in the general direction of a small convoy of German trucks. Two nights later he laid an ambush on the tertiary road between the small village of Bras and St-Maximin, but in the five hours the party stayed in position, only two cars passed.

It was now 18 August; the Anvil/Dragoon invasion force, elements of which had landed near Le Lavandou and dropped west of Le Muy, barely fifty kilometres away from St-Maximin, was already out of its beachhead and moving west, and Cinnamon had achieved nothing.

The following day Lespinasse took a party of *maquisards*, some two dozen strong, into the woods north of St-Maximin in response to reports that German troops were constructing defensive positions there. They were not, and perhaps his presence helped to convince them not to do so; if that was the case, it was the only really useful act he performed during the entire operation, save perhaps for some intelligence-gathering, although he does add that over the next three or four days, having by now made contact with the advancing Americans, he and the *maquisards* under his command 'got on with the job of guarding the villages and cleaning up the woods, where there were still groups of Germans'. On 24 August, having been in the field for just ten days, he reported to Brignolles, and from there, eventually, he and Marineau returned to their respective regiments.

Sceptre

Some way to the east, that same night of 13 August, team Sceptre was being inserted into the Var *département*, to a DZ known as Prisonnier, on the Montagne de Malay, fifteen kilometres north-west of the small town of Fayence and perhaps 120 kilometres away from the area in which it had been briefed to operate, along the Franco-Italian border. Once again, the field was unsuitable for bodies; the French liaison officer, Lt François Franceschi, who called himself Tévenac ('Intense') broke his foot, while the radio operator, Sgt Howard V Palmer ('Devoué') sprained a knee. Lt Walter C Hanna ('Vaillant') alone was unhurt. There was no transport available, and it soon became clear that a move deep into the Alpes-Maritimes was impossible.

Over the next three days, Hanna tells us, in a report remarkable for its terseness, Franceschi's broken foot was set, the team selected a campsite (near the village of Mons) and made contact with local *résistants* and an Allied Mission, Lougre, which had been dropped in to the same DZ two nights earlier (Lougre was charged with anti-sabotage operations in the very important naval base of Toulon; there is no explanation as to why it was dropped to a totally unsuitable site so far from its objective when it could have gone to Fantôme). It also 'collected 10 English parachutists and one injured English officer', who left the following day; it is unclear who these men were. There *were* other Allied parachutists in the area: OG Ruth, which had been dropped (by an RAF Stirling and without serious mishap) on to Prisonnier ten days earlier; no mention is made of them, but Hanna does mention three American parachutists – M/Sgt Howard Hachard, Cpl Albert De Shayer and Pvt Olin Hughes, who were not part of Ruth – who joined forces with Sceptre on 17 August and remained with the team, doing sterling work, until it was called to Brignoles.

Sceptre began patrolling on 17 August, and the following day planned an assault on Fayence; this was thwarted when Germans retreating from further east attacked Callians, east of the town, and Seillans, to the west, and the *maquisards* were called to defend them. A second attack was planned for 21 August, by which time De Shayer and Hughes had led partisan parties to destroy two bridges on roads leading out of the town. In the event, Hanna was able to send negotiators to persuade the German officer in charge of the Fayence garrison to surrender; 187 prisoners were taken, and over 200 weapons and four vehicles were handed over. The following day American paratroopers moved into Fayence, and Sceptre's work in the region was over.

Hanna and the others set out for Brignoles on 24 August, and kicked their heels there until 5 September, when they moved to Grenoble, picking up other redundant Jedburghs along the way.

Part Seven

THE SEINE BASIN

Harry and Isaac/Verveine

The second team which left Milton Hall on 3 June, together with Hugh, was to mount Operation Harry; it consisted of Maj Duncan Guthrie ('Denby'), Lt Pierre Dupont, alias Pierre Rousset ('Gapeau') and S/Lt René Couture, who took René Legrand as his *nom de guerre* ('Centime'). It was to be the evening of 6 June before they transferred from Hassells Hall to Tempsford and climbed aboard a Lockheed Hudson for the three-hour flight to the Morvan – an area of hills and valleys, covered with woodland interspersed with small farms – to the west of Dijon. Like Hugh, Harry was accompanied by two officers from 1 SAS, Lts Ian Stewart and Ian Wellsted, who made up the reconnaissance party for Operation Houndsworth, and similarly it was 'to assist them in establishing a base from which lines of communication [in this case the railway lines linking Lyon and the south of France and Paris, by way of either Dijon or Le Creusot and Nevers] could be cut'.

Also like Hugh, Harry was to be inserted 'blind', with no reception party. After circling the general area for half an hour, the pilot annouced that he was returning to base because he could not find the ground, near Le Vieux-Dun. Guthrie reasoned that it did not matter where they landed so long as it was in the approximate area; the pilot claimed to know where they were to within a few miles, and the party jumped, landing rather too close for comfort to a village – Rouvray – and the adjacent N6, one of the busiest roads in France, and some fifteen kilometres east of their target. The Hudson's unsatisfactory exit slide hindered some of the men, and Couture came to earth some distance away from the others; it was midday before he was located. They took no containers of weapons, but just the three with the equipment they would need; one landed safely, another, with one of the two Jedset radios, was destroyed, and the third, with the other radio, was never found; the team was thus isolated, with little in the way of personal kit.

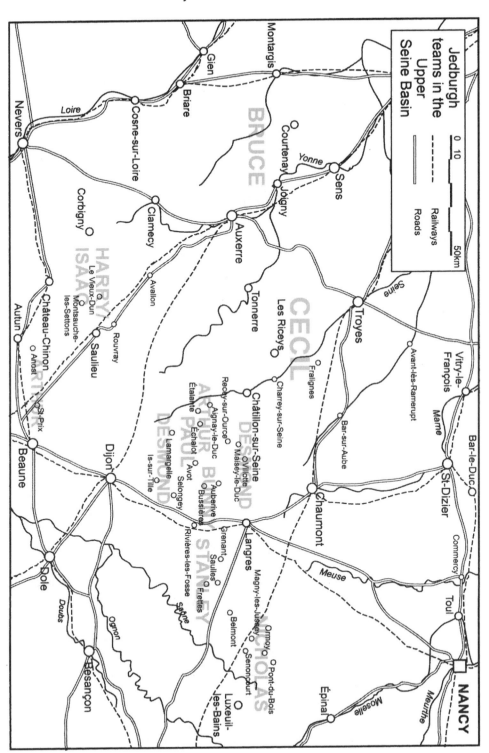

Jedburgh
teams in the
Upper
Seine Basin

On the evening of 7 June the party set off to meet an SOE agent near the intended DZ. He never appeared, and the following evening Rousset went to make contact with *maquisards*. At Le Vieux-Dun he was directed to the camp of the *Maquis* Camille, led by 'Grandjean' (Jean Longhi), the 'local' partisan band; as luck would have it, the DMR, 'Lemniscate' (André Rondenay) was also there.

The Houndsworth advance party arrived in the region two nights later; it, too, missed its DZ completely, and it was some days before all its members, and two men of Jedburgh team Isaac – Lt-Col James Hutchinson, who called himself John Hastings ('Télémètre') and his signaller, Sgt John Sharp – who had dropped with them, were all assembled. Isaac is usually numbered among the Jedburgh teams, but seems to have been destined from the outset to act as an Inter-Allied Mission, Verveine, and operate at a rather higher level, with wider responsibilities over a larger area. It never functioned as a 'normal' Jedburgh team, if there was such a thing, and its presence was to overshadow Harry. The third member of Isaac, its commander, a French colonel named Dubac who called himself Viat ('Diagramme'), did not join them until the first week of July, and later took over as DMR, following Lemniscate's arrest (in Paris as a black-marketeer; he had the bad luck to be identified for what he really was by a *milicien*, and was then shot out of hand).

Prior to the arrival of the Jedburghs and the SAS, and despite the efforts of the DMR, there was little co-operation or co-ordination between Resistance groups in and around the Morvan. Harry's first task was to contact them all, establish channels of communication and attempt to centralise command without being perceived as trying to take over. In fact, Guthrie was to be pre-empted before he had made much progress by the arrival of Diagramme, a Frenchman appointed by General Koenig and responsible directly to him, who clearly intended to lead from the front without fear of treading on anyone's toes – a luxury not permitted the Jedburghs.

The most pressing problem was the *maquisards*' lack of military skills, and Guthrie set up a week-long training course for group leaders and their seconds-in-command, based on the syllabus of the British Army's School of Infantry at Barnard Castle. The course was established in the forest south-west of the small town of Montsauche-les-Settons, where the *Maquis* Bernard, led by a gendarme from the town, had its base, and where 2 Troop of the SAS party and 'Col Hastings', together with a group of elderly ex-officers who believed themselves to be invaluable-but-overlooked additions to the Resistance movement, were also to be found. One of these ex-officers, 'Col Dubois' (Dufrenne), was co-opted as 'School Commandant'; Guthrie became 'Chief Instructor', and enlisted SAS troopers to assist him. The syllabus covered small-arms training on all the weapons available; the rudiments of handling an infantry company in both attack and defence; appreciation and orders; map reading and small-unit administration.

Soon after the leaders' course finished, Diagramme took charge of Resistance activities over the entire region, and Guthrie found himself sidelined; he lost his liaison officer when the DMR arranged Dupont's transfer to the Yonne to act as his representative there, but relates that this was no hardship, the young Frenchman having 'not co-operated at all with me, and not made himself very popular with the French'. From the time of Diagramme's arrival, Guthrie's contribution was largely limited to arranging supply drops; a plan to give him responsibility for organising *Groupements Mobiles* was proposed and fell through, scuppered, he believed, by 'Col Moreau' (Roche), originally the departmental leader of the rightist Liberation-Nord and now DMD.

Moreau was reluctant to accept the presence of the Jedburghs, and the situation was further complicated by the presence of 'Col Dupin' (Bertrand), whom we have already encountered in the Cher, to the west. Dupin had arrived in the Morvan as early as 21 June with documents issued by the Communist-dominated COMAC, appointing him to (military) command of all Resistance elements in the wider region comprising the *départements* of the Aube, Yonne, Nièvre, Haute-Marne, Côte-d'Or and Saône-et-Loire; Hutchinson, for one, took to him, perhaps in consequence of having been slighted by Moreau. Not unnaturally, Moreau refused to accept Dupin's credentials (or COMAC's right to issue them); eventually, on 3 July, the Jedburghs were instructed to disregard Dupin and support Moreau, and then two days later, to cease operating at all until Diagramme arrived. When he did finally appear he dismissed Dupin, who returned to the Cher.

Guthrie, left with no real job to do, spent most of his time compiling lists of equipment the *résistants* wanted (a simple task; they wanted anything and everything), though he did also continue to improve the *maquisards'* basic military skills. Later he participated in a failed attempt to evacuate SAS wounded by air, and also conducted a protracted campaign to persuade the Russians who made up a large proportion of the Château-Chinon garrison to surrender; this, too, proved largely fruitless.

This must have been a most frustrating time for Guthrie, a determinedly proactive officer with considerable leadership potential, for it seemed that London had virtually abandoned him, too. After 1 August, he tells us, he received just one radio message, and all his requests for resupplies of kit for himself and Couture went unanswered – all the more disturbing since this should have been a time of maximum effort. By mid-August, columns of German troops had started to appear on the roads running to the east, and by the third week of the month, with the Allied armies on the Seine, and along the north bank of the Loire as far as Orléans, the trickle had become a flood. For about three weeks a large part of the defeated German Army of Occupation streamed through the Morvan, but on Moreau's instructions, little or nothing was done to hinder or delay it despite the terrain being ideal for the mounting of ambushes.

On 12 September the Overlord and Anvil/Dragoon armies linked up near Châtillon-sur-Seine, and with that the war in the Morvan was effectively over. Guthrie and Couture made their way to Macon, and thence to 4 SFU HQ at Lons-le-Saunier, where they were debriefed. After a short stay in Paris, the pair returned to London on 27 September. Verveine was stood down at roughly the same time, and Lt-Col Hutchinson and Sgt Sharp also returned to London.

Aubrey

The next team dropped into the Seine Basin – this time almost within sight of Paris – did not leave the United Kingdom until the night of 11 August, more than two months after Harry and Isaac had been parachuted into the Morvan. Aubrey, which comprised Capt Godfrey Marchant of the Intelligence Corps ('Rutland'), Lt Adrien Chaigneau, who used the name Telmon ('Kildare') and Sgt Ivor Hooker of the Royal Armoured Corps ('Thaler'), was the first Jedburgh team to be deployed in civilian clothes. The men were inserted from Harrington to a ground near Le Plessis-Belleville in the Oise, less than forty kilometres from the outskirts of Paris, to work with SOE F Section's Spiritualist circuit, and met by the organiser, 'Armand' (René Dumont-Guillemet), who conveyed them to a safe house in St-Pathus while the substantial number of containers dropped with them were gathered up. The following evening they moved to the neighbouring village of Forfry, where Sgt Hooker succumbed to a mild case of mumps.

For the first week of their stay in France, Marchant was to operate as a sabotage instructor, working from a garage near the Boulevard de l'Yser in the 17th *Arondissement* in the north-west of Paris itself.

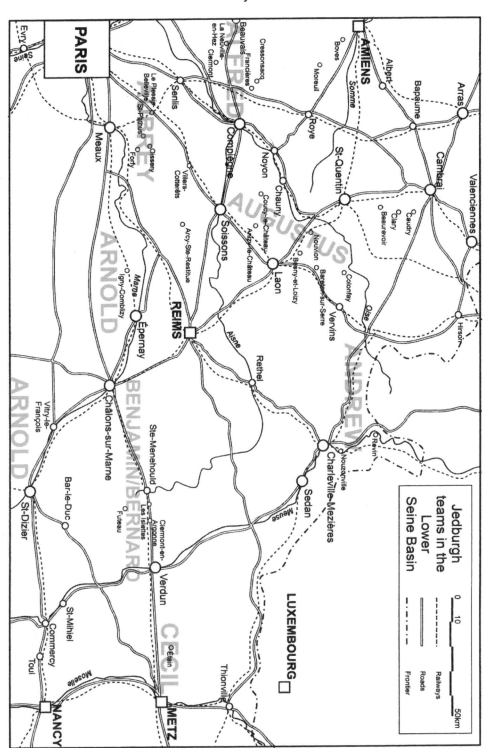

Jedburgh
teams in the
Lower
Seine Basin

Chaigneau acted as Armand's courier, which gave him the opportunity to meet the company commanders of the very large left-leaning guerrilla force the latter had built up in the eastern suburbs of the capital, and also maintained the link between Marchant and Sgt Hooker. On 21 August Marchant decided that his work in Paris was done, and set off on his bicycle to return to Forfry; the following day, 250 SS troops moved into St-Pathus, and 150 from the *Wehrmacht* arrived in Forfry, but all left on 24 August. The following day Armand ordered his *maquisards* to mobilise. By now the roads out of Paris were reasonably clear of Germans, and the plan was for the men to travel to St-Pathus in a convoy of lorries on the night of 26 August. Their ultimate destination was Meaux, to the south of there. Marchant and Sgt Hooker, now recovered, put on uniform for the first time that night, and they, too, took to the woods. It is not clear whether Chaigneau rejoined them that night or the next day.

The partisans' convoy – some twenty vehicles – arrived in St-Pathus around 0900 on the morning of 27 August, passed through the village and neighbouring Oissery, and drew up in a sunken lane beside a lake in woodland between there and Forfry; it had been involved in a skirmish en route from Paris, and had come off best, but it seems that the German had managed to maintain contact, for no sooner had the men begun to dismount than they came under effective fire from an armoured car and a light tank. The result, as Marchant describes it, was chaos:

> All the arms were still in the lorries, and no one seemed certain where anything was. Only two Brens were in working order, others being clogged with grease in the same condition as they had left the factory. There were four PIATs with twelve bombs, but no-one, with the exception of the three Jedburghs, knew how they operated …

The situation cannot have been quite that desperate, for in the fire-fight which followed, forty-five Germans are thought to have died (though French casualties – the Germans took no prisoners – were twice that). After about an hour, Marchant tells us, the order was given to disperse; he hid in a reed bed in the lake for eight hours and then made good his escape, but Chaigneau was less fortunate and was killed by fire from a Tiger tank while assisting a nurse to escape along the bed of the stream which fed the lake. Sgt Hooker, together with Armand got away, by that same route. They passed the night at the house of a *résistante* and met up with American troops the following day. On 30 August Sgt Hooker returned to Forfry, which was by then in American hands, to look for Capt Marchant. The two returned to London on 6 September.

Bruce

Team Bruce was deployed on the night of 14 August, in the Yonne, and found itself directly in the path of the German armies retreating from the Normandy battlefield. Composed of Maj William E Colby ('Berkshire'), Lt Camille Lelong, who took the name Jacques Favel ('Galway') and S/Lt Roger Villebois, who used Louis Giry as his *nom de guerre* ('Piastre'), it was to have been dropped to a reception committee provided by members of SOE F Section's Donkeyman network, but the pilot of the B-24 Liberator 'Slick Chick', which carried them from Harrington airfield, mistook a burning train for beacons, and dropped the team, in good order, over the outskirts of the town of Montargis, some thirty kilometres west of the desired spot.

By pure chance, the three men all landed in gardens, rather than on housetops, but the standard load of containers dropped with them was scattered widely, and the noise of them landing aroused the neighbourhood. The Jedburghs were soon assembled, and learned that there was a strong German presence in the town; abandoning their search for items of equipment, they cleared the area and retreated to the countryside, going to ground in a ditch where they spent all the following day, watching German search teams scouring the area for them and gathering up their kit:

> When dark came we moved off on a compass bearing towards our safe house contact. A storm came up and it became necessary to attach ourselves to each other by means of our pistol lanyards. After several hours of struggling through the mud in this fashion we heard voices ahead of us. The lightning flashes revealed a lone house so the attempt was made to contact whoever was in it in the hope of receiving aid. Lt Favel knocked on the door while the other two members of the party covered him. Our entrance was made and it was discovered that this was a resistance radio post with an operator who had come from London 8 days before ...

which perhaps begs a few questions of its own!

In any event, this happy encounter brought further good fortune in the shape of a ride in a *gazogène*-powered Citroën, the following day, as far as the team's safe house, and eventually they were put in touch with 'Roger' (Roger Bardet), who had taken over the Donkeyman network when its organiser, Henri Frager, had been arrested by the *Gestapo* a week earlier.

It was now 18 August, and the battle to consolidate the Allied grip on Normandy had passed its critical phase following Patton's break-out from St-Lô. In the south the Anvil/Dragoon forces were moving northward, having encountered very little opposition, and Hitler had already instructed *Armeegruppe G* to pull out of southern France. Gen Koenig had given the order to mobilise for guerrilla warfare at the start of the month, and stimulating it was of prime importance, the Donkeyman circuit having apparently gone to ground following Frager's arrest.

In fact, Roger (who was actually a German agent) was hedging his bets, playing a double game: on the face of it he was promoting Resistance activity most determinedly, but always seemed to find reasons why any particular *action* should not go ahead as planned. There was another factor to be considered, too. Colby makes no mention of it in his report, but in the same area 1 SAS was setting up Operation Kipling, and the previous night its party had been brought up to three officers and twenty-four other ranks, with five jeeps. It was in close touch with a faction led by 'Col Chevrier', who had been given overall responsibility for Resistance activity in the area by EMFFI. Kipling had orders to restrict open guerrilla activity in preparation for a massive airborne landing (Operation Transfigure), and had obtained Chevrier's support; eventually, however, the operation was called off, and the *résistants* were let off the leash again. Villages all over the area declared themselves liberated; sometimes German forces proved such confidence premature, but more often they lost little time in making their way eastward.

'On about 22 August American armoured units were reported at Courtenay,' Colby tells us, and thereafter the Jedburghs gathered and collated intelligence on German movements and concentrations and passed them on, while organising FFI units to guard their exposed right flank. This arrangement was formalised by a request to that effect from Gen Patton, which Colby received on a visit to 3rd US Army's advance HQ. On 26 August Chevrier's forces liberated Auxerre. As in the Vienne and Indre, to the west, partisan activity compelled the retreating Axis forces to concentrate into fairly large convoys, and thus, of course, they presented perfect targets to the Allied Tactical Air Force if they tried to move during the daytime.

By the end of the month the FFI had established a *cordon sanitaire* from Briare, on the Loire, as far east as Tonnerre. This line was pushed southward as the US Army's front expanded, and soon ran up against territory controlled by Diagramme from his new base in Auxerre. He had recently (6 September) been given responsibility by Koenig for the entire region, comprising the *départements* of Aube, Côte-d'Or, Haute-Marne, Nièvre, Saône-et-Loire and Yonne, and now began to exercise it more widely. As already noted, Diagramme was a forceful character, and with Chevrier subordinate to him, Bruce's work – which consisted in no small part of keeping him both in check and in motion – was effectively over. Colby returned to London, via Paris, on 26 September, the French members of the team remaining in France. William E Colby later became Director of the Central Intelligence Agency.

Andrew

The night after Bruce was deployed it was the turn of two teams who were to be dropped further north and east. Team Andrew was unique in that it had no French member; instead, its 'liaison officer' was Belgian, and this was entirely logical since it was to operate in the Ardennes, hard up against the Belgian border. The team was made up of Maj Henry Coombe-Tennant of the Welsh Guards ('Rupel'), Lt Édouard d'Oultremont of the Belgian Army ('Demer') and Sgt Frank Harrison of the Royal Armoured Corps ('Nethe').

Andrew was to liaise with an Inter-Allied Mission, Citronelle, under the command of 'Prism' (Cmdt Jacques de Bollardière), which had been in place since April 1944. Prism had taken until D-Day to establish any sort of fighting force, and then within weeks, thanks to impossibly lax security, it had been located and virtually destroyed in a series of raids. The few survivors were very short of equipment. The Jedburgh team was to be inserted with a party from 5 (Belgian) SAS who were to take part in Operation Noah, a purely Belgian operation; Andrew – which was forbidden to cross the border – had no further contact with it. They were accompanied by two junior French officers, supplementary personnel for Citronelle. The plan was for the SAS to jump first as a 'stick', the aircraft would then circle and make another run in, and the remaining five men and the packages would be dropped.

The aircraft arrived over the DZ near Revin at about 0100. The plan went awry when the ground party – which had been warned to expect two men plus containers – extinguished the beacons after the first stick was dropped, leaving the pilot with no point of reference when he came around again. To make matters worse, a cross-wind was blowing at around sixty kilometres an hour, and the results were predictable. The Jedburghs and the two Frenchmen landed two valleys away, in featureless, trackless woodland, with no clear idea where they were and little in the way of kit. It was the following afternoon before the five were reunited, at a cottage where they were able to obtain both food and news of Prism's whereabouts.

They walked all night, and reached Prism's camp at around 0600 the next morning, to be greeted by 'a light breakfast of champagne and dry bread, butter having run out for the time being'. That afternoon, somewhat rested, they met with Prism, and the full extent of the confusion started to become clear. De Bollardière had expected only the two French officers; the arrival of an SAS party – who were of no concern to him anyway – he accepted as just one of those things, but the Jedburghs – he had never even heard of Jedburghs, let alone of Andrew – were something else, for Tennant, obeying his instructions to the letter, duly announced that he was at Prism's disposal. According to Tennant's own account:

> I began to feel rather foolish, but d'Oultremont, whose blood is so blue that he never feels at a loss [he was the Comte d'Oultremont; his family had links to the House of Orange and the Hohenzollerns], began his explanation by saying 'Voyons, mon Colonel, nous disposons de notre propre flotte aérienne ... [Let's see, Colonel, we've got our own airforce ...]' The Colonel [de Bollardière had been promoted just a few days earlier] was obviously impressed and delighted at the possibility that we might be able to procure for him the arms and supplies which his own urgent and repeated demands had failed to produce ...

In the event, because Andrew was forced to use Citronelle's radio, there was so much confusion generated that London acted on none of its requests. The reason for this was simple: Citronelle's radio was linked, by reason of its frequency being crystal-controlled, to EMFFI. If Harrison used Andrew's codes, EMFFI simply regarded them as gibberish, and if he used Citronelle's codes his messages still made no sense. All this could have been avoided had EMFFI paid any attention to a signal Prism sent on 18 August, to the effect that Andrew had arrived and its operator would be using *his* radio to transmit the team's messages in *its* code, and would they please pass them to Jedburgh HQ for decoding? Tennant despaired of Andrew serving any useful purpose:

It was impossible to form fighting or sabotage groups without arms: the Colonel had none to spare. Therefore there was nothing left for us to do but to attach ourselves to his HQ and make ourselves as useful as possible about the place. Harrison was completely spare without his set. D'Oultremont could have done excellent work as liaison officer between the French and Belgian maquis groups if this had not been specifically interdicted. I was perhaps of some use as a clothes peg for British uniform; several of the French officers were kind enough to say that my presence showed the solidarity of Anglo-French relations … Mission Andrew was a failure.

In the early afternoon of 21 August, a small boy with a Belgian armband appeared at the campsite to report that his comrades had attempted an ambush on a main road just across the border. It had gone wrong; their leader was wounded, and the section pinned down. Could the Colonel help? The latter called two platoons to attention and set off, Tennant and d'Oultremont tagging along. In the action which followed, one of the platoon commanders, a Belgian himself, was mortally wounded, but otherwise the rescue mission was a success, with two prisoners and a quantity of arms and ammunition taken. The next day, however, just as the group was making ready to shift its campsite, they came under attack from three sides at once. Clearly outnumbered, and lacking in fire-power, they put up such defence as they could, but when mortar bombs started to rain down through the trees they pulled back, leapfrogging section by section. When they regrouped, some thirty men were missing and presumed dead, or captured, which amounted to the same thing. Among the dead were one of the French officers who had been inserted with Andrew, and an elderly colonel who served as a sort of Camp Commandant; Prism, d'Oultremont and one other officer were wounded, the latter two not severely.

Several days later, a message was broadcast by the BBC to alert Citronelle to a *parachutage* planned for that night. There was considerable excitement, since not only had some weapons been lost in the fire-fight at the campsite, but a great deal of ammunition had been expended. At about 0100 the distinctive sound of a four-engined aircraft was heard, the beacons were lit and Tennant commenced to flash the recognition letter, but after circling several times, the aircraft flew away. 'That was the last attempt made to resupply Citronelle,' said Tennant.

On 1 September, a messenger arrived from Nouzonville, a small town on the River Meuse, some twenty kilometres away, with a report that the German garrison there had pulled out hurriedly, leaving the bridge across the river intact. Prism, still suffering the effects of his wound, and Tennant set off to investigate, but when they arrived they learned that a German infantry platoon had arrived in the meantime, and had set up a defensive position. The local *maquisard* leader attempted to persuade Prism to try to drive them out; fortunately he was unsuccessful, for they proved to be the advance party of a reinforced battalion. Nouzonville became the scene of a pitched battle when American troops arrived in the area two days later. Andrew entered the town at the head of the relieving Americans, and remained there for some days before making its way to Paris, to SFHQ at the Hotel Cecil. Sgt Harrison then returned to London, while Maj Coombe-Tennant and Lt d'Oultremont travelled to Brussels to rejoin their respective regiments.

Augustus

Only three Jedburgh missions left no first-hand account of their activities. Two of them – Jacob and Martin – operated alongside either an SAS party or another Jedburgh team, and thus we know something of their adventures. The exception is team Augustus, which went into the field on the same night as Andrew, to be inserted seventy-five kilometres west-south-west of it; all three of its members were killed. Most of the information we have on Augustus comes from a report written by 'Lt Seigneur' of the FFI, and a brief account of the team's circumstances at the time of their deaths and the arrangements made for them thereafter, by an American investigator, Maj William Hornaday.

Team Augustus consisted of Maj John H Bonsall (Arizona), Capt Jean Delwiche (or Delviche or Delvichi), who took Dechville (or Decheville) as his *nom de guerre* ('Hérault') and Sgt Robert S Cote ('Indiana'). They were dropped on the night of 15 August to a DZ known as Fable, near the village of Colonfay, thirty-five kilometres east of St-Quentin and the same distance north of Laon, from which Delwiche originated, and were met by 'Gramme' (Jean-Pierre, a representative of the *Bureau d'Operations Aerienne*) and a *maquisard* leader, 'Raymond'. They were dropped across, rather than along, the DZ and since there were high winds that night in north-eastern France they were blown well away from the lights. They all landed safely, however, and the containers and packages dropped with them were recovered intact. Raymond was based near Nouvion in the Forêt de St-Gobain, the far side of Laon, and they set off in a car and a light truck, arriving safely around 0400 to be greeted with champagne (perhaps the region's best-known product) and talk of the mission's goals and objectives.

The following morning the DMR's liaison officer, 'Fontaine', arrived. It was decided that they should begin by operating near Caudry, which was a considerable distance – more than eighty kilometres – to the north, near Cambrai in the Nord *département*, and they set off once more in the Renault *camionette* for a farm near Clary, where they were to be accommodated. However, a meeting on 19 August at Beaurevoir, just south of the departmental border in the Aisne, at which all the local Resistance bigwigs were present, came to a different conclusion – that Augustus should move back south again, to Arcy-Ste-Restitue, twenty kilometres south-south-east of Soissons and something like 100 kilometres away. A young officer, 'Lt Seigneur', whose group was based at Arcy, was deputed to return to find accommodation and transportation for the Jedburghs, who had by now been provided with French identity cards (it is unclear whether they wore civilian clothes throughout the mission, but they certainly were doing so by this point), Bonsal becoming 'Joseph Porteval', a forestry worker from Anizy-le-Château, Delwiche 'Jean Derval', a timber merchant from Coucy-le-Château and Cote 'René Chabaud', a student from St-Quentin. Seigneur returned the following day with a *gazogène*-powered lorry loaded with rags and rabbit skins, under which the Jedburghs' kit and equipment could be concealed. With Delwiche and Cote in the cab beside the driver, and Bonsall, Seigneur and Fontaine reclining on top of the load, they set off to return to Arcy, arriving after numerous close calls – one quite literally, when they had to squeeze past a broken-down Panther tank – and an extended lunch-stop, at 2045 on 20 August. They were to remain at Arcy for eight days, Bonsall and Cote seldom venturing from the farm, while Delwiche went with Seigneur to liaise with other partisan leaders. By this time, most of the *résistants* in the area were armed – although supply drops were still being made – and were only waiting for the order to go over to open guerrilla warfare. Here, as elsewhere, it was part of the Jedburghs' responsibility to keep them in check.

Seigneur makes much of the heavy German presence in the area, and over the week which followed, this was to increase dramatically. Paris was officially liberated on 25 August, but much of the large German garrison there had begun to quit the city days earlier; many of them headed north-eastward, and took the main N2 road through Soissons. By the following weekend (26–27 August) the forward elements of the US 3rd Army were as close as Villers-Cotterêts, thirty kilometres away.

On 28 August Augustus, still accompanied by Seigneur, moved again, this time in the direction of Soissons. Some French sources suggest that Augustus had received instructions from SFHQ to move north in order to report on and help to secure river crossings (team Alfred certainly got a similar message, probably during its morning 'sked' on 29 August). According to American sources (which, however, suggest that it was not transmitted until the morning of 30 August) the message instructed the team:

> Take all possible steps to preserve following Somme bridges from enemy demolition. All bridges Amiens area, also at Moreuil, Boves, Fiquigny, Conde, Longpre. You should attempt to preserve these bridges for about four days after receipt this message. This is important task. Count on you for fullest cooperation. If you need arms can drop from low flying typhoons [i.e. Hawker Typhoons, ground-attack aircraft operated by the RAF].

This was, perhaps, something of a tall order. Seigneur's account makes no mention of the message in question, but he may not have been a party to all Augustus' doings. On the way the team made contact with an American armoured reconnaissance unit, and negotiated transportation to Laon, which was then at the forward edge of the battle area, and with that Seigneur returned to Arcy with the Jedburghs' kit. Augustus rejoined him the next morning, recovered their equipment and returned to Soissons, where they spent the night of 29 August at the Hotel de la Croix d'Or. At 1700 the next day they set out northward, first in a jeep, later aboard a tank. In mid-evening they reached the home of a farmer Delwiche knew at Besny-et-Loizy, just north of Laon, and asked for the loan of an inconspicuous vehicle in which they could cross the lines into German-held territory. German troops who had passed through the area that morning had left behind a horse-drawn cart, and the Jedburghs took that. The farmer accompanied them for some kilometres to set them on a back-roads route, and then turned back, the Jedburghs continuing on their way at 2200. Fifteen minutes later, the heavens opened. The rain was such as to reduce visibility to a few metres, and also made it impossible to hear much; that was to be a fatal combination. At around 2245 they came to a cross-roads at Bareton-sur-Serre, ran straight into a German roadblock, and apparently were surrounded before they had time to react. The kit found in the cart, including weapons and a radio set, sealed their fate. The Germans cleared the area some thirty minutes later, and people from neighbouring houses ventured out. They found 'Joseph Porteval' and 'Jean Derval' lying side by side on the road, and 'René Chabaud' a short distance away; all had been shot in the head. The three Jedburghs were later buried in the Communal Cemetery at Barenton-sur-Serre.

Arthur

Three teams – Arthur, Paul and Bunny – were dropped just to the east of the area in which Bruce was operating, on the night of 18 August. Arthur was made up of two Americans – Capt Cecil Mynatt ('Connecticut') and T/Sgt Albert Bacik ('Millième') – and S/Lt Xavier Hamblet, who used the name Louis Hache ('Smabrère'). They had instructions identical to those of Bill Colby and his colleagues save that they were to contact 'Ovale' (Cmdt Gauss) in the adjacent Côte-d'Or. It had been intended to drop Arthur and Paul to the same ground, but confused navigation led to the former going to a DZ known as Imprimerie, where they were not expected. Mynatt was also critical of the despatcher, blaming both him and the pilot who dropped them at too low an altitude as well as a faulty or badly packed parachute for a heavy landing which broke his back and left him incapacitated. It was almost a month before the actual extent of his injury was discovered, but Mynatt took no further part in the operation; he was moved to Paul's HQ and later, believing himself recovered, joined an Operational Group, but a fall soon put him out of action definitively. He was evacuated to the United Kingdom on 18 September.

Arthur was installed in a safe house in the village of Échalot, in the Côte-d'Or, forty kilometres north-north-west of Dijon, where a *maquis* hospital could give Mynatt at least rudimentary care. It was not until 22 August that Arthur got to meet Ovale, and then the team was left in limbo for three days more, until the DMR ordered Hamblet and Bacik to move south. Their exact destination is not precisely clear, but circumstantial evidence suggests it was near the south-eastern limit of the Morvan, north of Autun, that their sphere of activities extended into the heart of that area, as far as Château-Chinon, and that they co-operated with some of the Morvandiaux *Maquis*, including those of Anost and St-Prix, and also with SAS troops from Operation Kipling which had by then taken over from Operation Houndsworth in the region. The two Jedburghs seem to have been almost constantly on the move from one partisan camp to another over the following two weeks, trying in vain to persuade London to mount supply missions and organising ambush parties on minor roads. One such action provided a significant bonus; the lorry they stopped was carrying weapons recovered from a *parachutage* and 'we now own 6 Brens, 45 Stens and 30 rifles', which were distributed the following day.

On 8 September they heard that partisans from Montceau-les-Mines (with – although they did not know it – Maurice Stasse, of team Anthony, at their head) were marching on Autun, and hurried to participate. Hamblet's account of its liberation differs slightly from Stasse's; he states that the German garrison actually put up stiff, if fairly brief, resistance, their anti-tank guns repelling the few French tanks which had been diverted to give fire support and buying time for the Axis forces to make a semi-orderly withdrawal towards Beaune during the night.

By 14 September their work was done, and Hamblet and Bacik retired to Dijon; they travelled to Paris with Lt Vallée of team Paul, and from there made their way to London. Cecil Mynatt summed up the feelings of many Jedburghs in the conclusion to his report:

> Abandoned in the way of equipment by London, in France they did not realise our hopes of action which we had been led to foresee. We can only hope that in any future tasks that may have to be accomplished in any scene of operations, greater vision will be possible, and that those who will be sent to the field, will not be be left without help, and will be sent in more useful time, and not at the last minute as was the case for us in France.

Paul

Team Paul was composed of Maj Hugo Hood of the Somerset Light Infantry ('Shropshire'), Lt Michel Vallée, who called himself Cornier ('Ourthe') and Sgt Kenneth Brown of the Royal Armoured Corps ('Limerick'). Deployed by an RAF Halifax from Tempsford on the night of 18 August, they waited on the DZ, 'Anicroche', until 0500 for team Arthur, which was supposed to have preceded them, and spent the remainder of the night in an adjacent patch of woodland before moving to nearby Avot. When they were able to contact Ovale, four days later, he told them to remain in the area between Dijon and Châtillon-sur-Seine for a fortnight, organising and arming partisan groups there, and then be prepared to move south. In the event, the team remained roughly where it was until the end of its mission. The Germans moved against the *Maquis* Lucius at Avot some days later, and Paul shifted its command post some twenty kilometres to Étalante, to the west of Échalot where Arthur was still located. Here they were able to communicate more easily with *Maquis* Claude at Aignay-le-Duc, whose leader, Claude Monod, was a very influential figure locally. Capt Mynatt was later brought there, when Ovale ordered his colleagues to go south. Before moving, Hood was able to meet Capt John Wiseman of 1 SAS's Houndsworth party in the Morvan, who had established a satellite base just south of Avot, and was both arming the *maquisards* and mounting combat operations of his own.

The last week of August was spent meeting all the partisan leaders in the region and assessing their needs. Repeated requests for *parachutages* of arms and equipment were made to London, with no result, in contrast to resupply missions requested by the SAS, which arrived very promptly. In fact, when a *parachutage* did arrive it consisted of an additional Jedburgh team – Desmond – and Christopher, an Operational Group made up of fifty-five men, twelve of whom were officers. On 8 September the first supplies arrived, two Stirlings dropping forty-four containers and fourteen packages, and the team was able to arm a few hundred men. The following night a second OG, Adrian, made up of thirteen officers and eighteen ORs, was also dropped; the leader of the group, Capt Kielbowicz, was killed when his parachute's canopy was collapsed by a falling container. Three others were injured, and were taken to the *maquis* hospital at Échalot. That night the German garrison in Châtillon evacuated the town, and partisans, together with French and US troops from the forces which had landed on the Côte-d'Azur in Operation Anvil/Dragoon less than a month earlier, occupied it the next day. Dijon, the main city of the region, had been bypassed, and was not occupied until two days later, but with that, Paul's work was virtually over save for the usual run of small-scale mopping-up operations.

Hood tells us he 'installed himself in Dijon at an hotel working as a kind of ambassador to help English-speaking people' while waiting for a reply from London for a request that Paul be allowed to move eastward, towards Belfort. No answer came, and on 24 September 'I realised that the only way to get an answer from London was to go there myself, so having obtained petrol from the Americans Sgt Brown and I left Dijon the following morning by car'. The pair were in Paris by the evening, and the next day were reunited with Lt Vallée, who had left Dijon ten days earlier. After 'two days Jed reunion' they flew to London, to be debriefed and stood down.

Bunny

Team Bunny, the third to be deployed on the night of 18 August to assist Ovale, was composed of Capt JFD Radice ('Peso'), Lt Maurice Geminel, calling himself Gerville ('Yen') and Sgt James Chambers ('Drachma'). It was dropped to a ground known as Amaronde, near Selongey, ten kilometres east of Avot, and operated north of there in the vicinity of Auberive, in company with the *Maquis* Max. Neither Lt Geminel, who wrote the team's principal report, nor Sgt Chambers, who added a shorter and more personalised version, are critical of Max, but accounts from other sources are, suggesting that he was operating on the border between brigandage and resistance; gun battles between his men and those of other Resistance groups were not unknown. One of the complaints Hugo Hood had to deal with during his sojourn in Dijon involved members of this group having stolen several parachutists' personal kit.

A strong contingent from 2 SAS, engaged in Operation Hardy/Wallace, which eventually numbered seventy-seven all-ranks, was also established in the vicinity and elements of it remained to mount Operation Robey when the majority left to move eastward on 2 September. The Robey party stayed close to team Bunny of necessity, having no means of its own of communicating with London.

Bunny and its thirty containers of weapons and equipment was inserted successfully, and was soon in contact with Ovale, who told it to co-locate with Max near the Ferme de la Salle, eight kilometres east of Auberive, where a German garrison of around 200 was established. On 20 August Radice made contact with an SAS party under Capt Grant Hibbert, and two days later he and Geminel, together with Max, went to meet Col Claude (at an unrecorded location; it is unlikely to have been Claude's CP). On the return trip they came face to face with a German convoy drawn up in the main street of the small town of Longeau, and 'passed through ... machine gunning and throwing grenades at the enemy convoy'. Some fifteen Germans were killed or wounded, but so was Capt Radice, by a bullet which passed through both knees. He was taken back to the campsite and thence, next day, stripped of his uniform and any sign of his origins, to the hospital in still-occupied Langres. Because tourniquets applied to his legs to control the bleeding had never been loosed, he had contracted gangrene; his legs were amputated, but the infection had spread too far, and he died on 25 August.

The weapons Bunny had brought with them allowed the *Maquis* Max

to be expanded from its original twenty-five to around five times that
number (some of the newcomers, a small band in their own right under
a young lieutenant, 'Lamy', were already armed). They felt confident
enough to set up a checkpoint on the road between Auberive and
Langres and attacked a small German force, killing four, but more use-
fully were able to drive off a score of troops who had blocked the road
between Auberive and their campsite, killing or wounding a dozen of
them. On the night of 27 August they received their first *parachutage*, in
time to arm yet more men and take over Auberive when the German
garrison there evacuated the town on 29 August; they were joined by the
Robey party from 2 SAS the following day.

Maquisards and parachutists attacked a German fuel dump on the last
day of the month, keeping 5,000 litres – all they could carry – and
destroying the rest, but retribution came swiftly in the form of an attack
on Auberive during the night of 2 September by a force of 200 or 300
Axis troops, many of them conscripted Russian ex-PoWs. The partisans
by now numbered around 300 themselves, and were well-supplied with
weapons, including several MG42 general-purpose machine guns captured during the raid on the fuel dump, and were able to drive off the
attackers after fighting which lasted for several hours. Reports later
indicated that the Germans had lost twenty-one killed and perhaps
twice that number wounded. Geminel received a slight head wound,
twelve other partisans were injured and one was killed.

The next objective was Châtillon. The entire SAS party had been
involved in an attack on the garrison there on 30 August, employing its
3in mortar to good effect and leaving many of them dead and wounded,
but now the majority of the troopers had left the area to move into the
Vosges, and it was left to the *maquisards* to finish what they had started.
The assault on the town began on the morning of 8 September and
turned into a prolonged battle. Geminel took the remaining section of
SAS (the Robey party's leader, Lt Pinci, had gone to Paris to plead for
the intervention of an armoured column) and set up an ambush on the
route the garrison was most likely to take on leaving the town, the road
towards Chaumont, and was rewarded in the early afternoon by the
appearance of a convoy of motor vehicles. In the fighting which followed, he received a bullet wound to the leg and, when the time came to
withdraw, was inexplicably left behind, the SAS troopers apparently
believing him dead. He managed to crawl into cover, was overlooked by
German patrols searching the area and eventually discovered by
friendly forces, come to recover his body, at around 2000. He was taken
to the *maquis* hospital, which had by now moved up to Auberive, and a

doctor operated to remove the bullet. Châtillon was evacuated by 1630.

The first Allied troops arrived in Auberive on 12 September, the day the northern and southern armies linked up, and the following day combined partisan and regular forces launched an attack on Langres; this proved a tougher nut still, and it was well into the evening before the last Axis forces withdrew. The next day Geminel was moved to the hospital there, and on 15 September was transferred to Dijon; some days later Sgt Chambers received permission to withdraw, and returned to London, via Paris, on 20 September.

Benjamin and Bernard

The insertion of the next two teams, Benjamin and Bernard, was planned to take place on the night of 19 August, and they were called up from Milton Hall to London two days earlier, as was the custom. It was always envisaged that the two would drop together, and they had identical objectives: to assist the local *résistants* in conjunction with members of the Planète network, Benjamin operating in the eastern sector of the Meuse, Bernard in the western. In the event, they were to remain together from beginning to end, thanks largely to mishaps at the DZ, and are grouped with the Seine Basin teams by virtue of the fact that the stream which bordered the ground on to which they were dropped was actually the Aisne, just a few kilometres from its source and the watershed with the Meuse Basin.

Benjamin was composed of Maj Hubert 'Terry' O'Bryan-Tear, who used the name Forrest ('Stirling'; like Jim Hutchinson of team Isaac, he had been a senior figure in SOE, and feared that his identity was known to the German security service), Lt Paul Moniez, who took the name Marchand ('Ulster') and S/Lt Henri Kaminsky, who was known as Camouin ('Serre'). Team Bernard had Capt Jocelyn 'Jock' Waller of the Rifle Brigade ('Tipperary'), Capt Étienne Nasica, who used Prato as his *nom de guerre* ('Argens') and Sgt Cyril Bassett of the Royal Armoured Corps ('Lancashire'). The two missions submitted a joint report.

The Benjamin/Bernard report describes their briefing as 'good but not over-comprehensive; in particular no information was given at all on the existing state, numbers or location of maquis, and few contacts were given with the FFI in the department. There was also some difficulty in obtaining suitable maps', and one is left wondering just what the good part was. In the event, the aircraft carrying them – Stirlings, from

RAF Fairford – failed to find the DZ on 20 August, but they were dropped the following night to a DZ in the Forêt d'Argonne west of Verdun, close to Clermont-en-Argonne, without problems even though it was moonless. Unfortunately the reception committee had not been trained in the selection of DZs, nor in the management of a *parachutage*. The ground chosen was completely unsuitable – far too small, surrounded by woodland and criss-crossed by hedges and wire fences – and the reception committee compounded that error by siting the beacon fires just a hundred metres from one edge. The result was predictable: five out of the six men, and all the supplies – sixteen panniers and thirty-three containers – landed in the woods. The Benjamins and Capt Waller were soon reunited, but it was the following day before Nasica and Sgt Bassett were located.

> Two days and three nights were spent rounding up and collecting up the stores and parachutes, most of which were elegently draping the topmost branches of the tallest trees. During this time a fair proportion of personal equipment was lost to the depredations of the local inhabitants. And the enemy, who had inopportunely moved some troops to within 350 yards of the DZ at the last moment, sent a reconnaissance aircraft over the wood on the day after the operation. They were left in no doubt as to the cause of all the disturbance.

In fact, the situation was perhaps even worse than the report indicates. Arms and supplies enough for about a hundred men had been collected and cached, but the teams had only one working radio between them and virtually none of their personal kit; the fifteen *maquisards* who had met them were barely organised and their leader, 'Cmdt Laure' (Dulac), who completely lacked experience, had no clear picture of the situation or of the location of more senior figures. The BOA representative, Saulnier, was marginally better informed, however, and contacted one of Planète's liaison agents, who arrived the following day. He in turn located Planète's chief of staff, 'Col Aubusson', and the chief of the FFI in the Department, 'Cmdt Angelet', who arrived at the campsite on 23 August, and with that the Jedburghs could make a rough appraisal of the situation and begin to map out a programme of *parachutages* for the September moon period. Aubusson had brought word from Planète that he expected the Jedburghs to stick to the original plan, and operate one team each side of the River Meuse, to the east, and they selected three DZs in each sector, accordingly (though unless there is material missing from the teams' radio log, no message to that effect was ever sent to

London). That evening, the Resistance chiefs separated. Aubusson left for an unknown destination but Saulnier and Angelet returned to the village of Les Islettes; they would have been better advised to have remained in the forest, for the next morning they, and a number of other senior local *résistants*, were arrested in a raid mounted jointly by the *Sicherheitspolizei* and the *Milice*.

The Jedburghs had received 'vague news of enemy movements', and had evacuated the campsite, leaving a skeleton guard to watch over the well-concealed weapons cache, with instructions to observe and fall back if German troops should arrive in the vicinity. They did, and made straight for the arms dump, 'whose location must have been revealed by one of their captives'. The watching partisans opened fire, killing the *SS-Hauptsturmführer* leading the raid, and then made their escape in the confusion. Benjamin and Bernard gave up any thought of returning to the campsite, and moved off westward on foot, across the valley of the Bisme and deeper into the forest. Due to the density of the woodland, and the unsuspected presence of a large enemy ammunition dump, to which they gave a wide berth, it was three days before they were able to establish a new base, in the Forêt de Chatrice, south-east of Ste-Mene-hould, but at least Cmdt Laure was able to give them a DZ which had previously been reconnoitred.

From the radio log, it seems that the Jedburghs had heard – perhaps from Laure – of the presence of other parachutists in the area, for on 27 August they signalled London: 'Urgent – can you confirm dropping our parachutists south-east of Ste Menhould last two nights'. The following day they located the headquarters party of 2 SAS's Operation Rupert, and its commander, Maj Rooney, and discovered that he had called in a resupply mission to the same DZ they had intended to use. Next day they signalled London: 'On JOJO 30's operation [JOJO 30 was Rooney's callsign] send for us 2 planes with 2 loads A and B [these were standard fifteen-container loads with different mixes of weaponry and explosive stores]. 1 Jeep to enable Benjamin's move to east. 5 complete Jed kits with carbines. 1 Jed set and 2 silent stens [i.e., the Sten Mk 2S, with its integral silencer] for Benjamin. All stores including containers if possible to be marked to avoid mixup with SAS stores.' The stores would have put Benjamin/Bernard back on an operational footing, but unfortunately Rooney cancelled the *parachutage* at the last minute; he gives no reason in his own report, which in any event makes no mention of having even encountered the Jedburghs. Furthermore, he did not bother even to inform the teams that he had done so, and thus they were worse off than before, with more time lost and precisely nothing to show for their efforts.

Before he met the Jedburghs, Rooney had already encountered spearhead units of the advancing American Army; on 30 August Benjamin/Bernard received a message telling them to send guides to meet them, and the following day their campsite was overrun. Their task now changed to one of reconnaissance and information-gathering, but having had very little contact with *maquisards*, and no opportunity to build a clear picture of the local situation, they were scarcely well suited to it. Nasica was wounded in a skirmish with German troops near Futeau, south of Les Islettes on 31 August, and was evacuated to a hospital in Reims, and the following day Sgt Basset, Lt Kaminsky and Maj Tear were wounded when the truck in which they were travelling ran into an ambush; all five Jedburghs managed to reach safety, but only at the cost of leaving behind all their remaining kit, including the single Jedset the two teams had shared. Sgt Basset was later evacuated to an American field hospital (and both he and Capt Nasica were flown to the United Kingdom some days later).

Their lines of communication with SFHQ cut, there was little they could do save try to contact the Special Forces Detachment attached to US 3rd Army HQ, and this they did on 3 September, obtaining a new radio transceiver and scrounging such other kit as they could, while waiting for a new mission. It was to be ten days before they were reassigned, and moved south to Montier-sur-Der and then into the region east of Chaumont, to work alongside SOE's Pedlar (Maj Nick Bodington, q.v.) and team Arnold (see below) in their efforts to contain and mop up Axis troops who had not managed to clear the area. By now, however, the tempo of operations had slowed and they were clearly of little further use where they were. SFHQ did eventually come up with a tentative plan for the two British officers, plus David Nielson from team Cecil, Duncan Guthrie from team Harry, and all of team Maurice, to prepare for an operation in Germany. This project fell through, and the remaining members of Benjamin and Bernard returned to the United Kingdom via Paris on 2 October.

Arnold

It was a further four days after the departure of Benjamin and Bernard before the next team to be dropped into the Upper Seine Basin was finally deployed, due largely to continuing bad weather making air

operations impossible. Team Arnold consisted of Capt Michel de
Carville, who called himself Coudray ('Sussex'), Lt James Monahan of
the Royal Fusiliers ('Londonderry') and Sgt Alan de Ville of the Royal
Armoured Corps ('Escudo'). The team was to contact SOE F Section's
Pedlar or Diplomat circuits, and it was the organiser of the former, Maj
Nicholas Bodington, who controlled their reception. (He was something of a one-man fire brigade, dropped into France on three occasions
to sort out problems with different Resistance groups. A question mark
hangs over his name as a result of a too-close relationship with a French
operative named Henri Déricourt, who was almost certainly also
working for the *Abwehr* or *Sicherheitsdienst*.) They were dropped in civilian clothes from an RAF Halifax operating from Tarrant Rushton,
unusual in that Tarrant Rushton was an 'SAS field' from which the
Brigade's resupply operations were conducted, to a DZ near Igny-
Comblizy, west of Épernay, in the early hours of 25 August. A second
aircraft carried additional containers and panniers, and all were recovered, save for the pannier containing the teams' personal kit and
weapons, money, uniforms and the crystals for the radio, which was
never found. Bodington requested London to send replacements, but
they were never despatched, and Arnold was seriously hampered as a
result, particularly by not being in direct contact with SFHQ.

Bodington instructed Arnold to familiarise itself with the area
directly west of Épernay and contact local leaders there, with a view to
organising and arming an effective Resistance group. In fact, the
advancing American 7th Armoured Division was so close that there was
little time to do more than distribute weapons before they arrived on the
scene, on the morning of 28 August, and Arnold then spent the next
four days trying to recover those weapons, since the partisans had no
further legitimate use for them. On 2 September Arnold moved south-
east, to the vicinity of Montier-en-Der, south of St-Dizier in the
Haute-Marne. It soon became obvious that there was no work for it
there, and the following day it proceeded to St-Dizier, where it found
part-time employment assisting the well-organised local FFI elements
which were patrolling the surrounding area and rounding up small
groups of German troops who had been left behind when the main body
retreated. On 11 September the St-Dizier groups moved south, towards
Chaumont and Châtillon-sur-Seine. Finding that the latter town was
already in Allied hands, two days later Arnold led a reconnaissance
patrol to the outskirts of Chaumont, to learn that the town had been liberated that morning by elements of the French 2nd Armoured Division.

On 15 September they were alerted for a *parachutage*, organised at their request by 3rd Army, and received arms and ammunition (but no replacement kit, and no crystals for the useless radio transmitter they had been carrying around for three weeks), which were by then completely surplus to requirements. The next day was spent trying to find a safe home for the consignment, which was eventually put under guard in St-Dizier, and later collected by 3rd Army. The team made its way to Paris on 19 September, and negotiated five days' leave at Capt de Carville's family home in Normandy; it returned to Paris on 24 September, and three days later was back in the United Kingdom, having achieved, by its own admission, nothing of any import at all in its slightly-more-than-a-month in France.

Alfred

A second team dropped into north-eastern France that same night of 24 August, Alfred, had in fact been called up more than a fortnight before, on 9 August. Like other teams set to be sent into action at that time (see Cecil, below), it was delayed by bad weather, and was finally summoned from Milton Hall again on 23 August. An attempt to insert it that night was aborted over the DZ – after the containers and packages had been dropped – when the aircraft ran into a violent storm, but a second attempt the following night was more successful. Alfred was made up of Capt Leslie MacDougal ('Argyll'; his real name was Lewis MacDonald, and he used an alias because he had killed a guard during an escape from German captivity in 1940), Lt Jean-Pierre Herenguel, who called himself de Wavrant ('Aude') and Sgt Albert Key of the Royal Armoured Corps ('Wampum'). It is impossible to pin-point the location of the ground, but circumstantial evidence suggests that it was near La Neuville-en-Hez, between Beauvais and Clermont, in the Oise, about sixty kilometres due north of Paris. The *matériel* dropped the previous night was all to hand, save the pannier containing personal kit, which had been taken to a village some twenty kilometres away; it was not recovered until much later, and by then most of it had disappeared.

The next morning, Herenguel met the chief of the FFI in the *département*, Cmdt Dupont-Montura, who painted a fairly grim picture of an almost non-existent Resistance organisation, composed of a few hundred men armed with nothing better than sporting guns and a few old rifles. There were few effective leaders, communications were poor and the situation was exacerbated by a German presence in virtually every village. Clearly, the weapons dropped with the team would make very little difference to the overall situation, and there was an urgent need to arrange further *parachutages*.

On the morning of 26 August the team was forced to flee the farm where they were hiding when a contingent of Germans arrived and took it over; they moved to makeshift camp in a wood near Cressonsacq, and spent much of the following night waiting for a promised supply drop which never materialised. Forced to move again on 28 August, Alfred that evening received its first message from SFHQ, demanding to know the co-ordinates of DZs about which it knew nothing. The team countered by demanding *parachutages* for the best-organised of the vestigal Resistance groups, and was ignored. It then received an urgent message telling the men to do their best to safeguard 'the bridges over the Oise'. This they calmly disregarded for the moment, having made arrangements to mount two ambushes that night. One, near Francières, was a resounding success, considering the meagre firepower at the partisans' disposal, and halted an enemy convoy for some hours; the other, near La Neuville, remained undisturbed until the following morning, when a small party of German troops escorting thirty American PoWs appeared. The Germans were annihilated and the Americans freed.

That done, MacDonald set off, in a horse-drawn cart, and bearing letters of introduction to the Resistance chiefs in Amiens, to the Somme (whether to the river or the *département* is unclear from his account; evidently the earlier reference to 'bridges across the Oise' was a simple mistake, and it was the Somme – which runs through Amiens – that was meant). He got as far as Ferrière, and there met an American reconnaissance team, who told him that Ameins had already fallen to the British, whereupon he turned and retraced his steps to rejoin his team-mates. The next week was taken up with rather desultory searches for small groups of cut-off Germans and the organisation of a victory parade in Clermont, although MacDonald took time off to travel to the Pas-de-Calais to search out people who had helped him to escape in 1940. Before the end of the month the team was back in London, having been on active service in France for just a month.

Cecil

Team Cecil, which comprised Maj David Nielson of the Royal Fusiliers ('Delaware'), Capt Alfred Keser, who took the name Frayan ('Lys') and

Sgt Ronald 'Boxer' Wilde ('Centavo'), was originally alerted for insertion on 9 August, and travelled to London for its briefing four days later. Nielson reported an air of confusion at Devonshire Place, with too many teams present for either the house to accommodate or the staff to handle. Perhaps for this reason the team was five days in London, but when it arrived at Harrington it was told that flying operations were 'off', and was sent back to Milton Hall.

The men returned on the evening of 25 August, and were dropped, after some initial hesitation on the part of the B-24 Liberator pilot, at 0150 the next morning. The location of the ground is unclear, but circumstantial evidence places it not far to the north-east of the city of Troyes, in the Forêt d'Orient. The team's aircraft also carried twelve containers and eight packages, and was preceded by three other aircraft which dropped a further eighty-four items. The reception committee was big enough to handle the consignment, but had been poorly instructed in the use of the Eureka radar beacon; instead of placing it in the centre of the DZ – which was too small in any event, and surrounded by dense woodland – it was placed on the perimeter. The pilot dropped on the beacon, and as a result Keser, who was the first to jump, landed just inside the trees, and the other two Jedburghs fell into thick woodland. Sgt Wilde became hung up, and had to cut himself down, the fall causing a spinal injury from which he never fully recovered. It was some hours before the team were all assembled, and much of their personal kit was never found. Fortunately most of the containers and panniers were recovered, including the one which contained a million francs destined for 'Abelard' (Maurice Dupont, who was also known as Yvan), organiser of SOE F Section's Diplomat circuit, who had taken personal charge of the reception committee, as well he might have done, with so much cash expected.

The Jedburghs slept where they were until dawn, and then, with all containers located and weapons carted off, were taken to Avant-lès-Ramerupt, where they made their command post. Cecil's first task was to oversee the distribution of the large consignment of weapons dropped with it (though this came nowhere near supplying the needs of all the would-be *résistants* in the area; the team repeatedly requested additional *parachutages*, but none were forthcoming), and then turned its attention to surveying the Aube and Marne river crossings. Partisans under its control were able to safeguard no less than five of the eight bridges across the former between Arcis and Brienne, all of which had been readied for demolition, but were less well placed to protect those across the Marne. They were, however, able to pin-point locations at which the river could be forded at that time of year.

Just before the end of the month the team moved their base to Nogent-sur-Aube, to be closer to Abelard's CP. The armoured spearhead of the American army was still pressing eastward, but only on a relatively narrow front, and this produced a long salient, with more or less effective Axis forces on either flank. It was left to the FFI to guard these flanks, and French forces also secured the perimeter of Troyes to the south and east, where the countryside was heavily wooded, and German forces were able to operate with relative impunity. In the first week of September reports started to come in of a strong Axis force approaching from the south; in the event, these proved to be false – the Axis forces were actually moving east – but the American commander refused to believe reports from *maquisard* reconnaissance patrols which contradicted the rumours, and ordered the remaining bridges across the Seine in this sector to be destroyed quite unnecessarily, which made communication difficult.

It is not possible to follow Cecil's movements precisely, since Major Nielson's report, though very comprehensive, is completely lacking in chronological markers; one is left to make an informed guess by relating events he describes to accounts from other sources, but that is not always possible. Thus, we cannot be sure when he decided to distance himself from Abelard, and begin to work more closely with commanders appointed by the French authorities, but references to the appointment of Diagramme to command all Resistance forces in the region soon afterwards suggest it took place in the first week of September. The team moved into Troyes – which, though officially 'liberated' was not clear of German troops – and contacted Gen Koenig's appointee as the FFI leader in the Aube, 'Cmdt Montcalm'. A tour of the still-disputed area over which he had control, from Bar-sur-Aube in the east around to Les Riceys in the south, revealed that his forces were insufficient to bring matters to a satisfactory conclusion, and he refused to deploy the (over-large, in Nielson's opinion) 'garrison' he was maintaining in Troyes. The situation was soon exacerbated by the arrival in the south of the sector of more German troops retreating from the west, roughly along the line Auxerre–Tonnerre–Châtillon–Langres, and Cecil moved south so that Neilson and Keser could play a more direct part in running the FFI. After Châtillon fell (therefore some time after 8 September) they returned to Troyes to find that the situation there had deteriorated badly, that Montcalm's subordinates were on the brink of open mutiny, and that fighting had broken out between rightist and leftist factions.

Nielson appealed to London, and was directed to Diagramme, whose HQ was by then in Auxerre. The Jedburgh suggested that Montcalm be replaced by a stranger to the area, and that the three battalions of partisans still in and around Troyes should be reallocated, and Diagramme agreed. Montcalm was to go to Châlons-sur-Marne (now Châlons-en-Champagne) with one battalion; Abelard's battalion and that of the FTP, commanded by 'Cmdt Zaigue' would move south to Auxerre, with Zaigue in tactical command over both of them, and a regular army officer, Lt-Col Boudon, would take over in Troyes. Only Abelard dissented, and then only on a personal level, if Nielson is to be believed. He says he 'turned his battalion over to a French major and did not propose going to Auxerre with them. This, he explained to me, he considered the correct thing to do as, *not being a Frenchman himself* [italics added] and having been sent to the field as an organiser, he considered his mission now finished and proposed returning to England.' This is inexplicable, for Abelard was indeed French, and had been recruited at Agen, his home town in the Lot-et-Garonne, by George Starr. Once the changes were put into effect, the situation was rapidly resolved.

Cecil soon concluded that its mission, too, had come to an end, and set about locating Special Forces Detachment 11 at US 3rd Army HQ which, in the meantime, had moved to Étain, twenty kilometres east of Verdun. There was talk of the team redeploying to Germany directly from there (the possibility of Jedburghs working in Germany was raised quite frequently, but never came to anything), but it soon received orders from London to return there, via Paris. After three days in the French capital they managed to find seats on a Hendon-bound aircraft on 25 September.

Stanley

Stanley, which was composed of Capt Oswin Craster ('Yorkshire'), Lt Robert Cantais, under the name Carlière ('Meath') and Sgt Jack Grinham ('Worcestershire'), was despatched to the Plateau de Langres little more than a week before the Allied armies arrived in the region, on the night of 31 August, and found very little meaningful work to do during the fortnight it was to remain in France.

Its insertion was uneventful despite dropping from a considerable height on to a ground littered with rocks and small fir trees. Most of its containers and packages landed safely save, yet again, for the pannier containing personal kit and weapons, the parachute of which failed to open. The reception party was too small and had to work long and hard to clear the ground as a result. The DZ was close to the village of Riv- ières-les-Fosses, little more than ten kilometres from the farm where team Bunny was established (there is no mention in either team's report of any contact with the other), and there it remained for the night. The next day Craster met 'Jeneratrice' (sic, actually, 'Génératrice'), an FFI representative in the Haute-Marne, who, he tells us, requested him to move '25 kilometres north so as to join an actual formed maquis in the woods west of Bussières'. Before shifting its location, on 2 September, Stanley contacted London and requested two planeloads of weapons on DZ Hotel, where it had itself been dropped, and two more on another close by, known as Canapé, one of them to include a spare radio trans- mitter and replacement carbines. There is no evidence that these drops were executed, but it may be that they were rerouted, see below.

The 'formed maquis' Stanley found consisted of around 400 men from the region, including sixty gendarmes from Langres, forty-five rather unwarlike railway workers, and what Craster describes as 'the whole of the First Regiment of France. Formerly Pétainist but who had joined our maquis I think on 1st September'. The *Premier Régiment de France* – part of the *Armée de l'Armistice* which was not disbanded in November 1942 – has something of a mythic quality, and elements of it crop up regularly in the history of the liberation of France, at diverse locations. Stanley's report of the presence of the *Premier Régiment* prompted SFHQ to despatch another Jedburgh team, Nicholas, specif- ically to liaise with it.

On arriving at its new location, Stanley identified a new DZ, handily placed in the middle of the forest, close to the *maquisard* camp. Craster named it Zidor, and immediately asked for a large arms drop there. This request went unanswered until 8 September when 'to its amazement and intense disappointment', Stanley received a message querying the name of the DZ. It replied, and was ignored, but was then informed that a drop the following night would be made to yet another ground, Arthur, close to the village of Frettes, where there was a strong enemy presence. Craster was able to salvage a partial success from the opera- tion, however, for though two aircraft dropped on to Arthur, he was able to attract the attention of the other two by lighting straw fires along the roadside. The aircraft dropped accurately on them, and 'we quickly loaded our lorries and got away. The result of the night's work was forty containers'.

This additional weaponry enabled the partisans to begin a campaign of ambuscade on the routes through the region, on which traffic was now starting to build as the Allied armies arriving from the west and south began to make their presence felt by means of artillery and tactical airstrikes. On 11 September, after several local successes, they felt strong enough to take on the Axis forces established in three nearby villages – Grenant, Saulles and Belmont – but it soon became obvious that this force, which amounted to perhaps a thousand men, spread out along five kilometres of country road, with its command post dug in in the cemetery at Belmont, was more than the *maquisards* alone could handle. Craster sent an urgent message to SFHQ asking for a tactical airstrike:

> Three hours later four American fighters arrived. It was a magnificent sight, thirty trucks of ammunition were destroyed and 160 Germans killed. I did not know whether the arrival of the planes were the result of our message [frankly, it is unlikely; the procedural difficulties involved in relaying such a request were understandably enormous, and such a raid required a considerable lead time] but the results were 100 per cent and the Jed. stock soared. French troops belonging to the 7th Army [i.e. part of the Anvil/Dragoon force, from the south] arrived and there was a battle through the three villages. Our maquis helped mop up German stragglers in the woods and took over guarding the roads and the prisoners.

That was certainly the high point of Stanley's mission, but it was also its coda, for the following day the team received orders to travel to Paris, a journey which took three days, thanks to shortages of fuel and many punctures, in a borrowed car. Craster and Sgt Grinham returned to the United Kingdom on 20 September; Lt Cantais followed a week later.

Desmond

On the night of 4 September team Desmond – Capt William H Pietsch ('Skerry'), Capt Giles Maunoury, who called himself Bourriot ('Shetland') and M/Sgt Robert R Baird ('Hampshire') – was despatched to the Côte-d'Or, to the east of Dijon, alongside a fifty-five-strong Operational Group, Christopher. The relationship between the Jedburghs and the OG was almost bizarre:

Desmond was to have authority to recommend action to be taken by Christopher, but Desmond had no command function within the OG. Christopher was to maintain its own command channels and was to have complete authority to act according to the decisions of its commander. Although it was to accept advice from Desmond it need not follow up on this advice.

It took ten B-24 Liberators to carry the two parties and their stores, the aircraft leaving Harrington at ten minute intervals, with the Jedburghs in the lead plane. They were dropped at 'Anicroche' to a reception committee organised by René of the BOA and the *maquisard* lieutenant, Lucius, without serious mishap (one OG officer and one NCO suffered leg injuries, and were taken off to the *maquis* hospital at Échalot), and 'the OGs had a hearty meal and went to bed', while Pietsch and Maunoury spent the rest of the night formulating a plan of action. Ovale, the DMR, arrived the next morning, assigned a safe house to the OG and took Pietsch and Maunoury to Aignay-le-Duc to meet Col Claude.

Claude asked the Jedburghs to cross over into Allied-held territory, and attempt to obtain the help of an armoured column to support an attack on Châtillon-sur-Seine, which he believed to be the key to the region. They left at 0700 the following morning, taking with them the two injured GIs from Christopher, in a Buick Special which Ovale had siezed from a collaborator in Dijon. The trip from Aignay to Châlons-sur-Marne took eighteen hours, and finally brought them to US 3rd Army HQ, whose Special Forces detachment was unable to vouch for them, having no trace of team Desmond in its files. Eventually their identities were verified, and after considerable prevarication they obtained an agreement in principle that the US 106th Cavalry Squadron, a reconnaissance unit, would be assigned to assist them. They then returned to Aignay, where there was no sign of Claude, proceeded to Avot to pick up Christopher's commander, Capt Hjeltness, and returned to Aignay in time for dinner on the evening of 6 September.

Claude had planned his attack on Châtillon for the morning of 8 September, and the next day Pietsch and Maunoury returned in their Buick to the 106th Cav Sqn's CP near Fralignes, sixty kilometres from Aignay and the other side of Châtillon. Once all the details of Claude's plan had been passed to the Americans, and details for their role agreed, the two returned to Claude's CP, which had by now moved up to just south of Châtillon. Shortly before 0700 the next morning the mayor of the town contacted them to say that the Germans had left during the night, and

Pietsch tells how he, Maunory and Ovale 'proceeded into Châtillon on foot, tommy-guns at the ready. No Germans were left in the city and the party was received with hysterical joy by the liberated inhabitants', which hardly squares with team Paul's account …

Christopher arrived at the RV in the Jedburghs' absence. Hjeltness was all for taking his men into the city, perhaps to give them practice in liberation, but was eventually persuaded by Pietsch that the establishment of an ambush on the road the Germans had taken, in the direction of Larmagelle and Is-sur-Tille, to the south-east, should take precedence. A new RV at Échalot was agreed, and the Jedburghs set off to reconnoitre an ambush site, settling on one near Moloy. When they arrived at Échalot, early in the afternoon, there was no sign of the OG, and assuming that it had experienced more problems with its transport, they returned to the morning's RV in search of it. It was not there, either, having been persuaded that a contingent of perhaps fifty Germans who had got no further from Châtillon than Maisey-le-Duc, ten kilometres away to the east, would make an easy target. When they arrived at Maisey it was evident that there were far more than fifty dispirited Germans in and around the village. They found that Hjaltness had split his command into three components; one was actually in the village, one was in reserve to the south, and he himself was absent, having elected to lead a reconnaissance patrol in the direction of Villotte, to the north. In his absence none of the other OG officers would take any responsibility at all. Soon Claude arrived, and he, too, stressed the need for the OG to act, but once again its officers declined to take a decision. 'Desmond was faced with the problem of a unit that could [sic] not advance or withdraw,' Pietsch tells us. By now the situation was heating up nicely, with *maquisards* and German troops engaging in machine-gun duels; Pietsch decided that this was a job for the tanks, and set off towards Châtillon in search of the cavalry, whom he knew had arrived in the town in mid-morning. As he was clearing the area he met Hjeltness, who had lost a lieutenant to gunfire and had withdrawn his patrol in consequence. Pietsch encountered an armoured car patrol at a crossroads, two kilometres before the town, asked for their assistance and was refused; it took a visit to the unit's CP at Charrey, eight kilometres north of Châtillon, and a meeting with the regimental commander to 'persuade' the cavalry to intervene, and when they did it was almost dark; they fired a few rounds, and then promptly withdrew.

That night Pietsch and Maunoury returned to Avot. They had requested that jeeps be dropped to them, and learned that they would not be, but that an additional Operational Group, Adrian, had arrived.

When they met one of its officers, Capt Pitre, they were told that the group was not combat-ready, since 'the men were very tired, and all broken up by the death of Capt Kielbowicz, who had been held in very high esteem' (Kielbowicz had died during the insertion, when a rogue container collapsed his chute). The Jedburghs returned to Maisey, to find that Christopher had now pulled out, leaving the village to the Germans, who were dug in to strong defensive positions. The next morning Christopher tried to dislodge them, first with Bazooka rockets, fired from well outside that weapon's effective range, and then with high-explosive mortar bombs, which were equally useless. Pietch protested at the waste of precious ammunition, and was ignored. This was clearly the last straw:

> Desmond requested to be relieved of all responsibility for the OGs as they were not effective for this type of fighting.
> It was apparent that the only possible use for the OGs in this area was as a small combat infantry unit. They were not organised for this type of work.
> Since the Army was in the vicinity, Desmond requested that all OGs under his control [sic; they were not, of course …] be passed over to the control of SF HQ at 3rd Army.

Christopher was provided with transport to take it back to Avot, where it was united with Adrian and placed under Capt Pitre's command. The two OGs later returned to the United Kingdom by way of Paris, without ever being involved in more than skirmishes with small groups of lost Germans.

With his primary objective achieved, Claude now wished to move as soon as possible to Dijon, to ensure that the city passed into FFI control and not into the hands of the Communists, and he asked Pietsch and Maunoury to accompany him. They were barely in time – the local FTP commander had already installed himself in the prefecture – but the arrival of Gen de Lattre de Tassigny's First French Army (as *Armée B* had by now become) saved the situation. Claude then tried to enlist Desmond's assistance for operations around Vesoul and on to Belfort, but the team received orders to move to Paris, to await further instructions, and from there returned to London, arriving on 17 September. Bill Pietsch returned to Dijon briefly on 4 October, to oversee the securing of German files found in the prefecture and elsewhere (and which provided evidence pointing to the guilt of collaborators who were later brought to trial), and to gather up as many stray weapons as he could.

Nicholas

As a consequence of team Stanley reporting the presence of the *Premier Régiment de France* at Bussières, SFHQ hurriedly briefed team Nicholas, which comprised Capt John Maude ('Leicester'), Lt Henri Penin, calling himself Puget ('Breaknock') and Sgt Maurice Whittle ('Northumberland'), to liaise with it. The team was dropped on the night of 10 September to a DZ organised and manned by 2 SAS's Wallace party, together with two additional jeeps, three SAS troopers who had become separated from the rest of the patrol and had found their way back to the United Kingdom via the Houndsworth base in the Morvan and Normandy, and close on a hundred containers and panniers. There is no mention of the Jedburgh team in the very detailed report filed by Wallace's CO, Maj Roy Farran. 'Good drop, right place, right time. Reception committee well organised. Packages containing wireless set and two rucksacks were lost,' says Nicholas' report. Unfortunately, although they were indeed in the right place at the right time to be met by Wallace, they were at Pont-du-Bois in the Haute-Saône, over fifty kilometres to the north-east of the last known location of the *Premier Régiment de France* ...

The following day they met the *chef* of a small local *Maquis*, who knew of a bigger group near Magny-les-Jussey, twenty kilometres back in the direction of Bussières, and offered to conduct them there; he was also able to locate their missing luggage and radio. They set off at 0700 the following morning and arrived about an hour and a half later. At 0900 a large detachment of Axis troops reached Magny, debussed and began to form up for a sweep through the woods. As luck would have it, the Magny group was in the process of unpacking a substantial *parachutage* it had received some days before; the weapons were still packed with grease, as they had left the factory, and were, of course, unusable. Maude and Sgt Whittle made a run for it with the radio, while Penin helped the *maquisards* to disperse; the three were reunited on the afternoon of 12 September, in the Grand Bois near Senoncourt to the east, where there was another *maquisard* camp.

By now, Allied main force units were within forty kilometres, and the sounds of artillery could be heard quite distinctly, while retreating Germans were flooding eastward by every road; news came that they had established a temporary base at Jussey, and were preparing to defend Luxeuil-les-Bains, twenty kilometres to the east. All the Jedburghs could do under the circumstances was radio regular situation reports to London while waiting to be over-run. On 16 September they heard that a French reconnaissance unit was located at Ormoy, ten kilometres away to the north-west, and linked up with it that afternoon. With his original orders still in force, Maude enquired for news of the *Premier Régiment de France*, and was met with blank looks; he decided that the only course was to go and see for himself, and set off in borrowed transport, arriving at Bussières around 1600 to learn that the *Premier Régiment* had indeed been there 'but had left after a large scale action the previous Monday [i.e. five days earlier], for an unknown destination. We returned to the Grand Bois and sent a full report to London.' London responded by ordering them home two days later; they reached Paris on 20 September, and were back in the United Kingdom the following day.

Part Eight

THE SAÔNE VALLEY AND
THE FRANCHE-COMTÉ

Alan

It was mid-August before Jedburgh teams were parachuted into the Saône Valley, north of Lyon; the first of them, Alan, dropped from an RAF Stirling together with a party from 3 (French) SAS which was to participate in Operation Harrod. Alan landed without mishap near St Gengoux-le-National, about fifteen kilometres south-west of Chalons-sur-Saône, on the night of 12 August. Their instructions were to contact a French mission, Canelle, first to establish communications for the SAS parachutists, then to harass enemy lines of communication. The team was made up of Capt Stanley Cannicott ('Pembroke'), Lt Robert Toussaint, who took the name Gairaud ('Ariège') and S/Lt Robert Clause, who used the name Francis de Heysen ('Kroner').

Cannicott reported that they saw nothing of their primary contact, 'Goujon', after he had met them at the DZ and appropriated the contents of many of their containers. The team therefore ignored the instruction to liaise with Canelle and soon decided that the leader of the parachutists, 'Cmdt Conon' (actually Cmdt Pierre Château-Jobert, who took Yves Conan as his *nom de guerre*; he had wider responsibilities, having been named by Gen Koenig as commander of all FFI units in the area in addition to leading most of a battalion of SAS troops) 'was exerting no real influence in the region', which is a startling assertion. Instead they contacted a man described as 'the chief of the military of Saône-et-Loire, Cmdt Ferana ['Cmdt Ferent', (Capt de la Ferte)], who had a loose control of several Maquis in the area', and 'were invited to take charge of one of them'.

On the evening of 16 August they joined the *Bataillon du Charrolais*, also known as the *Batallion Claude*, after its creator, a regular army officer named Claude Ziegler, at its base west of Macon, and found it to comprise 600 men, divided into five companies, about half of them

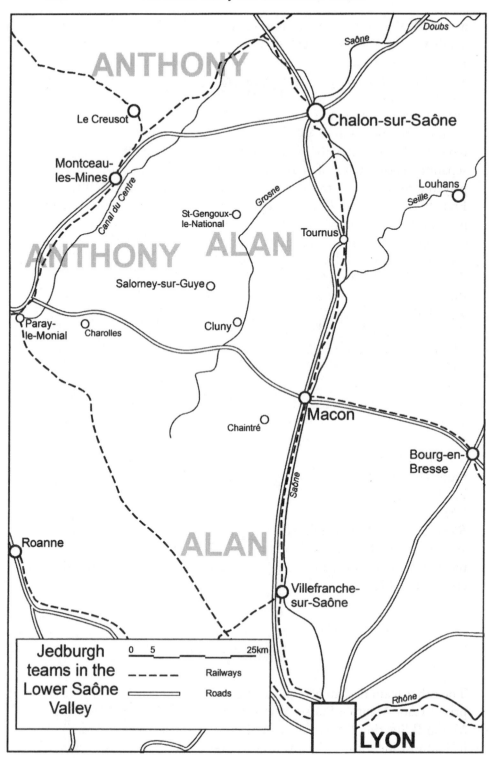

Doubs

Saône

ANTHONY

Le Creusot

Chalon-sur-Saône

Montceau-
les-Mines

Canal du Centre

Grosne

Louhans

Seille

St-Gengoux-
le-National

ANTHONY

ALAN

Tournus

Salorney-sur-Guye

Paray-
le-Monial   Charolles

Cluny

Macon

Chaintré

Bourg-en-
Bresse

Saône

Roanne

ALAN

Villefranche-
sur-Saône

Jedburgh
teams in the
Lower Saône
Valley

0   5   25km

- - - - -   Railways

———   Roads

Rhône

LYON

armed. By the last week of the month, by now relocated to Chaintré, just south-west of Macon, the battalion was in action regularly, cutting the Lyon–Dijon railway line, which was still in regular use, and mounting ambushes on the main N6 and secondary routes. It became even more effective from 2 September, after Cannicott had been able to obtain enough weapons to arm it fully, from an Allied Mission based at Cluny.

After the liberation of Villefranche, on 3 September – a simple collapse of the garrison there, says Cannicott, though Toussaint, in a separate report, talks of fierce and prolonged fighting in which he played a major role – the *Batallion du Charrolais* attached itself to the French *1ière Division Blindée* (1st Armoured Division). Unusually and irregularly, Jedburgh team Alan went with it, and Cannicott and Toussaint operated as infantry company commanders as they fought their way east from Dijon, across the Plateau de Langres and eventually to the vicinity of Belfort. Here, on 1 October, Cannicott received a serious shrapnel wound from artillery fire (Toussaint says sixteen of the *bataillon* were killed and thirty-five wounded in this engagement, at Magny-Danigon), but was fortunate to be evacuated to a medical aid station where a competent surgeon repaired lacerations to his intestine, kidney and liver. After rather haphazard post-operative care at a French military hospital in Lyon – on a diet of red wine and goat's cheese – he was returned to the United Kingdom aboard a Dakota on 23 October. Toussaint reported to SFHQ in Paris that same day, having remained with the *bataillon* until it had moved further north into the Vosges, almost within artillery range of the German frontier. S/Lt Clause, who had returned to the team, after being 'seconded' to 3 SAS, in mid-September, became involved in creating a tactical radio net for the *Bataillon du Charrolais*, using American radio transceivers supplied by *1ière Division Blindée*, with a lorry-mounted base station and four mobile units in armoured cars. He returned to London in January, 1945, by which time the battalion, by now completely integrated into the French Army, had crossed into Germany.

Anthony

The other team despatched on the night of 14 August, Anthony, comprised Capt Maurice Stasse, who called himself Deprez ('Perth'), Lt Mason B Starring ('Nebraska') and Sgt John L Bradner ('Pfennig'). It had almost identical orders to those given to Jude, save that it was to contact an SOE F Section network, Ditcher. The team left Keevil aero-drome in a Stirling at 2230 together with an eight-man stick from 3 SAS's Harrod party and was dropped without mishap to a ground near Salornay-sur-Guye, north-north-west of Cluny, to be met by a recep-tion committee and taken off to a nearby farm where 'Tiburce' (Albert Browne-Bartroli, organiser of Ditcher) and 'Jacquot', the Resistance leader in the area, were waiting. Later they met the leader of the *Régi-ment de Cluny*, 'Capt Laurent', and Cmdt Ferent, and it was decided that Capt Stasse should take command of a *maquisard* battalion (the *Bataillon de Sylla*) from Charolles, while Lt Starring and Sgt Bradner would remain with Tiburce. That was how the team operated, with Stasse leading a combat unit and Starring in an organisational and logistical role, though he also participated in reconnaissance patrols sent out to monitor traffic on the N6 and the adjacent railway line, and also oversaw liaison between the partisan elements and with team Alan, operating just to the south.

Additional sticks of SAS troopers, as well as containers of arms and equipment, were dropped over the following week, and both Stasse and Starring needed to take precautions against FTP elements in the area – who showed a marked lack of interest in fighting Germans – hi-jacking *parachutages*. By the end of August, the partisans were all armed; since a comprehensive training programme had been set up long before Anthony arrived on the scene, they represented an effective fighting force by the time it became possible to drive the Germans out, in the first week of September.

The sector allocated to Stasse's battalion was the area around Paray-le-Monial north of the N79 which links the Saône and Loire Valleys, and in particular the N70, which runs north from Paray to Montceau-les-Mines and the parallel route running north from Digoin through Gueugnon. His men were to work closely with SAS troopers, and achieved some spectacular successes. From 18 August the railway which runs alongside the N70 was cut in so many places and so frequently that it was scarcely usable, and by 21 August, some eighteen northbound trains were backed up at Paray; Stasse repeatedly requested airstrikes on the marshalling yards there, but none came. The small garrisons in vil-lages along the N70 all came under attack, too, but with less success since the road was heavily patrolled by German armour. Eventually, with the help of demolition experts from 3 SAS (though Stasse fails to mention that in his report), a culvert carrying a stream beneath the road and the adjacent canal was packed with explosives. The result was con-clusive: the canal bank was destroyed, and the road flooded for a considerable distance. By 3 September, Paray was surrounded, and its garrison cut off; in the afternoon regular French troops arrived, and when the Germans attempted to leave that night, they were annihilated. The next day it was the turn of Montceau; here the German resistance was more effective, but it, too, was overcome, and some 700 prisoners were taken before the *maquisards* continued northward, towards Le Creusot and Chalon-sur-Saône, both of which had been evacuated by the time they arrived. There was feeble resistance in Autun, but by the evening of 9 September, the whole of the Saône-et-Loire had been liberated, and it remained only to mop up isolated groups of German troops, most of whom were more than ready to surrender.

Anthony was reunited only in London, Starring and Sgt Bradner having returned there on 28 September, when Stasse arrived on 3 October.

Basil and Norman

Team Basil emplaned at Harrington in a rather less than calm atmosphere on the night of 25 August; its destination was the Jura mountains, south of Besançon, close to the border with Switzerland, where it was to operate under the orders of 'Ligne', (Lt-Col Broad), the DMR for the Franche-Comté. The tri-national team – Capt Robert Rivière, who took the name Raincourt ('Amblève'); Capt Thomas Carew ('Sutherland') and T/Sgt John L Stoyka ('Ore') – was dropped from little more than 100 metres altitude after the pilot had made six circuits of the ground and still failed to confirm the recognition letter. The American was stunned, and the Frenchman broke a finger. None of their personal kit had been loaded aboard the aircraft, and if a radio set had been, it was lost. 'We had only what we stood up in and our pistols. We were taken to [the Château de] Granges-Maillot and suffered from excessive hospitality', wrote Carew.

They reported 'finding' a B2 radio set in working order the next day and managed to contact London. They later met the senior *maquis* leader in that area, 'Col Lagarde' (Orcia) of the *Groupement Frontière*, and 'Col Boulaya' (Berthelet), from the region to the north. The situation was not promising; there were some 2,000 volunteers in the area, of whom only 300 were armed 'and then with a collection of which the British Museum would have been proud' but including a few Stens, some Brens, two bazookas and one PIAT. A signal asking for arms for

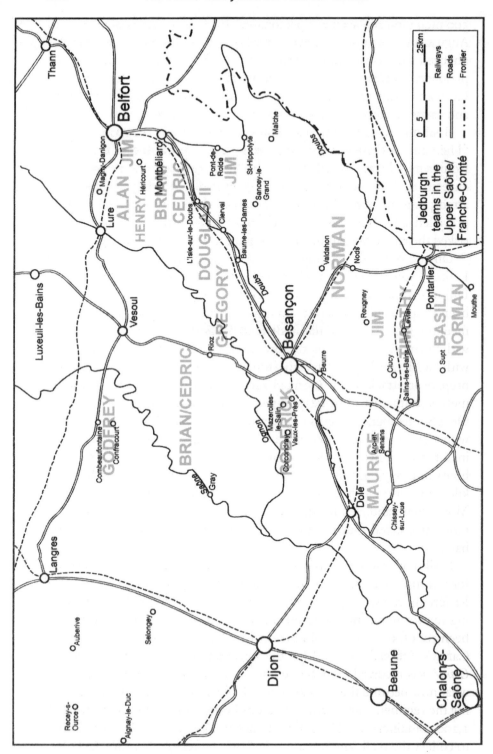

500 men (and replacement personal kit for themselves) was sent on 28 August, but was not even acknowledged. That same day the *résistants* attacked a convoy of horse-drawn vehicles, killing some, taking eleven prisoners and capturing some weapons and supplies, but as a result German troops garrisoned locally set out on a reprisal raid; Jedburghs and partisans retired into the forest.

Basil moved to Clucy, near Salins-les-Bains, later that day, and met 'Théodule', a British agent (other reports call him 'Albert', and are far from sympathetic towards him), who 'had great knowledge and influence in the area and resented our coming'. A potentially corrosive atmosphere of mutual distrust developed, but common sense finally prevailed, and after a few tense days the conflict – major enough to have risked the entire operation, according to Basil's report – was resolved.

On the previous evening, of 27 August, team Norman – Lt Marc Lautier, who called himself Bataille ('Washington'); Lt Konrad C Dillow ('Minnesota') and Sgt Lucien E Lajeunesse ('Tennessee') – had been despatched to operate alongside Basil, and Ligne, who came to meet the Jedburghs that night, divided the area between the two teams, with the newcomers taking the eastern sector. He told Basil to co-locate with Col Lagarde's HQ at Supt, fifteen kilometres south of Clucy, and prepare an attack on the German garrison at Mouthe, twenty-five kilometres south-east of there, and just a few kilometres from the border. On 4 September, elements of Lagarde's *Groupement Frontière*, together with regular French troops from the 3rd *Tirailleurs Algeriens*, a colonial infantry unit newly arrived from the south-west, took the town after two hours of heavy fighting. The next objective was Pontarlier, twenty-five kilometres away to the north-west, and astride a main road leading to Montbéliard and Belfort; the garrison here was bigger, and the fighting more prolonged, but by noon on 5 September it too was in French hands.

Basil now split up, Carew shifting to Salins to help turn the partisan force into something more formal, as the *Régiment Franche-Comté*, while Rivière moved to Pontarlier and concerned himself initially with policing the town and mopping up small bodies of enemy troops who had been cut off or failed to join the retreat, before starting similar work to Carew's. Official approval for the formation of the *Régiment Franche-Comté* was received on 8 September, and in addition to its work with what now became the 1st Battalion, Basil was given the job of overseeing the regiment's armament, weapons being dropped by air in a total of 1,200 containers to a DZ eight kilometres long. It took thirty-six hours to collect them all, and not a few had been rifled by the time the crews got to them. In the conclusion to Basil's report, this was described as 'a grandiose, but in reality a pathetic, gesture', since the regular lines of communication with Lons-le-Saunier and the Saône Valley had been established by then, and the consignment could have been delivered by road.

Norman had landed without mishap, and spent much of the rest of the night at the DZ waiting for team Maurice, which failed to arrive. (The plan called for the two teams to be dropped to the same ground, each one travelling in an aircraft of its own, with three more carrying only supplies; in the event, four aircraft arrived over the DZ, dropping team Norman, sixty containers and assorted packages. Maurice's kit had been loaded aboard Norman's aircraft, and vice-versa.) Norman's report stresses the high level of morale among the partisans, but reinforces Basil's appraisal of the general situation; it did have one major asset in the sector Ligne allocated to it, however: most of a battalion of Russians, who had deserted from the *Wehrmacht* taking all their weapons including heavy machine-guns and mortars and even one 4.5cm anti-tank gun, together with a large stock of ammunition.

Two days after the liberation of Pontarlier, Norman became involved in a fierce fire-fight in the village of Nods, some twenty-five kilometres north of the town, which German forces had evacuated a day earlier. The team had met up with a unit from the 3rd Spahis there that evening, but as Lautier and Dillow were getting into their car to return to their own CP they suddenly came under machine-gun fire: German mechanised infantry had re-entered the village and launched a spirited attack on the Spahis' command post. The unit's tanks were leaguered south of the village, but in the darkness they could not deploy effectively, and fighting continued until dawn, when the balance of power changed. Later that morning the Spahis, together with partisan elements and the Russian deserters, moved on the village of Valdahon, and the adjoining military encampment, five kilometres further north. Axis troops, including some armour, were installed in strong defensive positions here, and it took all day to dislodge them.

With that, the forward edge of the battle area moved out of Norman's operational area, and like Basil it now became involved with organising elements of the *Régiment Franche-Comté*, remaining with the 3rd Battalion located at Valdahon. Its report indicates that it made every effort to find itself a new mission, Dillow travelling to 7th Army HQ for the purpose, but to no avail, and on 22 September a signal from SFHQ 'suggested' it should return to the United Kingdom. The team arrived in

Paris on 24 September, and returned to London two days later. Basil followed Norman to Paris on 26 September, and it too returned promptly to London. Like all the other teams deployed at this time, Basil and Norman complained bitterly at having been sent into action far too late. It is true that those teams had been in training for seven months by then, and in the event saw only two or three weeks of combat action – but the reality of the situation was that the liberation of France actually proceeded far more rapidly, once the pivotal battle for Normandy was won, than any had dared hope.

Brian

Two other teams, Brian and Cedric, were despatched with Norman to the Franche-Comté region on the night of 27 August (Maurice should have gone too, but ran into difficulties). Team Brian consisted of Maj Francis Johnston of the Royal Armoured Corps ('Illinois'), Capt Roger Crétain, who took the name Francomte ('Orkney') and Sgt Norman Smith, also of the RAC ('Lira'). The trio was called up from Milton Hall on 14 August, but like other teams briefed at around that time, it was weeks before it could actually be sent into the field. In the end, Crétain says he lobbied Free French HQ in London, and room was found for the team – though not its containers of weapons – aboard one of the Fairford-based Stirlings that dropped a party from 3 (French) SAS, which was then engaged on Operation Abel, on the night of 27 August to a DZ near Montéchéroux.

Brian's orders were to assist an OSS officer known as 'Cmdt Pascal' (Capt Ernest Floege, who was also known as 'Maj Paul') to control the partisans he had assembled on the Plateau de Lomont, south of Montbéliard. Perhaps half of them were armed, and bringing in weapons for the rest was seen as a priority, so Crétain and Johnston spent their first days checking out possible LZs for Dakota operations; two were identified and their locations passed to London, but no aircraft ever came. On 5 September, Johnston's report says,

> 'Pascal decided to carry out an attack on the bridge at Lisle-sur-le-Doubs [sic] in the hope that he could hold it until the regular forces arrived. This attack was carried out by two companies of the Corps Francs assisted by the SAS. Cmdt Francomte also went on this attack. In its initial stages the attack succeeded but the enemy had time to call

up reinforcements and our troops had to withdraw under heavy mortar and machine-gun fire, when Francomte was wounded. After this time Francomte was hors de combat as far as the team was concerned ...

Next day Pascal's base on the Lomont Plateau came under attack from German mechanised infantry, supported by armour and self-propelled guns. French troops were by then within fifteen kilometres, but Johnston, uncertain whether they would get there in time, put in a request for close air support by radio. In the event the French tanks arrived before the German assault proper had begun, and the enemy broke off the action and continued on their line of march, towards Belfort.

It is clear from the team's report that Brian had very little to do at this point, but on 10 September it organised the reception of team Henry and two days later moved its base to Sancey-le-Grand, west of the plateau, and established a permanent command post for an Inter-Allied Mission, Étoile, 'who had lost their Jed team [Gregory] owing to casualties and who were obliged to travel about dictating policy to Groups who had already been overrun etc.' Étoile set about reinventing itself (as the co-ordinator of FFI forces preparing to push on into Alsace and Germany), and in the process it also defined a new role for Brian.

Brian had already gained an unofficial extra member – a young officer named Crowley, who had joined them on 31 August, and had assisted Sgt Smith with his radio; the report gives no indication of his origins, but he may have been a downed airman – and now grew to eight (Crétain being hospitalised) with the addition of five Frenchmen who were to act as liaison officers. The process of integrating the enlarged team into the mainstream of intelligence gathering was of necessity slow, and it was 12 October before it became properly operational again, although for some weeks prior to that it had been making daily reports to French 1st Army HQ.

By now much of the escaping German Army had already passed through the Belfort Gap, but the area east of Montbéliard, including the city itself, was still in German hands. The city was not as strategically vital as Belfort, but it was built on the River Doubs at its easternmost point, and was an important crossing; if its bridges could be kept intact, it would save considerable time and effort. Johnston had painstakingly built up a network of informers in Montbéliard, and had positioned some of the newcomers to the team with them; they had excellent channels of communications, including a radio-telephone link (made up by a Swiss amateur radio enthusiast). Now he put forward a plan to employ the *maquisards* to safeguard the bridges and to provide guides to lead the French armour and its infantry screen through the minefields in front of the city, and these two tasks were accomplished handsomely. Despite the partisans being under-strength and ill-supplied with weapons, they disabled the demolition charges on the bridges and then held off the German assault which followed, while other members of the group exposed themselves to fire in order to guide the regular forces through the obstacles and minefields into the city. Following the liberation of Montbéliard, Johnston tried to pursue his intelligence-gathering in the region beyond the Belfort Gap, towards Mulhouse, but found it much more difficult to operate in a region which had been extensively 'Germanised' since 1940. Later he and Sgt Smith moved north, to Nancy, to act as a communications relay for team Julian II during its operations in the Haut-Rhin. When Julian II was retasked they returned to London via Paris. Capt Crétain remained in France, and rejoined his original unit when he had recovered from his injuries.

Cedric

Team Cedric comprised the American Capt Douglas de W Bazata ('Vesdre'), Capt Louis Lesne, who took the name Chapel ('Dendre'), and Sgt Richard C Floyd ('Gulder'). They reported no problems during their insertion save that Bazata managed to get astride his static line and suffered what he called 'very serious injury' when it pulled taut; that must have been a cause of considerable concern to one who valued his reputation as a ladies' man. Due to German activity in the area (close to the main Besançon–Vesoul road, about ten kilometres south of Rioz), the team landed at a hastily prepared DZ on the far side of the River Ognon from the one originally readied to receive them; thanks to the efficiency of the organiser of the reception committee, 'Émile' (who had originally been dropped to work with Albert, but was now operating independently), this posed no problems. All their luggage and containers were recovered, and they were taken to a safe house for the rest of the night. Bazata does not tell us whether they dropped in uniform, but does say that it proved impossible to operate except in civilian clothes.

Émile described the situation in simple terms: the Germans were moving north-eastward through the area *en masse*, heading for Belfort and beyond, and Bazata decided to operate along the N83 between Besançon and L'Isle-sur-le-Doubs; when he met Ligne and Col

Boulaya, on 29 August, they instructed him to work further north, along the Vesoul–Belfort road, but he demurred. He and Lesne spent the next few days assessing the situation for themselves. Their most important asset was a group of some 650 Russian deserters located north of Vesoul, but requests to London for weapons to arm them went unanswered. On the night of 31 August, Cedric was surprised to hear aircraft circling a small, supplies-only ground only some hundreds of metres from its base, and more surprised still to discover that a *parachutage*, consisting of another Jedburgh team – Roderick – together with four plane-loads of containers was in progress; neither Cedric nor Émile had received notice of the new team's arrival, and there were no arrangements for disposal of the supplies. All they could do was put them alongside the containers they already had; the next morning German troops arrived and seized the lot. Roderick – whose report tells a somewhat different story – was eventually passed south, into the area where it was supposed to operate.

On 3 September the small partisan group to which Cedric attached itself cut the railway alongside the N83, and halted an artillery convoy on the road between Gray and Vesoul, further north, but the next day they had to watch impotently as what seemed to be an entire army, aboard commandeered civilian cars, passed along the minor road from Rioz towards Belfort. 'I firmly believe', wrote Bazata, 'that several thousand tyre bursters [miniature mines] covered by intermittent Maquis fire would have put this convoy into utter confusion.' By now the Jedburghs were desperate for weapons, so much so that when London announced that a special nine-man Mission ('Marcel') led by an American colonel would be dropped the next night to a DZ known as Onion, which proved to be right alongside the temporary home to a battalion of Germans, Bazata told them to hold the Mission but drop the containers they would have brought with them. Amazingly, the *parachutage* went flawlessly, and they were able to collect forty-six containers, the arms from which were distributed to the partisans operating along the N83.

It is clear from Cedric's report that communications with London were very poor, and much of the blame for that is placed squarely on the shoulders of the team's W/T operator. Bazata accuses him of falsely claiming that incoming messages were indecipherable, and as a result two other major *parachutages*, one of them involving 150 containers, were cancelled.

On 13 September, Cedric's CP was overrun by American forces, and from then on spent their time 'cleaning out pockets of Germans left by the advancing Allies, working Maquis agents through the lines, and doing the same ourselves'. Bazata was to be critical of the decision to insert the team so late – it should have been dropped in January, he asserted – but still believed the mission to have been a success. 'Certainly, our small and numerous ambuscades and attacks kept the Germans constantly in doubt as to our actual strength. Due to this fear their movements were definitely restricted and their tactics had to be altered daily.' Team Cedric returned to the United Kingdom on 6 October.

Maurice

Maurice – Capt Charles M Carman ('Utah'), Capt Hubert Reveilhac, who called himself Dumesnil ('Viriginia') and T/Sgt Francis J Cole ('Georgia') – was originally called up from Milton Hall on 14 August, with a substantial number of other teams, and like them was to suffer the frustration of enforced delays caused by adverse weather conditions. By 27 August the situation had improved, and the team was taken off to Harrington, together with Norman, for insertion that night; the five B-24 Liberators, one for each team and three more carrying stores, took off at ten-minute intervals, but due to poor navigation Maurice's failed to find the DZ, and circled the town of Dole, about thirty kilometres away, provoking its air defences into action, whereupon the pilot decided to abort the mission. As far as Maurice was concerned, disappointment apart, this was perhaps no bad thing, given the total incompetence, according to Carman's report, of the despatcher. They tried again on the night of 31 August, in an RAF Stirling from Tempsford, and this time the insertion, to a DZ near Chissey-sur-Loue, went smoothly; the reception committee gathered up the three men and the large quantity of stores dropped from a total of four aircraft, and by 0200 on 1 September the team was safe in the château at Arc-et-Senans.

Team Maurice's file in the London archive is by far the most complete of all the Jedburgh teams', but it has an extra distinction: the team's after-action report is both extremely detailed – it runs to twenty-four single-spaced foolscap pages – and mildly entertaining, since its author, Capt Carman, displays literary pretension, albeit at college level. It begins:

By the time we arrived in France, our state of mind was somewhat like that of a woman whose lover has left without saying goodbye. We had been led to expect that we would be sent in well before D-Day. Consequently, for three months we expected daily to be alerted. And for two weeks after we were alerted, the operation was daily postponed ...

The Jedburghs made contact with a reconnaissance platoon from the 3rd *Tirailleurs Algeriens* on their third day in France, and in the event, Maurice was to do good work in the period between the arrival of the first Allied troops in the area and its liberation, when the situation was at its most confused and the enemy perhaps at his most dangerous. For days, the actual circumstances were far from clear, with Axis troops constantly on the move, reoccupying villages and even towns which had thought themselves liberated, and disrupting their inhabitants' celebrations in no uncertain terms.

Maurice's only real taste of combat, skirmishes apart, came with the fighting around Besançon, the principal city of the area. Here they were able to supply American artillery units with the precise locations of German batteries, the rapid destruction of which persuaded the enemy, who occupied the city in considerable strength, to withdraw instead of trying to hold it. Later they accompanied *maquisards* who entered the city in the vanguard of the Allied forces, but 'from that point on [this was the evening of 7 September], practically nothing of interest happened to us. We stayed at Besançon another week, helping, where we could, to get the FFI organised'; much of their energy was devoted to collecting abandoned weaponry, of which there was an enormous amount. They withdrew to Dijon, to look for US 3rd Army HQ, on 16 September, moved north to Troyes, then to Châlons-sur-Marne (now Châlons-en-Champagne), then to Verdun, and finally succeeded in locating it. There they hung around for a further week in the hope of being allocated a new mission, and eventually returned to London on 26 September.

Roderick

Roderick, as briefly mentioned, dropped in unexpectedly on Cedric on the night of 31 August. The team was made up of Capt Jean Preziosi, who called himself Albert Paoli ('Nairn'), Lt William C Boggs ('New Hampshire') and T/Sgt Charles Mersereau ('Stronsay'). They, too, were to assist Ligne to organise the *maquisards* of the Doubs, and met him, and the FFI leaders, on the morning of 1 September. Operating to the west of Besançon, the team moved to a village named Corcondray on 4 September; they soon began gathering intelligence on enemy movements through the area, particularly on the main Besançon–Dole and Besançon–Lons-le-Saunier roads, and by the following day were able to mount ambushes on minor roads paralleling the main routes, with some success. That same day they heard reports of American reconnaissance units at Beurre, south of Besançon, and sent *maquisard* guides to assist them.

Next day, 6 September, the team and the partisans to whom they had attached themselves were surprised in their campsite by German infantry, and had to move hurriedly, leaving much of their kit behind; it was subsequently recovered, save for one haversack containing 15,000 francs. By now, it was clear that they were squarely in the path of the *Wehrmacht*'s 11. Panzer Division (which had left Toulouse for Provence in mid-August, and had fought a rearguard action up the Rhône and Saône Valleys, but was now in full – though largely disciplined – retreat towards the German border), and movement became increasingly difficult, despite the Jedburghs wearing civilian clothes. On 7 September the *maquisards* received an order to move up to Besançon, and did so that night, often intermingled with small parties of Germans, using minor roads and passing through Mazerolles-le-Salin and Vaux-les-Prés before joining the main road from Dole at Château-Farine, just west of the city, where they encountered elements of the US 3rd Armored Division. On 9 September Roderick took part in the attack on Besançon; the toll on the partisans alongside whom it was operating was heavy, and the team lost all its kit save for its radio. The following day it withdrew to Lyon, and within twenty-four hours was back in London, having been in France for barely ten days.

Gregory

In the light of the pictures painted by the Jedburgh teams dropped around Besançon at the end of August – which, while they may not match exactly, are roughly consistent and demonstrate that the area was largely liberated by mid-September – it comes as something of a surprise to discover that teams were still being sent there long after they could have been expected to carry out Jedburgh-style missions. In fact, four teams were despatched to assist Inter-Allied Missions Étoile and Orgeat, the latter having wide responsibilities over that entire area of eastern France, and being split into a number of parts, of which three – Sainfoin, Thym and Serpolet – were accompanied by Jedburghs.

Team Gregory, which accompanied the Étoile Mission, was the first of these to be despatched; it was on its second mission to France, having been briefly deployed as team Daniel in support of Mission Aloès in Brittany, in August. Its personnel were unchanged, with Capt Ed Bennett ('Apôtre') in command, with Lt Pierre de Schonen ('Argentier') and Sgt Ron Brierley ('Florin'). It was inserted together with the six members of Étoile (and a jeep) by C-47 Dakota, from Harrington to a temporary airstrip near Gex, in the Ain, north of Geneva. From Gex the party proceeded via Lons-le-Saunier to Baume-les-Dames; short of the latter, on 6 September, the small convoy – the jeep in the lead, followed by two civilian cars – came under fire from a German machine gun, and Bennet and de Schonen were both hit, as were two of the officers from Étoile. The party withdrew under fire. The wounded were cared for at an American dressing station and later evacuated, but Sgt Brierley remained with Mission Étoile, which now moved to safer ground at Pontarlier and then transferred to Paris in mid-October. He returned to the United Kingdom on 1 November.

Timothy

Team Timothy – Capt Louis Moutte, who called himself Ambel ('Nesque'), Lt Robert E Heyns ('Dyle') and Sgt Donald A Spears ('Escaut') – was assigned to Sainfoin, and left Harrington together with some elements of it on the night of 10 September. Its pilot refused to allow the Jedburghs to jump because he did not agree the recognition letter flashed from the DZ (though the members of Sainfoin, travelling in separate aircraft, did go), and they tried again, with the rest of the group, the following evening. This time things went smoothly and they jumped to a ground located north of the town of Levier, twenty kilometres west of Pontarlier; Lt Heyns broke his ankle on landing, and two nights later Lt Robert G Mundinger ('Marcelin') was sent to join the team, which soon moved to Besançon. After a brief period spent assessing the situation in the Doubs Valley between Besançon and Montbéliard, it became clear that there was nothing for the Jedburghs (or Sainfoin) to do in the area, and Capt Moutte was ordered to work up a plan to take his team to southern Alsace by way of neutral Switzerland. In the event this came to nothing, and after two frustrating weeks

Timothy was told that it was to be withdrawn. The American members arrived back in the United Kingdom on 1 October, but Capt Moutte remained in France and was reassigned, first to the *Groupement Mobile du Sud-Ouest*, under Col Schneider (which had actually ceased to exist by that time) and then to another 'flying column', this time made up of Alsatians.

Jim

Briefed to assist the Thym group of Mission Orgeat, team Jim – Capt Philip W Donovan ('Pennsylvania'), Lt José de Francesco, who took the name Jean Lavige ('Leitrim') and T/Sgt Michael F Henley ('Wexford') – was inserted by a Carpetbaggers' B-24 Liberator to a DZ 'a few miles from Reugney' in the early hours of 16 September; there were no mishaps, and Jim spent the rest of the night in a safe house. On 18 September they moved to Besançon, and two days later, by now apparently divorced from Thym, left for 'Plombiers' (actually, Plombières-les-Bains, sixty kilometres north-west of Vesoul, in the Vosges); on 21 September they joined the US 143rd Infantry Regiment 'at the front', and were with it when it crossed the River Moselle near Remiremont. That night they met Maj Oliver Brown of team Alastair, who briefed them on the situation immediately to the north. De Francesco remained with the American infantrymen while Donovan made his way to the headquarters of the US 36th Division, the spearhead of the 7th Army, to make a situation report but also to attempt to learn from London the whereabouts of team Jacob, which had been out of contact for some time. On 25 September, by now reunited with de Francesco, he was ordered to return to Besançon, moved from there back to Vesoul, and thence to Paris, a journey which took three days. The American members of the team returned to the United Kingdom on 5 October, Lt de Francesco remaining in Paris.

Douglas II

As its designation suggests, team Douglas II was also on its second mission to France; it too had been deployed in Brittany, and had operated there for three weeks during August in support of Aloès. This time the two officers – Capt Dick Rubenstein ('Augure') and Lt Jean Roblot, who called himself Ronglou ('Anchorère') – were joined by an American W/T operator, Pvt John Van Hart, Sgt John Raven having been incapacitated by what is described in the team's report as a self-inflicted wound (which cannot have been too serious, for Raven was soon back in action). Van Hart kept Sgt Raven's code name, 'Half Crown'. The team was inserted, together with the four officers who constituted the Serpolet group of Orgeat, to the ground south of Reugney, together with team Jim, and the two were whisked away while the large consignment of stores dropped with them – six B-24 Liberators were deployed altogether – were collected. Many of the packages, including much of Douglas II's kit and its radios, were destroyed thanks to chutes either failing to open or their static lines not having been attached. The Jedburghs and most of Serpolet remained at Reungey while the Mission's leader travelled to Besançon where Orgeat's commanding officer, Col Robert, had established his command post; he returned on 18 September to tell them that Serpolet was to be stood down, and that they would in all probability return immediately to London, there being no work for them to do.

In fact there *was* a requirement for a liaison Mission in the area, and while Serpolet's leader, Maj Gellard, found a new role elsewhere, its three remaining members and the attached Jedburgh team were redirected to L'Isle-sur-le-Doubs, and arrived there on 20 September, to operate to the east, towards Montbéliard, specifically to gather intelligence. The parent unit of one of the members of Serpolet and the French Jedburgh were in this region, and when the Mission was withdrawn, on 28 September, they remained behind. Rubenstein and Pvt Van Hart then made their way to Paris and thence to London, arriving on 4 October.

Henry

Even though the Allied advance into the Franche-Comté was fairly well advanced by 9 September and there were ten Jedburgh teams already in an area thick with retreating German forces, yet another team, Henry – Lt Raymond E Moore ('New Mexico'), Lt Stephane Jean-Montcler, who used Montcler as his *nom de guerre* ('Anglesey') and T/Sgt Vincent M Rocca ('West Virginia') – was dropped there that night; like Brian, they were to contact 'Pascal' (the OSS officer, Ernest Floege), and were inserted on the ground at Montéchéroux where they were met by Maj

Johnston of team Brian. Yet again, the pannier containing the team's kit had gone astray, and its radio was smashed. Sgt Rocca contacted London on Brian's set and asked for a replacement for his own.

Henry met up with Pascal the following day, and learned that the situation in the area – which was saturated with German troops – made operations by non-francophones (Moore and Sgt Rocca had no more than a very basic command of the language) impossible. Furthermore, Pascal told Moore, there was simply nothing for them to do, particularly as they had no radio, and passed them on to 'Cmdt François', Col Boulaya's chief-of-staff. François, in turn, passed them on to 'Cmdt Boulin', who had responsibility for the Belfort/Montbéliard sector. He was then located at Pont-de-Roide, due south of Montbéliard, which was still – nominally, at least – in German hands, but by the time Henry arrived there the following day, American forces were in the process of occupying the town.

On 14 September Brian was able to obtain a radio for them, and Maj Johnston suggested that they might find gainful employment to the north of Montbéliard, around Héricourt. He produced two liaison agents, 'Milou' and 'Vivanti', who had some knowledge of the area, but Montcler was not satisfied with their briefing, and Moore decided to contact the Allied advance HQ both in the hope of gathering additional intelligence and to learn what he could of the plans for the forthcoming attack on the Belfort/Montbéliard sector. He and Montcler travelled to Besançon the following day, 15 September, and there met with the Sainfoin Mission (and probably, though this is nowhere stated, with team Timothy, which was also trying to find something useful to do). They learned of the plan to send Timothy into the area behind the Belfort Gap by way of Switzerland, and became excited, briefly, at the prospect of joining them, but it soon became apparent that this scheme would come to nothing, and they returned to Montécheroux to pick up their W/T operator and their luggage in a car they had bought. By the time they returned to Besançon, on 20 September, Sainfoin had been disbanded, and its British members had left for London. Still not ready to abandon their mission, the team turned around and retraced their route to Maiche, then located Cmdt Boulin in St-Hippolyte; no sooner had they arrived in the town than they received a message from London telling them to stand down, and set off for Paris the following day. They had to abandon their car along the way, and arrived in the French capital during the early hours of Monday, 25 September, in the back of a truck, to discover that one of their rucksacks had been rifled, and their remaining operational funds stolen, on the way.

Godfrey

In late August, SFHQ worked up a plan to send a Jedburgh team into the Haut-Rhin, to the east of the Vosges mountains, to contact such Resistance groups as there were there (few indeed, in an area which had close affinity with Germany and bordered on it, and had seen substantial numbers of Austrians relocated there from 1940 onwards) but also to attempt to prevent the destruction of important power stations and electrical distribution plant. It was deemed impossible to insert a team here by parachute, and so Godfrey – Lt Ian Forbes, of the Field Artillery ('Rhode Island'), Lt Pierre Laval, who took the name Jacques Morhanges ('Roscommon') and Sgt Frank A Hanson ('Roxburgh') – was to be dropped into the neighbouring Haute-Saône. After a series of delays and false starts, it finally left Harrington aboard a B-24 Liberator on the night of 11 September. The pilot had no luck locating the DZ initially; eventually he found some beacons and a recognition signal which seemed to satisfy him, and the team jumped. They landed near Confracourt, twenty-five kilometres west of Vesoul, in the company of a small *Maquis* which had assembled to collect an arms delivery – sixty containers dropped some time before Godfrey appeared on the scene. The *résistants* were already somewhat stretched by the unexpectedly large *parachutage*, but helped Godfrey search for their containers and packages. They found the former, but of the luggage there was no sign until the following day, when some of the team's personal kit, and some civilian clothes, were found. There was no trace of their rucksacks or radios.

It soon became clear that it would be out of the question for Godfrey to attempt to move east into the area where they had been briefed to operate; it proved very difficult even to make local reconnaissance patrols. Lt Laval, dressed in civilian clothes, failed to cross the River Saône to contact the FFI chief in the *département*, Cmdt Beaumont, after having been stopped three times and having his bicycle 'confiscated', though he was later able to link up with the chief of the Vesoul-Nord sector. Out of touch with London and effectively cut off, there was little for Godfrey to do save work with the local groups, and over the days which followed they participated in the liberation of a handful of villages and, on 14 September, the small town of Combeau-fontaine, where they set up a command post. That evening the spearhead elements of the *11ère Division Blindée* rolled into the town, with Jedburgh team Alan in tow, and for the first time Godfrey was able to make contact with SFHQ, using the splendid communications centre which Alan's radio operator, S/Lt Clause, had set up for the *Bataillon du Charollais*. Godfrey spent the next four days in company with team Alan, and on 19 September received orders to make their way to Lons-le-Saunier. For no clear reason, they went south from there, to Grenoble, and thence to Valence, Orange and Avignon, where they were interviewed by Neil Marten. He sent them by train to Nîmes, and they eventually reached Toulouse by way of Montpellier before completing their unplanned circuit of France by heading for Paris by way of Brive, Limoges, Vierzon and Orléans. They arrived back in London on 7 October.

Part Nine

ALSACE-LORRAINE

Jacob

Jacob was despatched to work alongside a major operation, Loyton, mounted by 2 SAS. The team comprised Capt Victor Gough ('Arran'), Lt Maurice Boisarrie, who called himself Baraud ('Connaught') and Sgt Ken Seymour ('Skye'). Victor Gough it was who won the competition to design the distinctive 'wings' which were the closest thing the Jedburghs had to a badge or insignia.

Even before D Day, SHAEF had begun to press SFHQ to insert a Jedburgh team into this area, and by 8 June the British Army's commander of airborne forces, Lt-Gen Sir Frederick 'Boy' Browning, was writing to the commanding officer of the SAS, Brig-Gen Rory McLeod, telling him that 'SHAEF Special Ops are anxious to get a Jedburgh team with two SAS officers in there as soon as possible to carry out a full recce and report on possibilities. SFHQ are not very keen and would prefer to wait till mid July'. In the event the team, together with the Loyton advance party of seven SAS all ranks and a five-man Phantom patrol from GHQ Liaison Regiment, was not inserted until the night of 12 August. They used a DZ to the east of Raon-l'Étape, near St-Dié in the Vosges Mountains, and the drop was not a complete success; in particular, the containers of weapons were simply appropriated by *maquisards* under the local leader, 'Col Maximum' (Col Bourgeois), as a fee for the use of the ground, and the radios were lost.

Sgt Ken Seymour, who said he 'seriously damaged the big toe of my left foot which necessitated my moving around without a shoe' when he landed, was the first Jedburgh casualty. The parachutists were taken from the DZ to Col Maximum's base, some ten kilometres away 'on top of a mountain'; at around 0800 on 17 August, word of an approaching enemy force arrived, and the *maquisards* made preparations to move off in the other direction. The Jedburgh officers were near the head of the column which departed at 1000; Seymour, together with some *maquisards* who had been detailed to assist him, was near its centre. His account

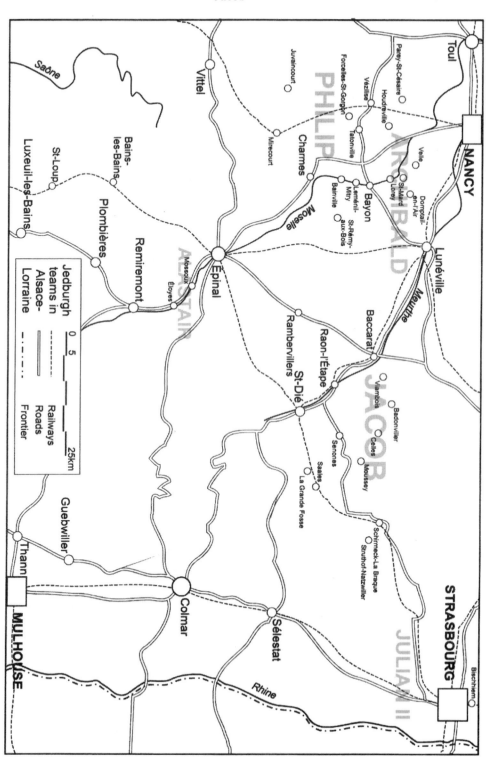

of what happened next has a rather artificial quality, and indeed, elements of it are contradicted by other reports. One should perhaps bear in mind that it was written some time after the event (in April 1945), and that Seymour had undergone much in the intervening period, but the suspicion that he was dissimulating in order to cover up his own malfeasance lingers:

At about 16.00hrs having descended the valley, we ran straight into more enemy troops coming from the other direction. We were proceeding along a narrow mountain path, single file … Firing started but from my position in the column I could not discover what was going on. The column left the path and endeavoured to scatter in the undergrowth. The enemy started to attack, whereupon the maquisards abandoned their arms and equipment and fled down the mountain side. That left me alone as owing to the twisted nature of the path, I could not see what was happening at the head of the column. I took cover behind a jutting out portion of rock and opened fire with my bren gun and when the ammunition was finished I took on [sic] my carbine and when the ammunition for that was finished I used my revolver. [This has been contradicted by one of the SAS officers who was present, who stated that Seymour did not fire a shot.] During this action I wounded several of the enemy who apparently did not know I was alone, they then made a careful advance on my position, about 15 of them advancing on me in a semi-circle. As they got closer they threw grenades at me and as I had no ammunition left I dived into a sort of cove [sic] mouth and destroyed my papers, wireless plan and cyrstals [sic] by burning them. [While it is theoretically possible to destroy crystals in this way, it would require a very large fire; it would have been far more effective simply to have smashed them. In the light of events to come, it would appear that Seymour did not, in fact, destroy either his radio plan or the frequency-controlling crystals.] During this time a grenade arrived and dropped near me but fortunately did not go off. Shortly afterwards a German appeared within about three yards from me. He shouted at me which I presumed meant to come out. As it was impossible for me to escape, I gave myself up. During this period I noticed a Captain of the SAS who appeared to have got away down the mountain side, but I have no knowledge of what happened to Capt Gough or Lt Baraud. I had no news of them until I reached the UK.

Seymour was the only man captured during Operation Loyton to survive the experience; all the others – thirty-three or thirty-four; there is a question mark over the events surrounding the death of one man – were killed, most within days of their capture, after they refused to answer questions. He was taken first to the command post of the unit which captured him, then, during the night, to the concentration camp at Schirmeck-La Braque, only twenty-five kilometres away, where he was threatened and deprived of food, but not physically maltreated during his interrogation by *SS-Obersturmbannführer* Wilhelm Schneider. 'Schneider, who remembers interrogating him, says that Seymour was not reluctant to give information,' says the report into the events surrounding Operation Loyton compiled by the SAS War Crimes Investigation Team, though post-war testimony from two of Schneider's men, Julius Gehrum and Marie Alphonse Uhring, suggests that he was in fact very forthcoming indeed, the latter saying that 'Schneider told me that the captured wireless operator had shown how to work the wireless set and the cipher'. Seymour's own account of that aspect of his interrogation contradicted that. Early on in his interrogation, he says, he was shown a Jedset radio, a Jedburgh one–time code pad and a 'silk' (a radio plan) and went on:

> I could not understand where these had come from, until they showed me a battledress blouse and asked me if it was mine. I discovered it belonged to the SAS Captain. He had apparently very carelessly left all his papers in his blouse which he had discarded. I expressed complete ignorance about these papers and then they asked me if I knew anything about the transmitter. I replied I knew nothing about wireless.'

He was later taken to Strasbourg, from there to a holding centre at Haguenau, some way to the north, then to Dulag Luft, the interrogation centre and transit camp for downed aircrew at Oberürsel near Frankfurt-am-Main, and was later incarcerated in a succession of PoW camps. Finally he was forced to participate in one of the 'death marches' around Germany in the final months of the war, in the course of which so many Allied PoWs died; was liberated by US troops at Bad Orb, near Frankfurt-am-Main, on 2 April 1945, and returned to the United Kingdom two days later.

Following Sgt Seymour's capture, Victor Gough continued to operate with Maurice Boissarie, although we have little information as to what, if anything, they were able to accomplish. A French source tells us, without even mentioning that he was a Jedburgh, that Boissarie took

command of a half-battalion of *maquisards* and was killed by a single
shot to the head during a pitched battle at a deserted farm named
Viambois, in the northern part of the Forêt des Reclos, north of Raon-
l'Étape, where they had their base, on 4 September. Thereafter Gough
operated alone, away from the Loyton party, and relied on *maquisards*
for support, passing messages for onward transmission to London by
Phantom and SAS signallers during occasional meetings with other
parachutists. He was seemingly captured at the end of September or the
beginning of October – his last radio message to London was transmitted from an SAS set on 18 September – but Lt-Col Brian Franks, the
commander of the Loyton party, reported seeing him in the company of
Col Maximum on the morning of 30 September. The next definite
sighting of him (by four Frenchmen who survived arrest and interrogation) was on 9 October. That day a small SAS party led by Lt David Dill,
captured near the village of Moussey, was handed over to an *Einsatz-
Kommando* commanded by *SS-Sturmbannführer* Hans-Dieter Ernst.
They were kept in a cell at the Maison Barthlèmy in Saales, and there
were reunited with three other SAS soldiers and with Victor Gough. By
the time Dill's party arrived at Saales, Gough had already undergone
prolonged interrogation and is said to have been badly beaten (though
he was in good enough health and spirits to have drawn a number of car-
toons while he was in captivity at Schirmeck, two of which were
reproduced in the SAS War Crimes Investigation Team's report on the
circumstances of his death).

The eight SAS ORs were later taken to a spot known as La Grande
Fosse, where a pit had already been dug to receive their bodies. They
were stripped naked and shot, and later Ernst reported to his superior,
SS-Standartenführer Dr Erich Isselhorst, that they had been killed while
trying to escape. The bodies of the eight men were recovered on 6
November 1945, and later re-buried in the Allied War Cemetery at
Durnbach near Bad Tolz in Bavaria. Lt Dill and Capt Gough – both of
whom had been notified to the Red Cross as prisoners of war – were
transferred to Schirmeck and thence to Rotenfels, a small holding
centre near Rastatt, between Baden-Baden and Karlsruhe, when the
concentration camp was evacuated on 22 November. They were shot in
a bomb crater at neighbouring Gaggenau on 25 November, along with
other captured SAS men and downed Allied aircrew. Their remains
were later recovered and buried at Durnbach.

Archibald

The next Jedburgh team to be despatched to eastern France, Archibald, fell foul of the adverse weather conditions of the second half of August 1944 but also, one suspects, to the general air of confusion which is manifested in the reports of other teams sent into action at this time. The tri-national team, which met up when its members were hospitalised after training accidents, comprised Maj Arthur Denning ('Cumberland'), Lt François Costes, who took Montlac as his *nom de guerre* ('Montgomery') and M/Sgt Roger L Pierre ('Sen'). Called up for 12 August, they finally got off, from Harrington, on the night of 25 August, and landed, safe and sound but in some disarray following the pilot's decision to fly across the wind, at a ground in the Forêt de Charmes on the border between the Vosges and Meurthe-et-Moselle. Many of their containers were smashed and weapons rendered useless (though Denning was later to describe how he worked alongside a Jugoslav captain 'who did remarkable work with hammer, cold chisel and pliers changing some 80 of the damaged arms into serviceable weapons, though perhaps not quite with Hythe [the British Army's School of Musketry] methods').

Another casualty was the team's radios, which were smashed beyond repair, but on a happier note, the thirty-five million francs they had brought for Planète, the DMR, was recovered intact. When an SAS party under Major Peter le Poer Power was dropped on to one of their grounds on the night of 27 August (to join Operation Loyton; it was dropped forty kilometres out of position), they were able to use its Jedset to ask for a replacement for their own, but 'presumably this direct contact [they had earlier sent messages by way of their liaison agent with SOE F Section's Pedagogue network, and also through Planète, and were to continue to do so as and when they could, though this was not a satisfactory arrangement] was responsible for London omitting to replace original sets'. Team Alastair also dropped on to the same field that night, but Denning makes no mention of that in his report.

Denning and Costes were involved in skirmishes with small groups of enemy troops as they moved around the region trying to assess the need and potential of the local Resistance groups – this was a relatively simple business, for only Capt Noël's group, which had met their insertion, proved at all serious – but on 30 August they received warning that a strong German force was on its way to sweep through the forest, and decided to move to Leménil-Mitry, a short distance to the north-west, across the River Moselle. The Germans, when they came, found no trace of the partisans, but burned the village of St-Rémy-aux-Bois anyway. Four days later, Costes led an assault on a German supply dump at Tantonville which saw the dump burned; eighty enemy died and nineteen were made prisoner, but at the considerable cost of ten *maquis-ards* killed and several, including the Jedburgh officer, wounded. He was later taken to a German military hospital at Luneville, 'an innocent caught in the cross-fire', and underwent surgery.

That same day Denning made contact with American forces to the west, but on his way back to Leménil he, too, was wounded, though less seriously. That night, in an attempt to safeguard its bridges, the partisans took the town of Charmes, but American forces were unable to come to their assistance, and the town was retaken four days later, with heavy casualties on both sides. By now the area between the Moselle and the smaller River Madon, which roughly parallels it, was effectively a no-man's-land, with both German and American forces mounting armoured patrols but with neither in a commanding position. East of the Moselle, the Germans were present in force, and Denning found movement there next to impossible; virtually all the bridges across the river in this sector had been destroyed, one of them – at Charmes – being blown up while a US armoured reconnaissance unit was crossing. Denning continued to try to gather intelligence to pass on to the American forces, but with very little success. Team Philip arrived in the area on 3 September, and Denning says that due to his immobility, its leader, Capt Jean Liberos, agreed to take over the area further north, towards Nancy; there are inconsistencies between his version of events and that of Liberos.

Towards the end of the first week of September, US forces made a renewed attempt to cross the Moselle, and got infantry companies across at three locations: Velles, St-Mard and Lorey. By now Noël's group had increased to well over a thousand men, all of them armed, and they were of real assistance, advancing to within a thousand metres of the Americans in the German rear and finally taking a key village, Domptail-en-l'Air, and holding it long enough for the Americans to arrive in strength. Denning's freedom of movement improved, but was soon curtailed, if only temporarily, when he was picked up by American security police; they refused to believe his story and whisked him off to Paris to be identified, but he was back the next day. His job was almost over, however; for ten days more he busied himself trying to keep Noël's enhanced battalion in one piece while at the same time seeking approval for a move further east, towards St-Dié, to continue his work as a Jedburgh. He was overtaken by events – a major conventional offensive towards the Meurthe – and before the month's end he and Sgt Pierre returned to London by way of Paris.

Alastair

Like Archibald, team Alastair – Maj Oliver Brown of the Buffs ('Kent'), who had been Chief Instructor at Milton Hall, Lt René Karrière, who used the name Mâitre ('Donegal'), and Sgt GN Smith ('Lincoln') – was supposed to have been deployed on 12 August; it finally got away on the night of 27 August, but it is clear that there was a mix-up of some proportions in despatching insertion missions that night. Alastair had been briefed to operate near St-Dié, close to where Jacob was working, but when they landed (and were joined by the stick of ten SAS men led by Maj Power) they discovered they were forty kilometres west of there. Of the aircraft carrying French officers who were to have operated with them there was no sign.

The Jedburghs left for Rambervillers, in the direction of St-Dié, the following day, dressed in civilian clothes and without identification papers of any sort, and moved twice more in the days which followed. At Mossoux, on their sixth day in France, they finally met 'Cmdt Didier' and 'Cmdt Étienne', the FFI leaders in the region, and mapped out with them an ambitious programme of supply operations, the first phase of which called for drops by three aircraft each on no less than fourteen grounds, all on the same night. The weapons dropped would be used to arm enough men to establish *cordons sanitaires* around zones earmarked to receive daylight drops, and these would be operations on a par with Cadillac or Zebra, bringing weapons enough to equip a guerrilla army of 25,000 men.

They moved again that night, to a village on the banks of the Moselle named Éloyes. Installed in their new safe houses, the supply plan was radioed to London, and Alastair settled down to wait for a response. It was a week in coming, and was negative; due to 'unforeseen circumstances and situations beyond our control', SFHQ decided it was impossible to send anything by night. Then they cancelled the daylight operations as well, Planète, who had obtained approval for them on a recent hurried trip to London, having 'failed to comply with some of the conditions'. During that week of enforced idleness, the general situation deteriorated to the point where it was impossible for the Jedburghs to move about the area – even going from one safe house to another was difficult – and eventually they were functionally useless, all contact with the Resistance lost. In fact, that may have been no bad thing from their point of view; security around the partisan groups was sketchy at best, and much of the extra local pressure was due to the arrival in the area of a strong contingent of *Waffen-SS*, tasked with rooting them out. Their primary objective in this sector was the area north of Éloyes (further east they targeted the farm at Viambois, where Maurice Boisarrie of team Jacob was killed), and when the attack came, the 300-plus *maquisards* encamped there, although warned of its likelihood, were unprepared. They were taking heavy casualties when fate, in the form of a flight of Allied ground-attack aircraft, took a hand; they strafed and bombed the German troops, and many of the *maquisards* were able to escape in the confusion. They were forced, however, to leave behind a significant number of dead and wounded, and the latter were, of course, all killed out of hand. This, coupled with the loss of most of their arms and equipment, demoralised them, and they were never again an effective force.

From then on, Alastair's task was restricted to gathering fragmentary intelligence, and by the end of the third week of September, it was clear that the team could achieve nothing more. Brown decided they should make their way to Allied lines, and they did so, meeting up briefly with team Jim on the way, and passing on such information as they had on the situation in the Moselle Valley north of Ramiremont to American troops before making their way to Paris and thence to London, arriving there on 3 October.

Philip

Team Philip – it was originally designated as Rupert; why or when the name was changed is unclear, though French sources say it was made the day the team landed in France – was made up of Capt Jean Liberos, who called himself De Rouen ('Kintyre'), Lt Robert A Lucas ('Caithness') and Spec. 3 Joseph M Grgat of the US Navy ('Leinster'). The team dropped on to a ground named Restaurant near the town of Mirecourt, close to the northern border of the Vosges, on the night of 31 August. The men landed safely, but two leg bags attached to a single parachute, and containing Liberos' and Lucas' personal kit, civilian clothing and carbines, were never found. It seems clear that, once again, the team was dropped in the wrong place; there were two Resistance groups to meet them, but little organisation and no sign of the DMR, Planète, or anyone representing him. On the evening of 2 September they set off for Nancy, where Planète was rumoured to be, but already that day Philip had met an American reconnaissance unit at Juvaincourt, just north of Mirecourt. They encountered more Americans along the way, and spent the night at Forcelles-St-Gorgon.

The following day, 3 September, they were taken to Leménil-Mitry; it is unclear whether they had been led to expect to find team Archibald there, but they did not, for the wounded Lt Costes had already been taken to the hospital in Luneville, and Maj Denning and Sgt Pierre had gone in search of American forces. Liberos tells us that the *Maquis* Noël was in action at Bayon and Bainville that day, trying to prevent the demolition of the river crossings there, but getting severely mauled in the process and that he took charge of the operations in the absence of the *maquisards'* leader, who had gone with Denning.

Liberos spent the next day gathering as much information as he could about the situation further north in the *département*, and at 1900 Philip set off for Nancy once more, in a truck, with three *maquisards* as guides. They had reached Houdreville, west of Vézelise and barely twelve kilometres from Leménil-Mitry, when they became aware that they were being followed by 'a platoon of motor machine-guns', which opened fire on them; they managed to gain the cover of some bushes, but Liberos and Lucas lost contact with Grgat in the process, and in the event, the 'enemy' proved to be an American reconnaissance unit. Philip's first priority now was to search for the missing NCO; there is a suspicion that Grgat's morale was deficient from the start – a French source, in describing his departure, talks of him 'losing his nerve and disappearing into the dark when things were getting tense'. Liberos seems to have had doubts about him, for on the night of 3 September, when he met Arthur Denning, he made an odd request of him regarding his radio operator:

> As he [Pierre] had been deprived of his radio equipment, which was destroyed in dropping, and as he was a better operator than Grgat, Major Denning was asked to give him to Team Philip (the two teams had a similar mission and were to work in the same department of Meurthe-et-Moselle). For personal considerations, Major Denning did not see fit to comply with this request.

Liberos and Lucas passed the night in woodland west of Houdreville, together with the American cavalry unit, and spent much of the next day, 5 September, looking for Grgat, to no effect. Towards evening they moved to Parey-St Césaire for security reasons, leaving the mayor of Vézelise in charge of the search. All day long there had been the sound of heavy fighting from the direction of Nancy, and next morning they began a wide loop around to the west, hoping to enter the city from the direction of Toul. On the way they made contact with another American advance unit, whose commander encouraged them to remain where they were for the moment; they passed another night in the forest, and reached Toul, newly fallen to American forces, just before noon the next day. It soon became clear that it would be impossible to enter Nancy, and instead, on 9 September, the pair moved to US 3rd Army HQ, to contact its Special Forces detachment; Liberos reports meeting Arthur Denning there, who was able to tell him that Grgat was safe, and being repatriated to London via Paris.

Liberos reported to Lt-Col Powell, the officer commanding the SF detachment, who had enough authority to issue new orders to the team: he and Lucas were to go to Verdun, where a new radio operator would be found for them, and arm the partisans there and at Conflans, to the east – a total of over 3,000 men – in order to establish a *cordon sanitaire* on the 3rd Army's left flank as it approached Metz. A radio operator was indeed provided, and during every scheduled transmission period over the next four days, between 11 and 15 September, Liberos asked London for weapons; there is no record of him even having received a reply and it seems likely that these transmissions were never received. By 16 September he was back with Lt-Col Powell again, and it seems to have been concluded that Philip's work was over, and that Liberos and Lucas should withdraw to Paris and await further instructions. They reached Paris on 18 September, and returned to London on the weekend of 23/24 September.

Julian II

The last Jedburgh team to be deployed in France, Julian II, had none of the personnel who had mounted Julian I in the Indre, and the reason it did not receive a new code name is unclear. It was led by Capt Jean-Paul Souquet, who called himself Kerneval ('Carnavon'), who had earlier led team Felix in Brittany, with S/Lt René Meyer, who called himself Robert Mersiol ('Yonne'), the radio operator from team Hugh in the Indre, together with a French subaltern named Scherrer who took the name Sauvage. It was thus, and uniquely, an all-French team. The original plan had called for the other two members of Felix, Capt Marchant and Sgt Colvin, to have accompanied Capt Souquet, but that was changed a few days after the team was first alerted, on 10 October, when the War Office withdrew permission for British personnel to be sent on missions to France. Meyer and Scherrer were chosen to replace them because they were both natives of Alsace, the region where the team was to operate; Souquet also knew it well, having been stationed there pre-war.

By the time the team was briefed, on 10 October, weather conditions over the Vosges mountains had begun to deteriorate, and the plan to parachute the men on to a DZ on the Rossberg, a mountain to the west of Thann, had eventually to be abandoned (the team later learned that *Sipo*-SD had infiltrated the *maquisards* who were to have met them, and that they, themselves, had made up the reception committee). When they were finally deployed, on 10 November, they were flown to Épernay aboard a Dakota, and then travelled to Nancy by road. Here they met Maj Johnston and Sgt Smith of team Brian, who were to relay messages for them, as well as senior FFI officers from Alsace. It was decided eventually – there is a marked lack of any sense of urgency in the affairs of team Julian II – that they should infiltrate into Alsace on foot, through the Raon-l'Étape forest, to Colmar, a distance of about a hundred kilometres. In the event, Strasbourg fell on 23 November, and then Mulhouse, two days later; there was no longer any need to infiltrate Julian II clandestinely.

This further change of plan, however, seems to have caused some confusion. Julian was first pulled back as far as Luxeuil, and then finally, on 13 December, ordered to Strasbourg. From there they were to have been infiltrated into the Colmar pocket, but it took a further fortnight to agree the details of their communications schedules and frequencies, and by the time they were ready to go, Colmar was sealed tight, and infiltration was impossible. On 1 January they were told to prepare to pull out.

That morning, the German forces which had been driven from Strasbourg mounted a strong counter-offensive; the city held out through the night and the following day, but in the early hours of 3 January, cracks began to appear in the defenders' morale. There was some panic, and fearing being surrounded, the American division covering the city pulled back to the west. By dawn, the liberated city was silent, the streets empty, as the Strasbourgeoisie waited for the Panzer divisions to return. In the event, a single German battalion entered the city, from the north, at Bischeim; elsewhere, men of the FFI, just two depleted battalions in all, were able to put on enough of a show of resistance to convince them that they had insufficient firepower to prevail. On 6 January the situation was saved when the 3rd *Tirailleurs Algerien* reached the city, but the respite was only temporary, for the Germans had recrossed the Rhine in force both north and south of Strasbourg, and First French Army was stretched dangerously thin. While Souquet and Scherrer laboured to integrate fresh recruits into the ranks of the FFI, Meyer and two additional operators worked every radio schedule, begging London to retransmit requests for arms drops to EMFFI in Paris. No response was forthcoming from EMFFI, and it was not until the end of the month that the situation along the Rhine began to stabilise once more, with the arrival of more French units and the return of American troops in large numbers. At that, team Julian II stood down, and Jedburgh operations in France came to an end.

AFTERWORD

For an endeavour essentially experimental in nature, the Jedburgh Programme was a considerable success. While it is impossible to quantify its results, even in an area where more or less reliable data, such as the numbers of weapons delivered, and the numbers of resistance fighters armed and trained, are available, it is clear that it made a considerable mark, especially when its relatively low start-up and maintenance costs are factored into the equation. One thing in particular stands out: the low cost in human lives for what was considered to be a very high-risk venture. It was made clear to volunteers that they could expect very high casualties, up to as much as fifty per cent, but in the event, out of the 280 Jedburgh deployments in France (including those who carried out multiple missions), only fourteen, five per cent, died, three of them as the result of accidents.

The performance of the support echelon, however, is another matter; serious criticism can be levelled at the degree of support the teams received while they were in the field, specifically in terms of resupply. Time and again, after-action reports record requests for supply missions going unacknowledged, and many which did arrive contained material which was at best of limited value. All too often, much of the material which did reach the right place at the right time was destroyed in the process, when the parachutes attached to the containers and panniers failed to deploy, usually simply because the static lines attaching them to the aircraft had not been hooked up correctly. While there is perhaps some explanation for supply drops failing to materialise, especially during the latter part of the period during which the teams were active (when there was concern at a high level that arms, in particular, were falling into the hands of men who were more interested in preparing for a factional struggle than they were in driving out the German invader), there is certainly no excuse for the aircrafts' loadmasters failing to perform a basic but undemanding task.

The other, almost ubiquitous, complaint the Jedburghs made concerned the timing of their insertion. As we have noted, only thirteen

Jedburgh missions were launched in June, with eleven more following in July; virtually all of the teams inserted later (and not a few of those twenty-four) complained that they arrived in their operational areas far too late, and that they could have accomplished much more had they been inserted earlier. The reluctance to put teams in place before Over-lord D-Day is perhaps understandable, given the fanatical determination not to take even the smallest risk in the timing, and more importantly, the location of the invasion being betrayed, but the delay in sending more teams in as soon as the landings had taken place is more difficult either to understand or justify.

There is little to criticise in terms of the Jedburghs' equipment itself; when they landed safely, the all-important Jedset and B2 radio trans-ceiver sets worked as well as had been expected, but it is clear that more attention should have been paid to the way they were delivered. In par-ticular, the practice of carrying a set in a leg bag, which was released while the parachutist was in the air, to hang at the end of a twenty-foot cord, and which then hit the ground at considerable speed, caused many sets to be damaged, often beyond repair. It appears that this method was not trialed in practice jumps; had it been, its fallibility would perhaps have been demonstrated. There was general praise for the way in which teams were delivered by the RAF, but some criticism of the way USAAF personnel performed; in particular, many American pilots flew across the drop zone beacons, instead of down the line of them, and some both failed to slow the aircraft and dropped from either too low or too high.

After their French operations were stood down, many of the Jed-burghs later transferred to the Far East (though some served in Italy, and Bill Colby – who was later to become Director of the USA's Central Intelligence Agency – took command of an Operational Group in Norway). The British contingent operated mainly in Burma and Malaya, as part of Force 136, the American chiefly in Burma and China (with excursions into what had been French Indo-China) as part of Detachments 101 and 202, and the French in Indo-China. Even less has been written about their exploits there than about their work in France. The first British team, which comprised Capt Thomas Carew from team Basil, Capt John Cox from Ivor and Sgt John Sharp from Isaac, went into action in the South-East Asian Theatre as early as 27 December.

Appendix A
FRANCE UNDER GERMAN OCCUPATION

Defeat and Occupation

German forces, which had invaded the Low Countries on 10 May 1940, crossed into France three days later. The French and their British allies fought a desperate rearguard action, but by 1 June the invaders were in Amiens, and by 11 June they were on the Seine and threatening Paris. By the time Paul Reynaud, prime minister since 21 March, was replaced by Marshal Philippe Pétain on 16 June, the majority of French people welcomed his order to the army to lay down its weapons, even though this meant some 1.6m French soldiers passing into captivity.

Under Axis rule the country was divided into nine zones, the two largest being the German-occupied zone and the *Zone Libre*, administered by Pétain's government from the spa town of Vichy. This situation endured until November 1942, when Hitler ordered Operation Attila, the occupation of the *Zone Libre*, after the Allied landings in North Africa (Operation Torch). The large area under Italian control also passed into German hands, after Marshal Badoglio signed a separate peace in September 1943. The only French terrestrial armed forces permitted under the terms of the June 1940 agreement were the *Armée de l'Armistice*, which was limited to 100,000 men, in metropolitan France, and the similarly sized *Armée d'Afrique*, which was increased first to 127,000 and later to 225,000 men but which was removed from the Axis ambit when North Africa fell to the Allies. The *Armée de l'Armistice* was permitted only light weapons, and was largely disbanded when the *Zone Libre* was occupied.

Forced Labour

The French prisoners of war were effectively hostages to the good behaviour of the rest of the population, but they became pawns in a larger game when Germany demanded that Frenchmen and women 'volunteer' for labour in Germany, and offered to release PoWs in the ratio of 1:3 as an enticement. Initially the *relève* (literally, 'relief') applied only to young men; it was extended to include all fit males between eighteen and fifty, and all single women between twenty-one and thirty-five, in September 1942. The initiative was quite successful to begin with, and a quarter of a million workers were enrolled by the year's end, in return for whom a total of 90,747 PoWs were eventually released. It was clear, however, that the supply – from what one author has described as 'the desperate and the marginal' in French society; most of them immigrants, many living alone, and few employed – would soon dry up, particularly when reports of the volunteers' living conditions, which were little better than those in the PoW cages, began to filter back. In January 1943 a new demand was made for a further 250,000 workers; the *relève* clearly would not supply such a number, and Pierre Laval, who had long pulled Pétain's strings but had been forced to assume power openly after Operation Attila, introduced *Service du Travail Obligatoire* (forced labour) in consequence.

The STO applied initially only to men in the classes of 1920, 1921 and 1922, who had avoided conscription in 1940. It was easier to implement than the *relève* because it was compulsory, and required all those eligible to register. Agricultural workers (and miners) were at first given exemption, but STO still cut deep into the rural village population for the first time, and has been cited as the root of rural resistance. Small numbers of village people left their homes and went to live, usually with relatives, in more remote areas, in order to escape deportation; but the majority of evaders actually stayed put and succeeded with the connivance either of the officials of the *commune* in which they lived or thanks to their employers claiming them to be indispensable, although this left them appallingly vulnerable. A similarly small minority of the urban workforce either went into hiding or fled the industrial towns for the countryside, where they were welcomed as a useful (and cheap) addition to the labour force in the agricultural areas. None the less, 646,421 Frenchmen and women were deported to Germany to slave in the factories and the mines by the end of 1943.

Some of those who left their homes to escape the STO were later to become *maquisards*, and at this point we must clarify the meaning of the term, as well as it origins. The word 'maquis' seems to have originated in Corsican dialect, and is used to describe the scrub or brush which covers much of the island; it was imported into French with the same meaning and was taken up by the men who took to the hills and forests to escape German repression. To be a *maquisard*, certainly at that time, did not equate to being an armed *résistant*. Most *maquisards* were simply *réfractaires*, which translates roughly as 'rebels' or 'conscientious objectors' denoting those who absconded to avoid the labour draft. Such men had no particular wish to fight the Germans, and their primary aim was to avoid being deported. Even in the summer of 1944, Jedburgh teams were to report that sometimes as few as ten per cent of the *maquisards* they encountered would have given 'to kill Germans' as the prime reason for their being with the bands. Indeed, as time went on there formed a natural division between those who had taken to the *maquis* in order to take up arms against the occupying Germans, and those who, to begin with, anyway, had fled their homes in order to escape deportation into forced labour; the former, perhaps inevitably, generally thought themselves superior.

The Mechanism of Oppression

German – or more accurately, Axis – forces stationed in France fell into two categories: there were combat troops, there primarily to defend against re-invasion, and there were occupation troops, whose task was to keep domestic order. The former, comprising units of both the *Heeres* (the German Army) and the military wing of the *Schutzstaffeln* (the *Waffen-SS*) were some of the best fighting men in the world, but the latter were largely of inferior quality, and many were actually captives – Russians, Ukrainians, Azerbaijanis, even Indian troops taken in North Africa – who had opted to switch sides rather than die slowly in the PoW cages. They were little more than cannon fodder, but none the less valuable for that, particularly since they were frequently characterised by a terrifying disregard for human life, and could be relied upon to carry out any order, no matter what its nature. Most of their officers and senior NCOs were German, of course, but as well as taking orders from their superiors in the *Heeres*, they were also subservient to the *Reichssicherheitshauptamt* (RSHA, the Reich Security Main Office), and in particular the intelligence and security service, the *Sicherheitsdienst* (SD*)*, and the *Sicherheitspolizei (Sipo)*, the latter widely known as the *Gestapo (Geheim*

Staatspolizei, State Secret Police), which formed the largest part of it. By early 1944, the *Sipo*-SD, which had always made very liberal use of informers, had been augmented by men (and not a few women) recruited from the far Right of French society: the *Milice Française*.

The *Milice*

Coincidentally, when Pierre Laval established the STO, he was also facing a serious shortfall in police numbers, and the situation was exacerbated by the need to enforce the new orders. He was presented with a solution by a right-wing activist named Joseph Darnand, a decorated hero of World War One, who had been one of Eugène Deloncle's Jew-hating, Jew-baiting, eventually Jew-murdering *cagoulardes* in the late 1930s. Darnand fought heroically again in 1940 and after the armistice became leader of an ex-serviceman's organisation known as the *Légion Française des Combattants* (LFC) in Nice. By mid-1941 he had created an élite within the LFC known as the *Service de l'Ordre Légionnaire* (SOL), and by the autumn he had taken the SOL so far to the right that it had lost all contact with the *Légion*. In January 1943 Laval transformed the SOL into the *Milice Française*, with the twin objectives of rounding up Jews, and those eligible for the STO, for deportation. Initially, the Germans eyed the *Milice* with suspicion, and it was not allowed to bear arms (nor even to exist, in the old Occupied Zone), and Darnand became increasingly frustrated. Then, in August, he – a man who had 'about as much political intelligence as a kerbstone', to quote Laval – had an inspiration: he swore a personal oath of loyalty to Adolf Hitler, and became a *Sturmbannführer* (Major) in the *Waffen-SS*'s *Charlemagne* Division. From then on the SS began to channel money and arms to the *Milice*, and the pistol holsters which used to be stuffed with paper now contained guns instead. It was split into two main parts: the majority were part-time volunteers, but some twenty per cent of its total force (of perhaps 30,000 by 1944), the younger, fitter members, were permanently mobilised and lived in barracks, and were known as the *Franc-Gardes*. The *Milice* was expanded to operate throughout France in December 1943, but was always more powerful in the south. Its chief strength lay in local recruitment – the *Miliciens* operated largely in the districts in which they had grown up; they knew their neighbours and their habits and were quick to spot newcomers or tell-tale changes in established behaviour patterns.

The Structure of Resistance

In a strictly formal sense, the French Resistance can be traced back to 18 June 1940, when forty-nine-year-old Brigadier-General Charles André Joseph Marie de Gaulle, the youngest and most junior general in the French Army (but also, if only briefly, the nation's junior war minister), who had been brought out of France by the RAF, issued his famous rallying cry to the French people courtesy of the BBC, which thought so little of it that it did not bother to record it for posterity. One of his first acts was to set up a small intelligence department, the *Bureau Central de Renseignements et d'Action Militaire* (BCRAM; it later lost the '*Militaire*' from its title, and later still split into two, with 'offices' in London and Algiers, which were known as BCRA(L) and BCRA(A) in consequence). He had been largely pre-empted by SOE, which had established its own F Section, and subsequently added RF Section, when de Gaulle accepted a broad proposal for co-operation between BCRA and SOE in mid-December 1941. Although BCRA was a poor relation in many ways, it did important work in its own right; its supply and agent delivery systems – the *Bureau d'Opérations Aériennes* (BOA) operating from the United Kingdom, and the *Service d'Aterrissage et Parachutages* (SAP) from Algeria – were an effective complement to those run by the British and Americans, though naturally they depended on them both for the supplies dropped and the aircraft which carried them.

The reality of resistance was more complex. The first acts of defiance were minor, personal affairs, carried out largely on the spur of the moment, and it was not until underground newspapers began to spring up that there was a unifying force in the movement. Even after resisters began to group together there was still the fractured nature of French political life, and a long-standing tradition of factional in-fighting, to be overcome. The divisions, not surprisingly, ran along the fundamental fault lines of French politics, separating Right from Left, and then further subdividing those basic factions (the Right in particular, de Gaulle's natural political home, was additionally split according to whether adherents did or did not accept the general's leadership). Even the Catholic and the Protestant churches had their own agendas. But by far the most important division was the chasm which separated the *Parti Communiste Français* (PCF; the Communist Party of France) and its puppet, the *Front National*, from the rest, and it is important to keep in mind that during the first year of occupation, until Hitler broke his pact with Stalin by invading the Soviet Union on 22 June 1941, the PCF officially supported the Germans.

Until unification was achieved, there was little that even the Special Operations Executive and later the Office of Strategic Services could do to help the resistance groups in a practical sense. It was through the efforts of men such as Pierre Brosselette, Christian Pineau and particularly Jean Moulin, the young *préfet* of the Department of Eure-et-Loir, that the Rightist factions agreed to pool their resources and form, first of all, the *Armée Secrète* (AS; Secret Army), on 2 October 1942, and then – and much more reluctantly, for by now the Communists were involved – the *Conseil National de la Résistance* (CNR; the National Resistance Council) in May 1943. After Moulin's arrest and subsequent death the following month the fragile union could easily have fallen apart, but it survived, and then developed into a truly national resistance movement, although when de Gaulle took a more direct hand in Resistance affairs, and declared that all individual groups would henceforth fall under the umbrella of the *Forces Françaises de l'Intérieur*, in February 1944, the Communists rebelled, and their *Franc Tireurs et Partisans* opted to remain independent.

By then, however, the movement had been augmented by a numerically small but influential group known as the *Organisation de Résistance de l'Armée* (ORA), formed from officers of the *Armée de l'Armistice*, who, long before the Germans occupied the southern zone, had begun secreting quantities of weapons and equipment against just such an eventuality. Originally Pétainist to a man, after the *Maréchal* had been marginalised by Laval they lined up behind de Gaulle's ineffective (even though he had American backing) Algiers-based rival for the leadership of Free French forces, General Henri-Honoré Giraud. By the time the amalgamation of all 'responsible' resistance groups into the FFI was being mooted, at the end of 1943, Giraud had accepted that he could not oust de Gaulle, and the ORA had switched its allegiance. It possessed important qualities that the *Armée Secrète* lacked – military experience, discipline and training, as well as those buried guns – and was in consequence welcomed into the ranks of the FFI, albeit rather grudgingly, since many already there both saw it as *arriviste* and mistrusted its leaders, reasoning that these were the very same men who had destroyed France by their inability to defend her in 1940.

No one knew then, and no one knows now, how many active *résistants*, ready to bear arms and engage in armed struggle, there were in France at any time during World War Two. Most of the figures which were produced at the time were politically-motivated guesses, and often bore no relation to reality, alhough we would do well to recall that some 24,000 *résistants* died during the liberation (and in total perhaps four times that number gave their lives). Dewaverin's office estimated that the *Armée Secrète* numbered around 125,000 in March 1943, around 210,000 in April and over 300,000 by the end of the year. Frankly, though, such estimates are meaningless, and anyway do not include the FTP groups, which were said by some to represent ten per cent of the total but have been put more recently, by revisionists, at anything up to five times that proportion. Even if the AS *could* have put a quarter of a million men into the field in the autumn of 1943, however, it could have armed no more than a very modest percentage of them.

The *Forces Françaises de l'Intérieur*

By early 1944, the French Resistance had achieved a solid status, but already serious questions were being asked of its leadership. Was the movement, born of and fostered by the middle and lower-middle class, but now with the working class as its foot-soldiers, to be hijacked by the very reactionary elements which had failed France so catastrophically in 1940? Not if the Communists had anything to say about it. The FTP vowed that it would not allow the remaking of the country to be entrusted to such elements. That it probably lacked the power to make such a proscription stick was irrelevant; it had structure and discipline, a lot of members and significant numbers of weapons – enough to ensure disruption, at least, and pose the terrifying threat of civil war for control of France after she had been liberated.

The habitually poor co-ordination of overall Resistance operations with post-invasion strategy was largely a reflection of the uncertain relationship of contending factions within and outside France with one another and with SHAEF. There was little in the way of general agreement, and the resulting power struggle frequently threatened to tear apart any small vestige of real cohesion. De Gaulle, intransigent as ever, insisted that the *Gouvernement Provisoire de la République Française* (GPRF; the Provisional Government of the French Republic), with himself at its head, and certainly not SHAEF, should decide the destiny of the French nation. In truth, de Gaulle probably had no more real confidence in the combat-effectiveness of the Resistance than did SHAEF, but he did appreciate the political capital to be accrued by at least paying it lip service, and exploited it to good effect during the post-liberation power struggle. When considering SHAEF's attitude to the liberation we should recall one thing above all others – its objective was the defeat of Germany, and the liberation of France, though admittedly important, was basically a side-issue. SHAEF's nightmare was the prospect of a potentially catastrophic civil war erupting in France before the war against Germany was concluded. The primary result of that consideration was to restrict the amount and type of weaponry made available to the partisans, but it also affected the decision not to call for a *levée en masse*.

De Gaulle himself had actually advocated general insurrection at one time, but by mid-1944 he was talking instead of a limited uprising, to be directed and managed by the GPRF through the FFI and regional leaders chosen by him, known as *Délégués Militaires Régionals* (DMR; Regional Military Delegates). They were sent into France from September 1943, and were later supplemented by departmental delegates (DMD); although they had no formal authority over commanders of individual resistance groups, and thus no stick with which to beat them into line, they offered very large carrots in their ability to organise supply operations. The CNR, however, with its own agenda, had pre–empted de Gaulle's attempts to take control of the Resistance by forming a Military Action Committee, COMAC (*Commission d'Action Militaire*) in February 1944. It might not speak for all the resistance movements, but it did have a powerful voice, and was equally determined to emerge as the only valid command authority. The CNR/COMAC appointees and those of BCRA were thus often at loggerheads.

SOE and OSS looked on, in mixed wonder and exasperation, at the machinations of the French Resistance. All they could do, finally, was supply it with arms, ammunition and explosives without any measure of control as to how, where, when or even if those munitions would be used. The only influence they could exert was by way of the organisers and instructors they inserted into France from 1941 onwards, and that depended essentially on the strength of character of those individuals. That most proved themselves to be outstanding is a tribute not only to them but also to the men and women who selected, trained and supported them.

It would be comforting to relate that once the invasion had taken place, the conflicts within and between the resistance movements resolved themselves, and that all were somehow magically united, but that, of course, was not the case. Not only did Right and Left remain at odds with each other, but individual warlords on both sides continued to dispute the leadership of their own factions. To that uncomfortable mix must be added the 'twenty-fifth hour men' who emerged from the woodwork as soon as the coast looked like clearing, to begin their self-imposed tasks of both seizing control and settling scores, as well as the even more dangerous criminal gangs who were to use patriotism as a cloak for pillage and murder.

Appendix B

THE JEDBURGH TEAMS

Operation/Team	Name	Rank	Workname	Codename	Nat	Location	Inserted
ALAN	Cannicott, Stanley M	Capt	Cannicott	Pembroke	UK	Saône-et-Loire	13 Aug
	Toussaint, Robert	Lt	Gairaud	Ariège	Fr		
	Clause, Robert	S/Lt	de Heysen	Kroner	Fr		
ALASTAIR	Brown, Oliver H	Maj	Brown	Kent	UK	Vosges	28 Aug
	Karrière, René	Lt	Maître	Donegal	Fr		
	Smith, G N	Sgt	Smith	Lincoln	UK		
ALEC	Thomson, George C	Lt	Thomson	Cromarty	US	Cher	10 Aug
	Bordes, Alain	Lt	Allet	Oxford	Fr		
	White, John A	T/3	White	Colorado	US		
ALEXANDER	de la Tousche, René	Lt	Thouville	Leix	Fr	Creuse	13 Aug
	Alsop, Stewart J	Lt	Alsop	Rona	US		
	Franklin, Norman R	T/Sgt	Franklin	Cork	US		
ALFRED	MacDonald, Lewis	Capt	MacDougal	Argyll	UK	Oise	25 Aug
	Herenguel, Jean-Pierre	Lt	de Wavrant	Aude	Fr		
	Key, Albert	Sgt	Key	Wampum	UK		
AMMONIA	Austin, Benton McD	Capt	Austin	Gaspard	US	Dordogne	10 Jun

Codename	Name	Rank					
	Le Compte, Raymond	Lt	Conte	Ludovic	Fr		16 Aug
	Berlin, Jacob B	Sgt	Berlin	Marcial	US		
	Verneuil, Jean	S/Lt	Verneuil	Marcellin	Fr		
ANDREW	Coombe-Tennant, Henry	Maj	Coombe-Tennant	Rupel	UK	Ardennes	16 Aug
	d'Oultremont, Édouard	Lt	d'Oultremont	Demer	Bel		
	Harrison, Frank	Sgt	Harrison	Nethe	UK		
ANDY	Parkinson, Ronald	Maj	Parkinson	Fife	UK	Haute Vienne	12 Jul
	Vermeulen, J	Maj	Verneuil	Carlow	Fr		
	Loosmore, Glyn	Sgt	Loosmore	Lundy	UK		
ANTHONY	Stasse, Maurice	Capt	Deprez	Perth	Fr	Saône-et-Loire	15 Aug
	Starring, Mason B 'Buz'	Lt	Starring	Nebraska	US		
	Bradner, John L	T/Sgt	Bradner	Pfennig	US		
ARCHIBALD	Denning, Arthur	Maj	Denning	Cumberland	UK	Meurthe-et-Moselle	26 Aug
	Costes, François	Lt	Montlac	Montgomery	Fr		
	Pierre, Roger L	M/Sgt	Pierre	Sen	US		
ARNOLD	de Carville, Michel	Capt	Coudray	Sussex	Fr	Marne	25 Aug
	Monahan, James	Lt	Monahan	Londonderry	UK		
	de Ville, Allan	Sgt	de Ville	Escudo	UK		
ARTHUR	Mynatt, Cecil F	Capt	Mynatt	Connecticut	US	Côte-d'Or	19 Aug
	Humblet, Xavier	S/Lt	Hache	Smabrere	Fr		
	Bacik, Albert V	T/Sgt	Bacik	Millième	US		
AUBREY	Marchant, Godfrey	Capt	Marchant,	Rutland	UK	Seine-et-Marne	12 Aug
	Chaigneau, Adrien	Lt	Telmon	Kildare	Fr		
	Hooker, Ivor	Sgt	Hooker	Thaler	UK		

Operation/Team	Name	Rank	Workname	Codename	Nat	Location	Inserted
AUGUSTUS	Bonsall, John H	Maj	Bonsall	Arizona	US	Aisne	16 Aug
	Delwiche, Jean	Capt	Dechville	Herault	Fr		
	Cote, Roger E	T/Sgt	Cote	Indiana	US	Aisne	
BASIL	Rivière, Robert	Capt	Raincourt	Ambleve	Fr	Doubs	26 Aug
	Carew, Thomas	Capt	Carew	Sutherland	UK		
	Stoyka, John L	T/Sgt	Stoyka	Ore	US		
BENJAMIN	O'Bryan-Tear, Hubert 'Terry'	Maj	Forrest	Stirling	UK	Meuse	21 Aug
	Moniez, Paul	Lt	Marchand	Ulster	Fr		
	Kaminski, Henri	S/Lt	Camouin	Serre	Fr		
BERNARD	Waller, Jocelyn 'Jock'	Capt	Waller	Tipperary	UK	Meuse	21 Aug
	Nasica, Étienne	Capt	Prato	Argens	Fr		
	Bassett, Cyril	Sgt	Bassett	Lancashire	UK		
BRIAN	Johnston, Francis	Maj	Johnston	Illinois	UK	Doubs	28 Aug
	Cretin, Roger	Capt	Francomte	Orkney	Fr		
	Smith, Norman	Sgt	Smith	Lira	UK		
BRUCE	Colby, William E	Maj	Colby	Berkshire	US	Yonne	15 Aug
	Lelong, Camille M	Lt	Favel	Galway	Fr		
	Villebois, Roger	S/Lt	Giry	Piastre	Fr		
BUGATTI	Fuller, Horace W 'Hod'	Maj	Fuller	Kansul	US	Hautes-Pyrénées	29 June
	de la Roche du Rouzet, Guy	Lt	Rocher	Hopei	Fr		
	Sigaud, Martial	S/Lt	Guillemot	Chekiang	Fr		
BUNNY	Radice, J F D	Capt	Radice	Peso	UK	Haute-Marne	18 Aug
	Geminel, Maurice	Lt	Gerville	Yen	Fr		
	Chambers, J	Sgt	Chambers	Drachma	UK		

	Name	Rank					
CECIL	Nielson, David	Maj	Nielson	Delaware	UK	Aube	26 Aug
	Keser, Alfred	Capt	Frayan	Lys	Fr		
	Wilde, Ronald 'Boxer'	Sgt	Wilde	Centavo	UK		
CEDRIC	Bazata, Douglas de W	Capt	Bazata	Vesdre	US	Haute-Saône	28 Aug
	Lesne, Louis	Capt	Chapel	Dendre	Fr		
	Floyd, Richard C	T/Sgt	Floyd	Gulder	US		
CHLOROFORM	Martin, Jacques	Capt	Martino	Joshua	Fr	Drôme	30 Jun
	McIntosh, Henry D	Lt	McIntosh	Lionel	US		
	Sassi, Jean	S/Lt	Nicole	Latimer	Fr		
CHRYSLER	Sell, Cyril H	Capt	Sell	Elie	UK	Ariège/Aude	16 Aug
	Aussaresses, Paul	Capt	Soual	Bazin	Fr		
	Chatten, Ronald E	Sgt	Chatten	Artus	UK		
CINNAMON	Lespinasse-Fonsegrieve, François	Capt	Ferandon	Orthon	Fr	Var	14 Aug
	Harcourt, Robert	Capt	Harcourt	Louis	UK		
	Marineau, Jacques	S/Lt	Maurin	Luc	Fr		
CITROEN	Smallwood, John	Capt	Smallwood	Anne	UK	Vaucluse	14 Aug
	Bloch, René-Clément	Capt	Alcee	Laurent	Fr		
	Bailey, Fred	Sgt	Bailey	Retif	UK		
COLLODION (LOCH)	Hall, Harold	Capt	Hall	Augustine	UK	Aveyron	7 Aug
	Marsaudon, Henri	Lt	Morgan	Benoit	Fr		
	Baumgold, Theodore	1/Sgt	Baumgold	Jules	US		
DANIEL	Bennett, Kemys 'Ed'	Capt	Bennett	Apôtre	UK	Côtes-du-Nord	6 Aug
	de Schonen, Pierre	Lt	de Schonen	Argentier	Fr		
	Brierley, Ron	Sgt	Brierley	Florin	UK		

Operation/Team	Name	Rank	Workname	Codename	Nat	Location	Inserted
DESMOND	Pietsch, William H	Capt	Pietsch	Skerry	US	Côte-d'Or	5 Sept
	Maunoury, Gilles	Capt	Bourriot	Shetland	Fr		
	Baird, Robert R	M/Sgt	Baird	Hampshire	US		
DODGE	Manierre, Cyrus E	Maj	Manierre	Rupert	US	Drôme	25 Jun
	Durocher, L T	Sgt	Durocher	Oswald	Can		
DOUGLAS I	Rubenstein, Richard	Capt	Rubinstein	Augure	UK	Morbihan	6 Aug
	Roblot, Jean	Lt	Ronglou	Anachorere	Fr		
	Raven, John	Sgt	Raven	Half Crown	UK		
DOUGLAS II	Rubenstein, Richard	Capt	Rubinstein	Augure	UK	Doubs	16 Sept
	Roblot, Jean	Lt	Ronglou	Anachorere	Fr		
	Van Hart, John T	T/Sgt	Van Hart	Half Crown	US		
EPHEDRINE	Donnart, Lucine	Lt	Rabeau	Julien	Fr	Hautes-Alpes	13 Aug
	Swank, Lawrence E	Lt	Swank	Gantor	US		
	Desplechin, Robert	S/Lt	Bourgoin	Leon	Fr		
FELIX	Souquet, Jean-Paul	Capt	Kernevel	Carnavon	Fr	Côtes-du-Nord	9 Jul
	Marchant, John	Capt	Marchant	Somerset	UK		
	Colvin, Peter	Sgt	Colvin	Middlesex	UK		
FRANCIS	Ogden-Smith, Colin	Maj	Ogden-Smith	Dorset	UK	Finistère	10 Jul
	Leborgne, Guy	Lt	Le Zachmeur	Durance	Fr		
	Dallow, Arthur	Sgt	Dallow	Groat	UK		
FRANK	Isaac, Idris	Capt	Isaac	Westmoreland	UK	Vendée/Loire-Inférieure	28 Sept
	Martelli, Alexandre	Lt	Massoni	Dumbarton	Fr		
	Henney, Thomas	Sgt	Henney	Cheshire	UK		

Team	Name	Rank	Field	Code	Country	Location	Date
FREDERICK	Wise, Adrian	Maj	Wise	Kinross	UK	Côtes-du-Nord	10 Jun
	Bloch-Auroch, Paul	Capt	Aguirec	Vire	Fr		
	Kehoe, Robert R	M/Sgt	Kehoe	Peseta	US		
GAVIN	Cabucca, Joseph J	Maj	Jeanclaude	Shilling	Fr	Mayenne/Ille-et-Vilaine	12 Jul
	Dreux, William	Capt	Dreux	Sixpence	US		
	Valentini, Paul	S/Lt	Masson	Halfpenny	Fr		
GEORGE I	Ragueneau, Philippe	Capt	Erard	Save	Fr	Loire-Inférieure	10 Jun
	Cyr, Paul	Capt	Cyr	Wigton	US		
	Gay, Christian	S/Lt	Lejeune	Rupee	Fr		
GEORGE II	Ragueneau, Philippe	Capt	Erard	Save	Fr	Deux-Sèvres	8 Sept
	Cyr, Paul	Capt	Cyr	Wigton	US		
	Gay, Christian	S/Lt	Lejeune	Rupee	Fr		
GERALD	Knerly, Stephen	Capt	Knerly	Norfolk	US	Morbihan	23 Aug
	L'Herbette, Claude	Capt	Beaumont	Suffolk	Fr		
	Friele, Berent E	1 Sgt	Friele	Selkirk	US		
GILBERT	Blathwayt, Christopher	Capt	Blathwayt	Surrey	UK	Finistère	10 Jul
	Carron de la Carrière, Paul	Lt	Charron	Ardeche	Fr		
	Wood, Neville	Sgt	Wood	Doubloon	UK		
GILES	Knox, Bernard M	Capt	Knox	Kentucky	US	Finistère	9 Jul
	Grall, Paul	Lt	Lebel	Loire	Fr		
	Tack, Gordon H	Sgt	Tack	Tickie	UK		
GODFREY	Forbes, Ian	Lt	Forbes	Rhode Island	US	Haute-Saône/Haute-Rhin	12 Sept
	Laval, Pierre	Lt	Morhange	Roscommon	Fr		
	Hanson, Frank A	Sgt	Hanson	Roxburgh	US		
GRAHAM	Crosby, Michael 'Bing'	Maj	Crosby	Huge	UK	Basse-Alpes	10 Aug

Operation/Team	Name	Rank	Workname	Codename	Nat	Location	Inserted
	Gavet, Pierre	Capt	Gouvet	Crispin	Fr	Basse-Alpe	
	Adams, William H	Sgt	Adams	Desire	US		Did not deploy
GREGORY	Bennett, Kemys 'Ed'	Capt	Bennett	Apôtre	UK	Vosges	5 Sept
	de Schonen, Pierre	Lt	de Schonen	Argentier	Fr		
	Brierley, Ron	Sgt	Brierley, Ron	Florin	UK		
GUY	Duron, André	Capt	Dhomas	Dronne	Fr	Mayenne/Ille-et-Vilaine	12 Jul
	Trofimov, A A E 'Troff'	Capt	Trofimov	Gironde	UK		
	Groult, George	S/Lt	Deschamps	Dordogne	Fr		
HAMISH	Anstett, Robert 'Bobby'	Lt	Anstett	Alabama	US	Indre/Cher	13 Jun
	Schmitt, Rene	Lt	Blachere	Louisiana	Fr		
	Watters, Lee J	Sgt	Watters	Kansas	US		
HAROLD	Whitty, Valentine	Maj	Whitty	Ross	UK	Vendée/Deux-Sèvres	16 Jul
	Jolliet, Pierre	Lt	Rimbaut	Tyrone	Fr		
	Verlander, Harry	Sgt	Verlander	Sligo	UK		
HARRY	Guthrie, Duncan	Capt	Guthrie	Denby	UK	Morvan	6 Jan
	Rousset, Pierre	Lt	Dupont	Gapeau	Fr		
	Couture, René	S/Lt	Legrand	Centime	Fr		
HENRY	Moore, Raymond E	Lt	Moore	New Mexico	US	Jura/Doubs	10 Sept
	Jean-Montcler, Stephane	Lt	Montcler	Anglesey	Fr		
	Rocca, Vincent M	T/Sgt	Rocca	West Virginia	US		
HILARY	Mautaint, Edgar	Capt	Marchant	Charente	Fr	Finistère	18 Jul
	Chadbourne, Philip H	Lt	Chadbourne	Nevada	US		
	Hervouet, Roger	S/Lt	Pariselle	Kopek	Fr		

Team	Name	Rank	Code	Field name	Country	Region	Date
HORACE	Summers, John W	Maj	Summers	Wyoming	US	Finistère	18 Jul
HUGH	Leclercq, Georges	Lt	Levalois	Somme	Fr		
	Zielske, William F	T/Sgt	Zielske	Dime	US		
	Crawshay, William	Capt	Crawshay	Crown	UK	Indre/Vienne	6 Jun
	L'Helgouach, Louis	Capt	Legrand	Franc	Fr		
	Meyer, René	S/Lt	Mersiol	Yonne	Fr		
IAN	Gildee, John J	Capt	Gildee	Oklahoma	US	Vienne	21 Jun
	Desfarges, Alexander	Lt	Deslorme	Maine	Fr		
	Bourgoin, Lucien J	Sgt	Bourgoin	Mayo	US		
ISAAC	Dubac	Col	Viat	(Diagramme)	Fr	Morvan	10 Jun
	Hutchinson, James	Lt Col	Hastings	Télémètre	UK		
	Sharp, John	Sgt	Sharp		UK		
IVOR	Cox, John	Capt	Cox	Monmouth	UK	Cher	7 Aug
	Colin, Robert	Lt	Dantec	Selune	Fr		
	Goddard, Lewis F	T/Sgt	Goddard	Oregon	US		
JACOB	Gough, Victor A	Capt	Gough	Arran	UK	Vosges	13 Aug
	Boissarie, Maurice	Lt	Baraud	Connaught	Fr		
	Seymour, Ken	Sgt	Seymour	Skye	UK		
JAMES	Singlaub, John K	Lt	Singlaub	Mississippi	US	Corrèze	11 Aug
	Le Bel de Penguilly, Jacques	S/Lt	Leb	Michigan	Fr		
	Denneau, Anthony J	T/Sgt	Denneau	Massachusetts	US		
JEREMY	Hallowes, George McL	Capt	Hallowes	Aimable	UK	Haute-Loire	17 Aug
	Giese, Henri-Charles	Lt	Fontcroise	Dur	Fr		
	Leney, Roger	Sgt	Leney	Ferme	UK		
JIM	Donovan, Philip W	Capt	Donovan	Pennsylvania	US	Jura	16 Sept

Operation/Team	Name	Rank	Workname	Codename	Nat	Location	Inserted
JIM	de Francesco, José	Lt	Lavige	Leitrim	Fr	Jura	16 Sept
	Henely, Michael F	T/Sgt	Henely	Wexford	US	Jura	
JOHN	Stern, David	Capt	Stern	Beau	UK	Tarn-et-Garonne	17 Aug
	De Galbert, Maurice	S/Lt	Le Rocher	Lucide	Fr		
	Gibbs, Donald	Sgt	Gibbs	Silence	UK		
JUDE	Evans, William	Capt	Evans	Glamorgan	UK	Rhône	15 Aug
	Larrieu, Jean	Capt	Lavisme	Rence	Fr		
	Holdham, Alfred	Sgt	Holdham	Guinea	UK		
JUDE II	Evans, William	Capt	Evans	Glamorgan	UK	Rhône	7 Nov
	Larrieu, Jean	Capt	Lavisme	Rence	Fr		
	Holdham, A E	Sgt	Holdham	Guinea	UK		8 Nov
JULIAN	Clutton, A H	Maj	Clutton	Stafford	UK	Indre-et-Loire	11 Aug
	Vermot, Marcel	S/Lt	Brouillard	Vermont	Fr		
	Menzies, James	CQMS	Menzies	Essex	Uk		
JULIAN II	Souquet, Jean-Paul	Capt	Kernevel	Carnavon	Fr	Alsace	19 Nov
	Scherrer	S/Lt	Sauvage		Fr		
	Meyer, René	S/Lt	Mersiol	Yonne	Fr		
LEE	Brown, Charles E	Capt	Brown	Pice	US	Haute-Vienne	10 Aug
	Angoulvent, Paul	Lt	Viguier	Sous	Fr		
	Pierat, Maurice	S/Lt	Chevalier	Reis	Fr		
MARK	Thévenet, Johanes	Lt	De Thévenet	Sympathique	Fr	Tarn-et-Garonne	17 Aug
	Conein, Lucien E 'Lulu'	Lt	Conein	Intrépide	US		
	Carpenter, James J	Sgt	Carpenter	Lester	US		

Code	Name	Rank	Field surname	Field name	Country	Region	Date
MARTIN	Mellows, Thomas	Capt	Mellows	Blasé	UK	Gers	17 Aug
	Redonnet, Georges	Lt	Remond	Substantif	Fr		
	Carey, Neville	Sgt	Carey	Placide	UK		
MASQUE	Guillot, Nelson E	Capt	Guillot	Harmonieux	US	Isère	28 Aug
	Bouvery, Jacques	Lt	Gramont	Succulent	Fr		
	Poche, Francis M	1/Sgt	Poche	Ideal	US		
MAURICE	Carman, Charles M	Capt	Carman	Utah	US	Doubs	1 Sept
	Reveilhac, Hubert	Lt	Dumesnil	Virginia	Fr		
	Cole, Francis J	T/Sgt	Cole	Georgia	US		
MILES	Allen, Everett T	Capt	Allen	Libre	US	Gers	17 Aug
	Estève, René	Asp	Fourcade	Lumineux	Fr		
	Gruen, Arthur	T/Sgt	Gruen	Fidèle	US		
MINARET	Hartley-Sharpe, Lancelot	Maj	Hartley-Sharpe	Edmund	UK	Gard	14 Aug
	Cros, P	Capt	Mutin	Hector	Fr		Did not deploy
MONOCLE	Ellis, John W	Sgt	Ellis	Arsene	UK		14 Aug
	Fiardo, Jacques	Capt	Tosel	Immense	Fr	Drôme	14 Aug
	Foster, Ray H	Lt	Foster	Solide	US		14 Aug
NICHOLAS	Anderson, Robert J	T/Sgt	Anderson	Raieux	US		
	Maude, John	Capt	Maude	Leicester	UK	Côte-d'Or/Haute-Marne	10 Sept
	Penin, Henri	Lt	Puget	Breaknock	Fr		
	Whittle, Maurice	Sgt	Whittle	Northumberland	UK		
NORMAN	Lautier, Marc	Lt	Bataille	Washington	Fr	Jura	28 Aug
	Dillow, Konrad C	Lt	Dillow	Minnesota	US		
	Lajeunesse, Lucien E	1/Sgt	Lajeunesse	Tennessee	US		

Operation/Team	Name	Rank	Workname	Codename	Nat	Location	Inserted
NOVOCAINE	Gennerich, Charles J	Lt	Gennerich	Mathieu	US	Hautes-Alpes	7 Aug
	Pronost, Jean-Yves	Lt	Le Lann	Hérve	Fr		
	Thompson, William T	1/Sgt	Thompson	Gilles	US		
PACKARD	Bank, Aaron	Capt	Bank	Chechwan	US	Lozère	1 Aug
	Denis, Henri	Lt	Boineau	Fukien	Fr		
	Montfort, Marcel	S/Lt	Montfort	Formosa	Fr		
PAUL	Hood, Hugo	Maj	Hood	Shropshire	UK	Côte-d'Or/Jura	19 Aug
	Vallée, Michel	Lt	Cormier	Durthe	Fr		
	Brown, K J W	Sgt	Brown	Limerick	UK		
PHILLIP (RUPERT)	Liberos, Jean	Capt	De Rouen	Kintyre	Fr	Meurthe-et-Moselle	1 Sept
	Lucas, Robert A	Lt	Lucas	Caithness	US		
	Grgat, Joseph M	S3C	Grgat	Leinster	US		
QUENTIN	Fenton, Ronald	Capt	Fenton	Cornwall	UK	Loire-Atlantique/Vendée	28 Sept
	Raux, Jean	Lt	Lasserre	Wicklow	Fr		
	Rawson, David	Sgt	Rawson	Merioneth	UK		
QUININE	Macpherson, Tommy	Capt	Macpherson	Anselme	UK	Lot	9 Jun
	de Bourbon-Parme, Michel	Asp	Bourdon	Aristide	Fr		
	Brown, Arthur 'Oscar'	Sgt	Brown	Felicien	UK		
RAYMOND	de Hosses, R	Capt	Waguet	Waterford	Fr	Deux-Sèvres	28 Sept
	Cadilhac, H H L	Lt	Chaulais	Gloucester	Fr		
	Adams, Walter	Sgt	Adams	Kincardine	UK		
RODERICK	Preziosi, Jean	Capt	Paoli	Nairn	Fr	Doubs	1 Sept
	Boggs, William C	Lt	Boggs	New Hampshire	US		
	Mersereau, Charles	T/Sgt	Mersereau	Stronsay	US		
RONALD	Deseilligny, Georges	Lt	Dartigues	Boutton	Fr	Finistère	6 Aug

Operation	Name	Rank	Trumps	Boursier	Nat	Region	Date
SCEPTRE	Trumps, Shirley Ray	Lt	Esch	Pound	US	Alpes-Maritime/Var	14 Aug
	Esch, Elmer B	T/Sgt	Esch	Pound	US		
	Hanna, Walter C	Lt	Hanna	Vaillant	US		
	Franceschi, François	Lt	Tevenac	Intense	Fr		
	Palmer, Howard V	Sgt	Palmer	Devoue	US		
SCION	Grenfell, Osborne	Maj	Grenfell	Scintillating	UK	Drôme/Isère	30 Aug
	Gruppo, Roger	Lt	Revard	Vif	Fr		
	Cain, Thomas 'Cobber'	Sgt	Cain	Vibrant	UK		
SIMON	Fouere, Maurice	Capt	Fontaine	Fernard	Fr	Vendée	28 Sept
	Coomber, Anthony	Capt	Coomber	Coustard	UK		
	Somers, Claud	Sgt	Somers	Stephane	UK		
STANLEY	Craster, Oswin E	Capt	Craster	Yorkshire	UK	Haute-Marne	1 Sept
	Cantais, Robert	Lt	Carliere	Meath	Fr		
	Grinham, Jack	Sgt	Grinham	Worcestershire	UK		
TIMOTHY	Moutte, L	Capt	Ambel	Nesque	Fr	Doubs	12 Sept
	Mundinger, Robert G	Lt	Mundinger	Marcelin	US		
	Heyns, Robert E	Lt	Heyns	Dyle	US		
	Spears, Donald A	1/Sgt	Spears	Escaut	US		
TONY	Montgomery, Robert E	Capt	Montgomery	Dollar	US	Vendée	18 Aug
	Paris, Lucien	Lt	Devailly	Écu	Fr		
	McGowan, John E	T/Sgt	McGowan	Quarter	US		
VEGANIN	Marten, Neal	Maj	Marten	Cuthbert	UK	Drôme/Isère	9 Jun
	Vuchot, Claude	Capt	Noir	Derek	Fr		
	Gardner, Dennis 'Jesse'	Sgt	Gardner	Ernest	UK		
WILLYS	Marchal, Georges	Capt	Granier	Simon	Fr	Ardèche	29 Jun
	Montague, John	Capt	Montague	Honan	UK		
	Cornick, Ted	Sgt	Cornick	Chansi	UK		

INDEX